GLOBALIZATION AND HUMAN RIGHTS

[illegible] of women working in the garment industry is a case in point. Low-skilled labor with low wages, long hours of work and lack of job security are typical of the feminization of labor in unorganized sectors. The state generally [illegible] the [illegible] and [illegible] violation of the labor laws. It is clear that the women are being exploited, but they [illegible] their [illegible] against the sexual harassment they [illegible] face in the work place.

WOMEN IN AGRICULTURE

[illegible]

GLOBALIZATION AND HUMAN RIGHTS

DR. ANIL DUTTA MISHRA
DR. P.V. SARMA
DR. SOHAN RAJ TATER

REGAL

REGAL PUBLICATIONS
New Delhi

GLOBALIZATION AND HUMAN RIGHTS

ISBN 978-81-8484-415-3

Typeset by
RAHUL COMPOSERS
New Highway Apartments, Lakshmi Niwas
760, Pocket-D, Lok Nayak Puram, New Delhi - 110 041

Printed in India at
MAYUR ENTERPRISES
WZ Plot No. 3, Gujjar Market, Tihar Village, New Delhi - 110 018

Published by
REGAL PUBLICATIONS
F-159, Rajouri Garden, New Delhi - 110 027
Phone : 45546396, 25435369
E-mail : regalbookspub@yahoo.com, regaldeepbooks@yahoo.com

Contents

Preface

Globalization and Human Rights are buzz words in contemporary world. All the discourses in Political Science, Economics and Social Sciences are dominated by the theme of Globalization and Human Rights. Liberalization, globalization and privatization have changed the world, its people and their mindset. Small is being replaced by mega. Man is being replaced by machine. One can see development everywhere. Women, dalit and downtrodden are occupying high posts. Dictatorship is no longer in commanding position. Democracy and demand for good governance is echoed world over. Technology is being used as an agent of change. Shrinking space, shrinking time and disappearing borders are linking people's lives more deeply, more intensively and more immediately than ever before. It is not just the integration of the economy but culture, technology and governance. People all over globe have become happier and prosperous. Individual and community are integrated with the world through social media. The global markets, global technologies, global ideas and global solidarity are enriching the lives of people everywhere, greatly expanding their choices. The growing interdependence of people's lives calls for shared values and a shared commitment to the human development of all people. This era of globalization is opening many opportunities for millions of people around the world. Increased trade, new technologies, foreign investments, expanding media and Internet connections are fuelling economic growth and human advance. Today we have more wealth and technology, and more commitment to a global community than ever before.

But reality is totally different. Recently, there has been increasing disillusionment among policy-makers in several parts of the world and some fundamental questions are asked. These are: Who want globalization? Globalization for what and for whom? Why is globalization of human resource not taking place? Do people want globalization? It is said that the issue of globalization is receiving considerable attention but no work is being done on the social costs involved (in terms of poverty, inequality, unemployment and tensions) nor on the growing marginalization of people in India as well as in other developing countries. The progress in areas like health, education and other social sectors are slowed by the diversion of precious human resources for national security and in combating terrorism and separatist movement. In fact present day globalization is based on domination, hegemony, exploitation, alienation, concentration of knowledge, wealth and power. On the few top TNCs of the developed nations have increased their profits manifold, on the one hand, a very significant majority of people around the world are still struggling for their basic needs and existence. The people of Asia, Africa and Latin American regions are still not part of the globalization. Globalization is a calculated imperialist design of hegemonization in economic, political, ecological and cultural terrains, threatening loss of economic, self-reliance and political sovereignty, erosion of democratic structures and damaging of plural cultural identities.

As a culmination of the unbridled, unrestrained 'multinational' capitals, globalization leaves the poorer counties behind in global competition, as the clear objective of capital mobility is profit, prestige and power for its owners and not the well-being of the people at large. This is confirmed by historical and empirical evidence. It is intrinsic to the nature of capital, as articulated by Lenin most vociferously, to more towards exploitable resources. As investments capital has moved and modernized, it has also in the process exploited people and natural resources and often left behind pollution, poverty, inequality, injustice, crime, corrupting and a general degradation of environment—a record not much different from the imperialist history of aggressive capitalism, obsessed with growth.

Globalization is a totalizing process in terms of both hegemonization and homogenization, and extended and subtler American version of European colonial/imperialist ambitions of domination, expropriating and transforming the world in its own image. Ideologically also, it is a derivative of the earlier conceptualizations of 'progress' and 'modernization', premised on the Westcentric view of civilization, materialism and economies glorification of the 'invisible hand' of the market, growth-observed industrial industrialism, objectification of nature and an instrumental treatment of humanity.

The humanity today faces the problem of Human Rights of global dimension, which has threatened the very survival of mankind. In the name of modernization and development it ultimately leads to consumerism and violation of Human Rights. The more dangerous thing is happening in the neo-liberal political world is that in the name of protection of Human Rights the mightiest west is violating the human rights of the innocent citizens of other countries around the globe. One must keep in mind that no technological intervention, however, brilliant, no socio-economic reform, however profound will be able to save us from the impending catastrophe, unless and until we radically change our life-style and learn to live in harmonious relationship with nature. We must learn to protect the Human Rights of downtrodden, voiceless, and powerless irrespective of caste, creed, sex, region and country. The real development will take the society from Vikriti (perversion) to Sanskriti (culture). It is not going back, but going in the right direction. Equity and justice are the *sin-qua-non* of sustainable development. It is four dimensional : (1) Equity among nations—rich nations, poor nations, developed nations, developing nations; (2) Equity with countries—between regions, social classes, genders, sectors of activities; (3) Equity between generations; and (4) Equity between economics and ecology and science and spirituality.

Basic needs of all human beings; i.e food, clothing, shelter, education, health, security, and self-esteem must be met adequately. Priority must go to these needs. Level of these needs will be determined by natural and technological resources available and the global socio-economic context. The great failure of the world community of government is not just that they have been unable to guarantee underprivileged people's social, economic and cultural rights. Underprivileged people's right to peace, livelihood, development and equality are the prime issues in this high tech society world over. The growth of nationalist, secessionist and ethnic conflicts which threaten all regions of the world with violence and bloodshed has armed opposition groups to adopt similar methods of repression and terror in pursuit of their goals. People have been killed, women are raped, and ill-treated or taken hostage by armed opposition groups in all regions of the world.

Human rights for underprivileged, as for all individuals, are protected in international law. Yet underprivileged people suffer the full range of human rights violations known to the modern world in the name of development. Tribals, farmers and women face human rights violations solely or primarily because of their deprivation of land and forest by state and industrial houses. This is leading to overall increase of violence.

The United Nation's Universal Declaration of Human Rights proclaims: "All Human beings are born free and equal in dignity and rights". Yet there is violation. Even there is inequality in UN Security Council. The Five permanent members in the Security Council can veto any resolution. The only and most appropriate way to solve the problems of underprivileged is to change the position of underprivileged in society and make her equally responsible for the well-being of the social order. 'Basic Human Rights', Henry Kissinger said 'must be presumed and cherished and defended if peace and prosperity are to be more than hollow technical achievements. Human rights are the very essence of a meaningful life, and human dignity is the ultimate purpose of government.'

The international community can play a decisive role in protecting human rights through vigilant and concerted action. Important steps towards protecting underprivileged people's human rights worldwide include documentation of human rights violations, publicizing them to press, government and authorities for an end to the abuses. At the same time the transformation of human rights from underprivileged perspective is crucial to addressing global challenges to human rights in present day world.

The problems of human rights are consequence of follies of greed, exploitation and domination. Therefore, present exigency demands that one acquires the basic wisdom of nature that is to follow its laws and learn to manage according to its principles. Therefore, the present developmental crisis demands a different world view on Gandhian line that is to give up the present lifestyle and reduction in consumerism. The message is simple and very clear. People have no choice but to heave towards a secure future and that it has to keep note of the imperatives as well as the potentials of sustainable environment and sustainable consumption for protection of human rights. We cannot stop violation of human rights on the foundation of materialistic culture. If mankind is to live and want to live in peace and harmony with nature, it has to eschew materialistic culture and has to develop a way of life anchored in the philosophy of simplicity and integrated lifestyle based on four purusharthas—Dharma, Artha, Kama and Mokshya. We should be cautious of those who want to reach heaven by creating a hell on earth. It is high time for the individual to change the chemistry of thought and action by adopting human values in our daily life.

ANIL DUTTA MISHRA
P.V. SARMA
SOHAN RAJ TATER

List of Contributors

Dr. Anil Dutta Mishra, Deputy Director, National Gandhi Museum, New Delhi and Hon. Professor, Centre for Gandhian Philosophy and Human Development Gayatri Vidya Parishad College (Autonomous), Visakhapatnam (A.P.).

Dr. Biraja Shankar Rath, Reader & Head, P.G. Department of Political Science, F.M. Autonomous College, Balasore (Odisha).

Dr. D. Venkateswara Rao, Professor and Head, P.G. Department of Public Administration, Sri Y.N. College, Narasapur (A.P.).

Dr. G.N. Trivedi, Associate Professor, Department of Political Science, Motilal Nehru College, University of Delhi, Delhi.

Dr. Ghanshyam Roy, Associate Professor, Department of Political Science, G.M.R.D. College, Samastipur (Bihar).

Dr. Haripriya Behara, MBA Final year student at Andhra University Campus, Visakhapatnam (A.P.).

Dr. Madhukar Patnaik, Professor, G.V.P. Degree College (A), Visakhapatnam (A.P.).

Dr. Malbika Talukdar, Assistant Professor, University Law College, Gauhati University, Gauhati, Assam.

Dr. Manish Sharma, Chairman, Department of Gandhian and Peace Studies, Panjab University, Chandigarh.

Dr. Manohar Lal Sharma, Professor, Department of Gandhian and Peace Studies and Honorary Director, Gandhi Bhawan, Panjab University, Chandigarh.

Dr. Pravin Kumar, Associate Professor, Shyam Lal College, Delhi University, Delhi.

Dr. Prem Anand Mishra, Assistant Professor, Peace Research Centre, Gujarat Vidyapith, Ahmedabad (Gujarat).

Dr. Rajiv Bhattacharya, Assistant Professor University Law College, Gauhati University, Gauhati, Assam.

Dr. Sadhana Thakur, Associate Professor, Sri Arvind Mahila College, Patna (Bihar).

Dr. Seema Thakur, Guest Faculty, Department of Gandhian and Peace Studies, Panjab University, Chandigarh.

Dr. Shivraj B. Nakade, Former Vice Chancellor, Marathwara University and President of Indian Society of Gandhian Studies.

Surinder K. Shukla, Professor of Political Science, Panjab University, Chandigarh.

1

Globalization

A Conceptual Analysis

ANIL DUTTA MISHRA

"The real wealth of a nation is its people. And the purpose of development is to create an enabling environment for people to enjoy long, healthy and creative lives. This simple but powerful truth is too often forgotten in the pursuit of material and financial wealth".

—Human Development Report, 1990

INTRODUCTION

Globalization is not new but the present era has some distinctive features such as shrinking space, shrinking time and disappearing borders are linking people's lives more deeply, more intensively and more immediately than ever before. Globalization is a process integrating not just the economy but culture, technology and governance. Globalization is considered to be neo-liberal. Its normative base is the celebration of the market. In other words it is a triumph—not only over so-called global "historic alternatives" [F. Fukuyama (92), The End of History and the Last Man] but also over unions and Keynesian states. In fact, elites on behalf of the states are real authors of globalization.

Globalization has become the current Mantra or even panacea to solve all human problems. It is believed that the achievements of globalization would make the people all over globe happy, prosperous and contended and that there would be no conflicts, no poverty and inequality, no violation of human rights, no malnutrition, no illiteracy, and no disease, etc. Each individual and community would be so integrated with the world that the benefits would flow both laterally and vertically so smoothly that no one would remain untouched by prosperity. There would be nation-state without boundary. It is said that global markets, global technologies, global ideas and global solidarity can enrich the lives of people everywhere, greatly expanding their choices. The growing interdependence of people's lives calls for shared values and a shared commitment to the human development of all people. This era of globalization is opening many opportunities for millions of people around the world. Increased trade, new technologies, foreign investments, expanding media and Internet connections are fuelling economic growth and human advance. All these offer enormous potential eradicate poverty in the 21st century. Today we have more wealth and technology—and more commitment to a global community–than ever before.

But reality is totally different. Recently there has been increasing disillusionment among policy-makers in several parts of the world and some fundamental questions are asked. These are: Who want globalization? Globalization for what and for whom ? Why is globalization of human resource not taking place? Do people want globalization ? It is said that the issue of globalization is receiving considerable attention but no work is being done on the social costs involved (in terms of poverty, inequality, unemployment and tensions) nor on the growing marginalization of people in India as well as in other developing countries. The progress in areas like health, education and other social sectors are slowed by the diversion of precious human resources for national security and in combating terrorism and separatist movement. It is also said that the culture of consumerism is the product of globalization. Almost all the consumer items that are being promoted to sustain the economic growth have significant impact on nation and society directly or indirectly. The concept of globalization and the culture of consumerism are antithetical for all that Indian culture stands for. The new information technology and advances in telecommunications have tended to erode the heterogeneity of national lifestyles, social and economic values and even cultures. This is visible in the standardization of consumer tastes in favour of fast foods (evidenced by the omnipresence of Mc Donald's and Coca Cola) and American films and soap operas. Consumerism is based on domination, hegemony, exploitation, alienation, concentration of knowledge, wealth and power. On the Few top TNCs of the developed nations have increased their profits manifold, on the one hand, a very significant majority of people around the world are still struggling for their basic needs and existence. The people of Asia, Africa and Latin American regions are still not part of the globalization.

In the present scenario, globalization is irreversible and unstoppable. Most of the countries of the world, willingly or unwillingly, have already accepted it and others may have to accept it. However, it is mostly agreed that globalization should be introduced with human face for the benefit of the poor and needy. The challenges arising out of globalization require total newness on all fronts–from government to NGOs levels. In this article an attempt has been made to analyse the broad concept of globalization and its effects on people in terms of growth and productivity, poverty and income distribution, as well as employment.

GLOBALIZATION : A CONCEPTUAL ANALYSIS

Globalization means different things to different people according to their ideology and perception. The word globalization is used in two ways. In a positive sense, it is used to describe a process of increasing integration into the world economy. In other words, it means the expansion of economic activities across national boundaries. It is also used to prescribe a strategy of development based on a rapid integration with the world economy and view it as salvation. In other words, globalization is a process associated with increasing economic openness, growing economic interdependence and deepening economic integration in the global economy. In negative sense, it is seen as domination by developed nations over developing nations. In most of the countries, particularly those belonging to the developing world, liberalization policy has not been evolved indigenously. It has been adopted under World Bank-IMF combine conditionality of which internal and external liberalization policies are integral part.

Globalization is not new. Recall the early sixteenth century and the late nineteenth. But this era is different:

New markets—Foreign exchange and capital markets are linked

		globally, operating 24 hours a day, with dealings at a distance in real time.
New tools	—	Internet links, cellular phones, media networks.
New actors	—	The world trade organization (WTO) with authority over national governments, the multinational corporations with more economic power than many states, the global networks of non-governmental organizations (NGOs) and other groups that transcend national boundaries.
New rules	—	Multilateral agreements on trade, services and intellectual property, backed by strong enforcement mechanisms and more binding for national governments, reducing the scope for national policy.

According to the World Development Report (2000-01) five actions are necessary:

- Promoting global financial stability and opening the markets of rich countries to the agricultural goods, manufactures and services of poor countries.
- Bridging the digital and knowledge divides, thus bringing technology and information to people throughput the world.
- Providing financial and non-financial resources for international public goods especially medical and agricultural research.
- Increasing aid and debt relief to help countries to take actions to end poverty within a comprehensive framework.
- Giving a voice to poor countries and poor people in global forums.

The key features of globalization are: (a) Economic features: Growth in Trade; Growth in FDI and Capital Flows; Global Production and consumption; Global competition; Trade and Investment Liberalization Policies, (b) Non-Economic Features: Loss of National Sovereignty; Standardization of values and cultures. In other word, a major feature of globalization is the growing concentration and monopolization of economic resources and power by transnational corporations and by global financing firms and funds and globalization of national policies and policy-making mechanisms. National policies (including in economic, social, cultural and technological areas) that until recently were under the jurisdiction of States and people within a country have increasingly come under the influence of international agencies and processes or of big private corporations and economic/financial players. This led to erosion of national sovereignty and narrowed the ability of governments and people to make choices from options in economic, social and cultural policies. Governments now have to implement policies that are in line with the decisions and rules of these international institutions. The key institutions concerned are the World Bank, the International Monetary Fund (IMF) and the WTO.

The other fundamental premise of globalization is the relatively unhindered flow of goods and capital (but not people) across national boundaries. There are three economic manifestations of this phenomenon–international trade, international investment and international finance. Globalization requires country's openness to the world economy. There are four elements that are conventionally considered in determining a country's openness to the world economy. There is, most importantly, (i) the proportion of a country's gross domestic product (GDP) that is involved in the international trade of goods and services. Than there is (ii) the related element of the level of tariffs, which speaks to the degree of protection accorded to local production against imports from the world economy. Beyond trade there is (iii) the element of the degree of transnationalisation of production, that is, the extent to which exchange of capital takes place for purposes of production; for the less developed countries, it refers primarily to the import of foreign direct investment (FDI). Transnationalisation of production stands on a different footing from international trade, even though trade is involved prior or subsequent to the production process. Essentially, while in the area of international trade during the era of globalization the relevant actors treat the world as a global market, in the internationalization of production the relevant actors treat the world as a global factory, the different constituent parts or division of which are located in several countries, yet from a single production system. Finally, but not unrelated to the previous elements, in (iv) the extent of state controls on capital movements

It is very common to hear the words privatization, globalization and liberalization. In fact, privatization and globalization are inherent in liberlization. The theoretical foundations for the policy of liberalization including privatization are provided by several interrelated strands of literature mainly contributed by New Right Schools of Thought, Property Rights Literature, the Principal-agent Relationship and Organization and Management Literature. In all there are four New Right Schools of Thought. These are : (i) the Chicago School led by Friedman; (ii) the Austrian School led by Hayek; (iii) Public Choice School led by Buchanan, Tullock and Niskanen; and (iv) the supply side Economics School led by Laffer, Gilder and Wanniski. The New Right Schools of thought, in spite of intellectual differences, broadly maintain that state involvement leads to increasing monopoly, increasing budget and suppressing of entrepreneurial behaviour, limiting choice, over production of unwanted services and encouragement to waste and inefficiency. In view of this the New Right has forcefully argued retrieval of the State as a regulator and producer. Therefore, deregulation/liberalization and privatization are amongst six-point reform agenda of the New Right. The other measures are the reduction of inflation, lower taxation, increasing role of market forces in the provision of public services and institutional and constitutional reforms. The aim of these reforms is to promote competition between rival bureaucracies, reduce the influence of interest groups and corporatist institutions and impose a constitutional upper limit on the public expenditure as a proportion of the gross national product.

The theoretical base of globalization is directly rooted in the principle of comparative advantage, specialization in the production of goods and services based on factor endowment and competition results in benefits to all countries in international trade. In the open economy model (i.e. economy having linkages with global market), international trade leads to factor price equalization and optimum pattern of resource allocation globally.

Globalization is a calculated imperialist design of hegemonization in economic, political, ecological and cultural terrains, threatening loss of economic, self-reliance and political sovereignty, erosion of democratic structures and damaging of plural cultural identities. Not only this, employment of protectionist policies, discriminatory trade-conditions, direct intervention in the domestic affairs of LDCs regarding their intellectual property right amount to virtual 'trade war' and destabilization of the fragile economies and strife-ridden politics of the latter. Globalism would remain an idle fancy in the absence of genuine 'inter-nationalism' that is, egalitarian interaction among nations.

As a culmination of the unbridled, unrestrained 'multi-national' capitals, globalization leaves the poorer counties behind in global competition, as the clear objective of capital mobility is profit, prestige and power for its owners and not the well-being of the people at large. This is confirmed by historical and empirical evidence. It is intrinsic to the nature of capital, as articulated by Lenin most vociferously, to more towards exploitable resources. As investments capital has moved and modernized, it has also in the process exploited people and natural resources and often left behind pollution, poverty, inequality, injustice, crime, corrupting and a general degradation of environment—a record not much different from the imperialist history of aggressive capitalism, obsessed with growth.

Globalization is a totalizing process interims of both hegemonization and homogenization, and extended and subtler American version of European colonial/imperialist ambitions of domination, expropriating and transforming the world in its own image. Ideologically also, it is a derivative of the earlier conceptualizations of 'progress' and 'modernization', premised on the West-centric view of civilization, materialism and economies glorification of the 'invisible hand' of the market, growth-observed industrial industrialism, objectification of nature and an instrumental treatment of humanity.

The specter of mass resistance and political movements is on the anvil in a majority of third world societies that have set out in the direction of globalization, constantly haunting and scaring to generate chaos and degeneration of whatever little is achieved by these societies. It appears that eventually globalization will prove to be a disaster for the developing societies that will push them into the oblivion of anarchy and instability reminiscent of the Hobbesean state of nature.

THE REALITY OF GLOBALIZATION

The end of 20th century witnessed ushering in of an epoch of New World Order in which the idea of globalization found expression and flourished under the auspices and blessings of Breton Wood institutions—notably the World Bank and International Monetary Fund—paving a way for the neo-capitalist hegemony and subjugation in a more vigorous but civilized manner. As a matter of fact globalization is a latest dream selling exercise on the part of U.S. promising a transparent, free and rational world order, which will ultimately culminate into an ideal Global Village.

Liberalization, privatization and globalization are the buzzwords in contemporary world. All goals end here. Privatization worldwide began in 1980's because of rising debt and low commodity prices. Eastern Europe, Russia, Ukraine, Argentina, Brazil, Hungry, Mexico, Poland have already gone through the process. In support of privatization it is said that direct state involvement in commercial activities conflicts with its other roles. The real picture of liberalization, privatization and globalization is quite different and complex.

Uruguay Round agreement brought the WTO into existence. WTO agreements appears to be based on the hypothesis that liberalization is the panacea for all ills in the economy, trade & commerce for the society The Uruguay Round agreement not only reduced trade barriers—by an average of 40 percent—but also laid down rules for what kinds of policies governments can make on matters such as intellectual property and investment, making its impact more complex, more expensive to employment and more difficult to predict. It is generally advocated that the free trade would lead to higher rates of economic growth. But the fact is that economic globalization and trade liberalization have concentrated power in the larger entities we know as transnational corporations. It is the TNCs which have benefitted the most in the era of globalization. Small farmers are unable to compete in the global economy and are being driven off their land, leaving the doors wide open to the corporations. Free trade has enslaved the hungry rather than freed them. Trade can help to achieve food security, but only if it is democratic and free from corporate control; only if it helps rather than hinders the poor. Further, about one-third of the global trade conducted by the MNCs is instrumental in liquidating national economies. In the political sphere, the nation-states find themselves increasingly constrained, as new enters of power emerge to delimit political sovereignty in terms of foreign aid, IMF loans, deregulation, etc. Growing concentration of economic 'resources and political power has also aggravated social schisms and conflicts.

The modern world has corporate-managed trade rather than free trade. The trade liberalization has failed the poor and stands in danger of giving trade as a whole a bad name. The poor are going hungry because of the way the trading system is working. Trade liberalization—'free' trade, trade without barriers—is harming, not helping them. The trade liberalization that the WTO oversees appears to be failing the poor, hindering rather than helping them, and handing power to transnational corporations.

India urged that developing countries be allowed greater autonomy in establishing and supporting domestic agricultural policy. A purely market-based approach might not be appropriate for developing countries, it said; for some countries, it might be necessary to adopt a market-plus approach, in which nontrade concerns such as the maintenance of the livelihoods of the agrarian peasantry and the production of sufficient food to meet domestic needs are taken into consideration... [W]hile it may not be possible to immediately ensure that developing countries are able to produce at least a minimum percentage of their annual food requirements, this is a goal that has to be pursued.

Globalization has an adverse effect on poor developing countries with an inadequate national capacity. Almost all the countries of the Third World have signed the WTO. While most have gained, the poorest, 800 million hungry people, have lost. Any society, national or international, will ultimately be judged on whether its systems, rules and regulations assist the most needy. By that criterion, the current international trade system is failing. People go hungry because they are too poor to grow enough or to buy enough food. On the other hand, in the late 1990s the world , as a whole, spent more than US $500 billion to combat the supposed 'millennium bug'—ten times more than rich countries give to the poor each year in development assistance. By contrast, the amount needed to have world hunger free by 2015—a target agreed at the 1996 World Food Summit—would be US $60 billion dollars over 15 years, or US $4 billion per year in increased spending, hardly an excessive amount.

Globalization is transforming trade, finance, employment, migration, technology, communications, entertainment, the environment, social systems, values, ways of living, patterns of thinking, cultures and patterns of governance. Unemployment, poverty, inequality and alienation are increasing, partly as a result of globalization. Crime, drugs, terrorism, violence, civil wars, diseases and environmental destruction are becoming globalized. Capital, technology and advanced skills dominate the more reality dispensable factors: unskilled labour and the environment. Cost reductions are carried out and labour and nature suffer. Globalization offers great opportunity for human advance—but only the stronger governance.

The globalization of production is weakening state-centric schemes for implementing economic, social and cultural rights, most dramatically in the wealthier countries of the Northern Hemisphere. It does not however seem to be creating viable alternative mechanisms. Semi-permanent unemployment, attributable in part to the development of increasingly global mechanisms of production and exchange, has already led to a modest shrinking of the welfare state in many countries in Western Europe.

In any case, the impact of globalization on economy, society and polity extends beyond external openness in respect of foreign trade, tariff levels, transnationalisation of production and capital controls. The existing attraction of globalization as well as international pressures, such as from the WTO, encourage domestic policy changes in an effort to bring about greater institutional convergence with the more advanced economies. These policy changes in turn, are likely to have additional impact on economy, society and polity.

Globalization is very uneven process, with unequal distribution of benefits and losses. This imbalance leads to polarization between the few countries and groups that gain, and the many countries and groups in society that lose out or are marginalized. Globalization, polarization, wealth concentration and marginalization are therefore linked through the same process. A World Bank study finds that the poorest 40 percent of people in developing countries have seen their incomes fall since liberalization began. The evidence is powerful and it discredits the claims of Western government ministers that trade liberalization lessens poverty. The rapid growth of the global economy in recent decades is perhaps most clearly shown by the fact that in 1970 the total number of Transnational Corporations (TNCs) was about 700, but grew by 1998 to at least 53,607 TNCs that were contracted with at least 448,917 foreign subsidiaries. The six largest corporations in the world (Exxon, General Motors, Ford, Mitsu, Daimler-Chrysler, and Mitsubishi) have combined revenues larger than the combined budgets of 64 nations that include 58 percent of the world's population (including India, Indonesia, Brazil, Russia, Pakistan, Bangladesh, Nigeria, and Mexico). Only seven nations have budgets larger than Ford, Exxon or General Motors: namely, France, the United Kingdom, Italy, China, Japan, Germany, and the United States. Size of individual corporations in comparison to nations is impressive. However, their growing influence based on their growing number makes them even more powerful.

The world has become more polarized, with the gulf between the poor and rich of the world widening in recent years. From 1970 to 2000, the share of the poorest 20 percent rose from 70 percent to 85 per cent. Uneven globalization is bringing not only integration but also fragmentation, dividing communities and nations. In the aftermath of liberalization, manufacturing by license has given way to competitive manufacturing. Free trade is merely the global manifestation of the division of labor. The forces of global integration and technological advance can and must be harnessed to serve the interests of poor people. In 2000, of the world 6 billion people, 2.8 billion live on less than $2 a day and 1.2 billion on less than $1 a day. Six infants of every 100 do not see their first birthday, and 8 do not survive to their fifth. Of those who do reach school age, 9 boys in 100 and 14 girls do not go to primary school. These conceal extra-ordinary diversity and variations.

Globalization has divided the world into several factions that may be called Davos, Seatlle, Moscow, Beijing, Tehran and Okinawa factions. The Davos faction includes some 1000 state and corporate elites that annually meet at Davos, Switzerland, to chart the course of globalization. It represents the interests of the Global 1000 largest TNCs and OECD group of rich nations. The Seatle Faction consists of those in the advanced capitalist countries protesting against World Trade Organization in Seatle last year, because their lives have been dislocated by globalization. The Moscow Faction is composed of those countries that by reason of their own failures or discrimination are being left out of the globalization bandwagon. The Beijing faction consists of those countries that have more or less successfully jumped on the bandwagon in the hope of benefiting from its fruits. As a Crossroad of Japanese, Chinese, Southeast Asian, and Western civilizations, the Tehran Faction could be interpreted to include the Islamic militant movement protesting against the economic, political and cultural domination of a western world order. The most eloquent spokesperson for its views happens to be but a secular Christian Palestinian nationalist, Edward said.

Globalization is thus affecting different categories of countries differently. This process can broadly be categorized as follows: growth and expansion in the few leading or fully participating countries; moderate and fluctuating growth in some countries attempting to fit into the globalization/liberalization framework; and marginalization or deterioration experienced by many countries unable to get out of acute problems such as low commodity prices and debt, unable to benefit from export opportunities. The UNCTAD report also warns of the risks, stating "the process of globalization and liberalization can also give rise to a number of potential negative consequences and challenges to development". It gives details of the following three problems: lose of policy autonomy (the range of policy instruments available to developing countries has narrowed as a result of economic liberalization policies and stringent multilateral disciplines); financial openness and the risk of sentiments of external investor; and the phenomenon of marginalization (in which some developing countries, specially LDCs, are unable to benefit from or meaningfully participate in globalization due to structural supply-side weakness and debt.)

The uneven and unequal nature of the present globalization process is manifested in the fast-growing gap between the world's rich and poor people and between developed and developing countries, and in the large differences among nations in the distribution of gains and losses.

A large number of people in the developed and developing nation have strong reservations about the benefits of globalization to the poor nations and they have shown their resentment through protests on various. In advance of Seattle meeting, more than 1200 NGOs from nearly a hundred countries—from environmentalists to labour unions, Third World development groups to consumer organizations-signed a 'stop the WTO round' petition. The international trading system, said the petitioners, is 'inequitable, untransparent and in conflict with national and international regimes that promote high environment and development standards'. They proposed a fundamental review of the system, and the development of 'an alternative, humane and sustainable international system of trade and investment relations'. And they urged governments to 'move away from the habit of shaping their international trade policies around offensive interests of large Transnational Corporations'. The recent meeting of WTO in France was also protested by the large number of people.

INDIA AND LIBERALIZATION

The aim of structural reform programme was to attain a higher rate of growth on sustainable basis through efficiency and productivity originating from relaxation of government controls over production, investment and prices in the domestic economy and progressively opening up of the Indian economy to foreign trade, capital and technology. The structural reform measures constitute the core of the economic liberalization.

Liberalization in India has two dimensions—internal and external. The domestic liberalization policy encompasses all facets of the Indian economy. However, thrust areas are industry, public enterprises, taxation, financial and infrastructure sectors.

The industrial sector has witnessed far-reaching reforms. The New Industrial Policy, 1991 abolished compulsory licensing for all except a few industries. The reform has enabled the taking out of the licensing system for more than 90 percent of the industrial sector. In case of existing units all major expansions are exempted from licensing. The existing and new units are provided a new broad banding facility with a view to enabling them to produce any article without an additional investment.

In the area of public enterprises five major reforms have been introduced. First, monopoly of the state sector has been drastically reduced from seventeen to four. That is, thirteen industries have been opened to private sector, which was hitherto monopoly of the state sector. This is known as disguised privatization. Within existing public enterprises, sweeping changes favouring increasing role of market forces are in progress. These include performance improvement through a memorandum of understanding (MOU) system, referring of sick enterprises to the Board for industrial and Financial Reconstruction (BIFR) for the formulation of revival /rehabilitation schemes or closure and enhanced autonomy to select public enterprises for enabling them to become global and domestic players.

Privatization has not been explicitly referred to in the NIP, 1991. Initially, the word privatization, it seems has been avoided partly due to political considerations. In the first budget (1991-92) immediately after the announcement of NIP, 1991, limited selling of government equity under the name of disinvestments policies was mentioned. The selling of government equity below 50 percent continued till late nineties. It is during October 1999 budget that a full-fledged privatization policy was announced. Under privatization policy, 13 public enterprises and 21 hotels owned by the government have already been privatized.

Based on the recommendations of Chelliah Committee and Raikhi Committee tax reforms comprise of moderate rate of taxation, broadening the tax base, simplification in compliance and extension of modified value added tax (MODVAT) to other areas.

Financial sector reforms consist of slashing of Statutory Liquidity Ratio (SLR) and thus increasing the availability of funds with banks, allowing private banks to expand, encouraging new entrants, simplification and rationalization of the interest rate structure. The Government has also opened insurance sector to private sector. The capital market is undergoing similar reforms.

The infrastructure sectors particularly telecommunication, power and roads which were traditionally monopolies have also been opened to the private sector.

External liberalization (i.e. globalization) in India has covered areas such as trade, foreign exchange, capital and technology. The major initiatives include current account convertibility of rupee, allowing exchange rate of rupee to be determined by the market forces in foreign exchange markets, abolition of import through licensing except for consumer goods, drastic reduction in import duties overtime, automatic approval of Reserve Bank of India for foreign equity in select high priority industries, the provision of automatic approval for technology agreements in select high priority industries. In addition, Foreign Institutional Investors (FIIs) registered with RBI are permitted to operate in the capital market. Large number of incentives are provided to Non-Resident Indians (NRIs) and Overseas Corporate Bodies (OCB) to invest in India. Indian firms are also allowed to raise capital from International market through Global Depository Receipts (GDRs) and Foreign Currency Convertible Bonds (FCCBs).

Scarcity of income distribution data, obviously, makes it very difficult to arrive at precise assessment of the impact of Globalization on income inequalities, but it is clear that even after nearly one decade of advent of Globalization in India a vast gulf exists between the different income-earners with, as per *World Development Report*, 1999, top 20% of the population accounting for 39.3% of the total income while share of the bottom 20% was only 9.2%.

The point about retailing the foregoing data about persistence of individual-level poverty is that it gives rise to doubts about the positive pay-offs of Globalization as far as the regional inequalities also are concerned. While data sets about income inequalities at individual or percentile and decline levels are relatively scarce, a number of regional or inter-state inequalities data-sets have been generated making it possible to assess the impact of Globalization on a real disparities.

According to Economic Times Research, the annual data show that over the period 1996 to 2000, 38 per cent of the companies declared losses at the net level in 2000 as compared to 16 per cent in 1996. In the period of economic reforms does the loss making companies whose percentage has increased represent the cost of liberalization.

The cost of economic reforms is also reflected in the number of cases with the Board for Industrial and Financial Reconstruction (BIFR). BIFR till the year 1998 has compiled figures about sick companies on the edge of closure. A total net worth of Rs. 17,815.56 cr. Has been wiped out two and half times over by accumulated losses amounting to Rs. 7,159.54 cr. Over 2,454 units across 19 industries are affecting around 15 lakh workers. The extent of human disaster is particularly acute in industries like textiles, metallurgy and jute etc.

The various Rounds of Surveys conducted by the National Sample Survey Organization (NSSO) reveal that the average annual growth rate of overall employment (in both the organized and unorganized sectors) was 2.73 percent annum in the period 1972-73 to 1977-78 but declined to 1.54 per cent per annum in 1983 to 1987-88 to 1993-94. As per the 55th Round (July 1999-June 2000) of the Survey on employment conducted by the NSSO overall employment grew by about 1 per cent per annum during 1993 = 94 to 1999-2000. Employment in absolute numbers has risen from 303 million on 1983 to 374 million in 1994 (2.04 per cent) and to 397 million in 2000 (0.98 percent). The labor force participation rate deceleration in the growth of the labor force from 2.29 per cent per annum in 1987-88 to 1993-94, to 1.03 per cent per annum in the period 1993-94 to 1999-2000.

A more detailed scrutiny of the inter-state variations in the growth-pattern (UNDP, 1999) shows that two states with high per capita income in 1980-91 viz. Punjab and Haryana lost momentum in the nineties while Maharashtra and Gujarat overshot them indicating that during the Globalization era the Green Revolution lost steam while industry-based growth of Maharashtra and Gujarat was gathering speed. In case (and the probabilities of this being the case are high) economic momentum of Punjab and Haryana declines further the inequalities between the different states of the Indian federal system would certainly be aggravated significantly. In more specific terms, states like Tamilnadu, Kerala, West Bengal, Madhya Pradesh, Andhra Pradesh and Karnataka would continue to stay at their current GNP ranks while Panjab and Haryana would decline and Guajrat and Maharashtra forge ahead while Uttar Pradesh, Bihar and Orissa would continue to remain at the bottom unless those associated with "public governance" address this issue of persisting areal imbalances directly rather than letting the markets (read: MNCs) adopt their basic policy of "Betting upon the strong."

Thus, a worrisome aspect of the impact of Globalization upon the state economies is revealed by the fact that there are not only wide-ranging areal differentials in terms of decline of poverty in India but the "Green Revolution" states are finding it difficult to sustain their (low) poverty-shares. While Punjab and Haryana had, till recently taken giant strides in poverty reduction, but, Haryana has already begun to slip with its BPL share in population rising from 0.92% in 1983-84 to 1.83% in 1987-88 and then dipping but still remaining higher at 1.37% in 1993-94 than 1983-84. More recent Planning Commission data updated to 1999-2000 has shown that Haryana has regained its `quit poverty' momentum but, in a paper prepared as recently as October 2001, Jeffery Sachs, Anupam Bajpai and Annabhi Ramiah have noted that following the Green Revolution high growth occurred in Punjab and Haryana and also, to a lesser extent, in other adjacent states of Rajasthan, Gujarat and Maharashtra, but populous eastern states like U.P. and Bihar failed to take advantage of Green Revolution and this factor can be regarded a cause of "divergence" or enhancement in inter-state inequalities during the Globalization process in India.

One of most visible manifestations of what one might call a "Globalization failure" pertains to the strategic front of inequalities, a failure which assumes great poignancy in the case of ROI since elimination of inequalities, individual as well as areal, was one of the most prominent items on the manifesto of its long "freedom struggle"; the Indian National Congress, which enjoyed pre-eminent dominance for the first four decades of the short ROI history and which is even now in control of as many as 14 states spread in all corners of its vast territory, is also committed to this goal making monitoring of the economic dispersion of the gains (and losses) of Globalization in terms of the territorial contours of the Indian political system an urgent necessity as the political parties which evolve the "correct" policies of public governance on this score is likely to gain better territorial acceptability.

Even the father of the nation Mahatma Gandhi, who was fond of and always emphasized for 'Swadeshi' set tone of globalization as early as in *Young India*, June 1, 1921, when he said that "*I do not want my house to be walled in an all sides and my window to be stuffed. I want the cultures of all lands to be blown about my house as freely as possible. But I refuse to be blown off my feet.*"

Mr. Manmohan Singh advocated greater interaction with the world and warned that "*if our economy is not equipped to absorb, assimilate, and to adopt this technical change which is taking place, all over the world, I think we will be marginalized. Many developing economies are already being marginalized in the new global economic system that has emerged.*"

If the prevailing political and administrative environment continues, the possibility of recurring crises in the near future is not ruled out. The symptoms have already started appearing. Sluggishness in exports in spite of gradual devaluation of rupee via open market, increasing fiscal deficit, downgrading in international credit rating of India, bearish trend in the stock market, non-preparedness of the Indian people particularly the elite to pay more taxes, etc., are signaling towards another crisis. Liberalization, privatization and globalization policies seem irreversible in India. India should strive to manage these mega trends to the best of its advantages.

SUMMING UP

Human Development Report champions the agenda of the world's weak, those marginalized by globalization, and calls for a much bolder agenda of global and national reforms to achieve globalization with a human face. It cautions that globalization is too important to be left as unmanaged as it is at present, because it has the capacity to do extraordinary harm as well as good.

Liberalization, privatization and globalization policies have been exercising considerable influence on people and government. In developing countries like India, governance has responded both slowly and unevenly to economic liberalization. It is mainly due to the fact that liberalization policy in India has not evolved indigenously through the participation of political, bureaucratic and other institutions of governance. The liberalization policy is mainly adopted under the influence of World Bank-IMF combine. In case of India the institutions of economic governance have responded very quickly to economic liberalization. The post liberalization phase has witnessed amendments in many economic laws as well as introduction of economic laws to deal with changed environment.

Supremacy of economic institutions particularly finance ministry accompanied by erosion in the role of Planning Commission in Economic Policy-making is another outcome of economic liberalization. Setting of new institutions such as Ministry of Disinvestments, Disinvestments Commission, Expenditure commission and regulatory authorities in the field of telecom, power and insurance have increased the jurisdiction of economic administration in the Indian economy. Very fast growth of economic administration in response to liberalization, however, has not succeeded in achieving its goals such as a higher rate of growth on sustainable basis accompanied by improved efficiency and productivity in the Indian economy.

Further, these initiatives have covered mainly those services and areas, which cater to the elite. The areas of social concern such as poverty, unemployment, regional disparities and sectoral imbalance which have borne the burnt of liberalization policy have been kept out of these initiatives. This combination of coverage and neglect, if continued on the one hand would help the elite to consolidate its advantaged position and become partner of the ruling coalition of politicians and bureaucrats. On the other hand it would alienate further the disadvantageous groups, sectors and regions from the mainstream.

Competitive markets may be the best guarantee of efficiency, but not necessarily of equity. Liberalization and privatization can be a step to competitive markets-but not a guarantee of them, and markets are neither the first nor the last word in human development. Many activities and goods that are critical to human development are provided outside the market—but these are being squeezed by the pressures of global competition. There is a fiscal squeeze on public goods, a times squeeze on care activities and an incentive squeeze on the environment.

In order to widen their policy options in the future and to strengthen their bargaining power, developing countries have to organize themselves to strive for a more democratic global system.

Grater collaboration among regional institutions of the South (for example, ASEAN, SAARC, SADC, Mercosur, Caricom, etc.) especially in sharing of information and coordination of policies and positions, would be beneficial.

The developing countries should have more rights of participation in decision-making processes in the IMF, World Bank and WTO, which should also be made more accountable to the public and to the local and poor communities.

In the 21st century, much more focus has to be placed on changing economic policies and behavior in order that the patterns of consumption and production can be made environmentally sound. What need to be discussed is not only the development model of the South but much more the economic model of the North and of course to international economic order.

There is also a need to strive for governance at a national level that combines economic development, environmental concern and social justice. In both North and South, the wide disparities in wealth and income within countries have to be narrowed. In a situation of improved equity, it would be more possible to plan and implement strategies of economic adjustment to ecological and social goals.

As globalization becomes the new mantra of the powerful on the planet with the unholy Trinity—the IMF, the World Bank, and the WTO–claming that it will solve all the economic problems of the world (including poverty and deprivation), it is time for the countries of Asia, Africa and South America to pause, take stock and critically appraise the whole process, examining the true and only options available to them.

The developing countries must be provided with a range of options regarding when, how and to what extent they should open their economics. For this, they must press their case in international forums and institutions where decisions on the global economy are made. Failure to do so would mean that they are subjected interminably to policies that further development prospects and options as well.

The developing countries should have more rights of participation in decision-making process in the IMF, World Bank and WTO, which should also be made more accountable to the public and to the local and poor.

There is also a need to strive for governance at a national level that combines economic development, environmental concerns and social justice. In both North and South, the wide disparities in wealth and income within countries have to be narrowed. In a situation of improved equity, it would be more possible to plan and implement strategies of economic adjustment to ecological and social goals.

We are aboard a train, which is gathering speed, racing down a track on which there are an unknown number of switches leading to unknown destinations. No single scientist is in the engine cab and there may be demons at the switch. Most of the societies are in the caboose looking backward.

References

Alternative Economic Survey, 2000-01, New Delhi, Alternative Survey Group, 2001.

A.S. Bhalla (Ed.), *Globalization, Growth and Marginalization*, London, Macmillan Press Ltd., 1998.

Beyer, P. (1994), *Religion and Globalization*, London, Sage.

B. Ramesh Babu (Ed.), *Globalization and the South Asian State*, New Delhi, South Asian Publishers, 1998.

B.R. Nayar, *Globalization and Nationalism: The Changing Balance in India's Economic Policy, 1950-2000*, New Delhi, Sage Publications, 2001.

Dieter Bos, *Privatisation: A Theoretical Treatment*, Oxford: Clarendon Press, 1991.

Louis De Allesi, "The Economics of Property Rights: A Review of the Evidence", *Research in Law and Economics*, Vol. 2, 1980.

Peter Aucoin, *The New Public Management: Canada in Comparative Perspective*, Montreal, Canada: Institute for Research on Public Policy, 1995.

Prahlad, K. Basu *et al.*, *Governance and Government: Emerging Scenarios in the 21st Century* (Report for FCPC), New Delhi, 1996.

Robert, J. Holton, *Globalization and the Nation-State*, London, Macmillan Press Ltd., 1998.

V.S. Sheth (Ed.), *Globalization and Interdependence: Africa and India*, Mumbai, Allied Publishers Ltd., 2000.

Kurian, N.J., "Widening Regional Disparities in India: Some Indicators", *Economic and Political Weekly*, February, 12, 2000:538-50.

Dollar, David, *Globalization, Inequality and Poverty Since 1980*, Washington, D.C. World Bank, Mimeo, 2001.

World Bank, *World Development Report*, Washington, D.C., World Bank, 2001.

Ahluwalia, M.S., *"The Economic Performance of The States in The Post-Reform Period"* in Rakesh Mohan (Ed.) Facets of The Indian Economy, New Delhi, OUP, 2002.

Adarsh, Kishore, "*Globalization, Living Standards and Equity: Recent Progress and Continuing Challenges: National Experience—India*", Paper presented at the Workshop for G-20 Members, Sydney, May 26-28, 2002. Mimeo.

UNDP, 1999, *Diversity and Disparities in Human Development: Key Challenges for India*, New Delhi.

Eisenstadt, S.N., *Modernization: Protest and Change*, Delhi, Prentice Hall, 1969.

Fukuyama, F., *The End of History and the Last Man*, New York, Free Press, 1992.

Hirst, P.Q. and Thompson, G., *Globalization in Question*, London, Cambridge, 1996.

Magdoff, Harry (1992), *Globalization: To What End?*, New York, Monthly Review Press, 1992.

Rostow, W.W., *The Stages of Economic Growth: A Non-Communist Manifesto*, London, Cambridge University Press, 1960.

2

Globalization and Indian Economy

Towards Understanding Changing Agriculture

SURINDER K. SHUKLA

This paper is an attempt towards understanding the changing agriculture in the context of India and more especially in the state of Punjab. In this context there is an attempt to reflect on certain parameters of the evolved economic situation in India—from politics of macroeconomic policy in general to failing agriculture and marginalization of peasantry at the regional level. It is important to note that the economic policy is not free from political calculations and choice thereby making it difficult to adopt Gandhian alternative in the changing agricultural scenario. Yet Gandhian perspective appeals to the mind and enjoins the human beings to exercise this choice even in the fast changing world economy scenario. This paper is divided into three parts:

Part I dwells on a brief overview of globalization,
Part II deals with the Gandhian approach, more especially the trusteeship theory, and
Part III links up the former two parts with Indian Economy in general and at state-level

I. GLOBALIZATION IN THE HISTORICAL PERSPECTIVE

At the end of twentieth century, as the sense of transformation grew, three kinds of narratives achieved wide currency. The accounts of these three narratives overlapped and they are partially related to each other.

(1) First idea was that of post-modernity.
(2) Second idea was that of post-Cold-war World.
(3) Third idea was that of globalization.

1. *Post-modernity*—At the core was the denial of the certainties of the modern world. Post-modernism challenged all traditional models of understanding. As a result, intimate links of post modernity to modernity were proposed.
2. *Second idea was that of a post-Cold War World*—This reflected the apparently dramatic significance of changes in international politics. At the centre of post-Cold War narratives was the idea that winding down political and military conflict between blocs world involve fundamental transformations of political—and hence perhaps social and cultural—relations in general.
3. *The third idea, of course, was globalization*—This emphasized technical, economic and cultural transformations that were having impact on even boundaries of nation-states. This narrative was often presented as a new certainty. Its proponents suggested that, indeed, it reflected unstoppable forces, Jaques Derrida (1997) as a result of questioning, agreed that the political phenomena to which he was referring was what is conventionally called globalization.

Post-modernity and globalization both began to emerge as serious concepts of change in the 1970s. This was the decade of the détente, the period in which Cold War rivalries appeared to have relaxed, yet the crisis of post-war boom produced great global economic instability and there was a widespread sense of dissolution of traditional cultural and social relations.

In the 1970s, however, although there was widespread sense of crisis and dissolution after the relative stability of earlier post-war decades, there was not yet a strong feeling of transition. Indeed, the Second Cold War of the early 1980s reinforced awareness of a definite world structure, after the loosening of the previous decade. It was only when this faded, in the middle of 1980s, that the sense of transition came into its own. It is from the point onwards that we can trace the definite influence of narrative of change.

Today we are living at the threshold of new global civilization. As the whole world is an indivisible whole, its parts are interrelated and interdependent so that what happens to one part ultimately affects the whole. Progress in one cannot succeed unless it ultimately spells progress for the whole.

Globalization is essentially a process of unification, unity, convergence and uniformity. This, indeed, is a new phenomenon, but the process of unification of people coming together, of ideas merging with one another, has been going on from time immemorial. Evolution from a diversified world to a global village was made possible with help of technological breakthrough, dramatic and drastic reduction of distances, universalisation of electronic media and other powerful means of communication.

As a global village or as a network system, everyone in the four corners of the world is expected to follow the global stereotypes, which for the most one dictated or circulated by the developed countries. The current trend towards globalization is estimated to create the necessary infrastructure for individual and nations to interact with each other and mutually benefit from such a process. A globalised world is one in which political, economic, cultural and social events become more and more multidirectional yet interconnected, and also one in which they have more impact.

Globalisation is taking place at all levels—it is integrating economies, changing the face of families universalizing the nation of human rights, environment, and education and changing the role of governments. It is about restructuring the society in a fundamental manner.

But in this restructuring game there are some winners and some losers. For the winners, there is much that is attractive about the prospect of world of constant travel and multimedia communication in a networked global village and global marketplace. For the losers it is a whole of global village in which the gap between the powerful and powerless, rich and poor, privileged and underprivileged continues to widen.

II. GANDHIAN APPROACH

Gandhi was a many sided personality. He was at once a saint and politician, an educationist and a journalist, a humanist and a social reformer. This little man, so frail in appearance was a giant among men, measured by the greatness of his soul. His profound sincerity and spirit, his freedom from hatred and his mastery over himself, his human-friendly, all embracing charity, his strong conviction which he shared with great ones of history—and which he successfully put to test in many dramatic situations—show the impact of religion on life. The impact of eternal values on the shifting problems of the present world need to be analyzed in the Gandhian paradigm.

Gandhi looked at politics not as a struggle for power and wealth, but a persistent and continuous effort to enable the submerged millions to attain good life, to raise the quality of human beings, to trans them for freedom and fellowship for spiritual depth and social harmony. In fact, Gandhi saw a very close relationship between religion and politics. He condemned politics which was bereft of religion on the ground that it makes a man corrupt.

For our relevance, let us visualize Gandhi's views on ends and means. He rejected Machiavelli, Hitler, etc. who celebrated power by saying that 'ends justify the means'. Gandhi was against this concept and he held diametrically opposite views and that is, that it was neither possible nor desirable to detach ends from means. If means are wrong, how can ends be good he logically argued? If you sow neem plant (botanical name: azadirachita indica) which has bitter tasting leaves, you cannot expect mangoes (botanical name: mangifera indica) having sweet and juicy fruit from the plant. The logic is simple.

Referring to Gandhi's views on Trusteeship we can see that he had an alternative even in the times in which he lived. The relevance of his alternative methods has become a subject of study at the other universities, including the famous American University Harvard. Gandhi emphasized the ideal of a simple life and insisted that a person should only possess what is absolutely essential for his day-to-day life and attainment of self-realization. He was against the unnecessary accumulation of wealth and goods. Gandhi's trusteeship theory was designed to point a way towards the painless extinct of capital and property that were a source of inequality and consequent violence and exploitation in social relations. Gandhi recognized that acquisitions and ownership property in any form go with the excessive of certain functions and qualities which must not be used for selfish ends, but for the good of community. He thought that it was possible to inspire capitalist (or the man of property) to use, for the good of the society, his intelligence and talents that are responsible for the acquisition and ownership of capital and property. Capital is the result of the labour and cooperative efforts of the society.

Therefore, Gandhi argued, that the wealth producing power embodied in capital must be held in trust for the good of community, nor for acquiring power over often men, and using it for anti-social ends or misusing it in other ways.

'Let the society benefit by the power that capital creates and by the intelligence that the capitalists possess and the workers lack'. Trusteeship is desired from the basic Gandhian concepts of non-violence, swaraj and equality which are all interlinked with one another. He wrote: 'A society based on non-violence cannot mature any other ideal'. Further, 'the more we are committed to achieve the goals of equal distribution the more we will lay the foundation of a non-violent society'.

Gandhi said rich should be made to feel that they have no justification for keeping surplus wealth with them. He summed up his concept of trusteeship thus in six principles–

(1) Trusteeship provides a means of transforming the present capitalist order of society into equalitarian one; it gives the present owning class a chance of reforming itself. It is based on the faith that human nature is not beyond redemption.

(2) It does not recognize any right of private ownership of property except as it may be permitted by society for its own welfare.

(3) It does not exclude legislative regulation of ownership and use of wealth.

(4) Thus, under state-regulated trusteeship, on individual will not be free to hold wealth in disregard of the interest of society.

(5) Just as it is proposed to fix a decent minimum living wage, even to a limit should be fixed for the maximum income that could be allowed to any person in society.
The difference between minimum and maximum must be reasonable and equitable and variable from time to time. (I draw your attention that the present globalization does not allow this and this is the crux of the problem).

(6) Under Gandhian economic order the character of production will be determined by social necessity and not by present greed.

Though trusteeship does not preclude state action and legislative steps to bring it into existence the method or approach will largely remain one of persuasion, non-violence and mass satyagraha.

This is a powerful alternative based on logic and appeals to the spiritual aspect of human life. This alternative is important and assumes special significance in present times that are drive by corporate governance and where stress levels are indeed very high.

III

The third part of my paper looks at present Indian economy in the contest of globalization and makes a presentation of Gandhian alternative is assimilated in the land where he was born.

Indian economy is viewed from various points of view and is considered: Underdeveloped, developing, dualistic and mixed. Contributing to underdeveloped economy is the factor of 64% of population being dependent on agriculture. And which there is nothing wrong with being agricultural the problem lies with the techniques of production that are not advanced in the agricultural sector all thought they sustain 2/3rd of the population.

On the other hand, the industry sector has become pervaded by modern techniques of production, but they are less advanced than those in use in the developed economies.

- 38% of population lives below poverty line. The problem of mass poverty is complementary to income inequalities.
- Private enterprise in India has failed to play a prominent role in development and there is one of the single major factor behind India's underdeveloped status.
- Scarce availability of capital is another major setback to the country's' development plans. Less than 40% of total resources are with the government channels while roughly 60% lies private sector. This is an alarming statistic and goes give one crude jolt. Referring to the Structural Aspect of Indian economy.
- A glance at statistics will reveal that the share of agriculture and allied sectors in India's economy has come down over the years. The industry sector's share of GDP (including mining, manufacturing, electricity supply and construction) has witnessed a rise since 1960s. It stood at 31% in 1996-97.

The service sector (including trade, hotel, transport, communication, finance, real estate, personal services contributed about 48% to the GDP (2000-01).

Referring to the Quantitative Aspect of Indian economy—a study of national income trend over past year from 1950-57 to 1993-94 it has grown 10 times. Though national income has not been rising at a steady pace, its rate of increase has been higher than the rate of population growth. So per capita consumption has seen some improvement and capital accumulation has been possible to some extent. Per capita income has shown a growing trend from Rs. 3687 in 1950-51 to Rs. 10,254 in 2000-01.

Progress in financial sector has been in terms of better money organization, capital markets and establishment of specialized industrial set-ups related to finance. The banking sector has witnessed growth in banking service mainly through commercial banks and cooperative credit societies.

Dualistic Nature

Indian economy reveals dualistic nature—it exhibits features of a modern economy as well as a traditional one. While traditional sector is associated with agriculture or small industries, and has variable technical production co-efficient and labour-intensive methods of production, the advanced sector has large industries fixed technical coefficient production and capital-intensive methods of production.

In agricultural and handicrafts sectors, there has been slow technological progress but in the industrial sector, technologic development is noticeable.

Mixed Economy

Another feature of Indian economy has been 'mixed economy'—a special kind of planned economic that was adopted by India at the behest of Prime Minister Jawaharlal Nehru, soon after independence. Mixed economy is an economic system in which both the state and private sector direct economy, reflecting characteristics of both market economies and planned economies. Most mixed economies can be described as market economies with strong regulatory oversight, in addition to having a variety of government-sponsored aspects.

The basic plan of the mixed economy is that the means of production are mainly under private ownership; that markets remain the dominant form of economic coordination; and that profit-seeking enterprises and the accumulation of capital would remain the fundamental driving force behind economic activity. However, the government would wield considerable indirect influence over the economy through fiscal and monetary policies designed to counteract economic downturns and capitalism's tendency toward financial crises and unemployment, along with playing a role in interventions that promote social welfare.

There is not one single definition for a mixed economy, but the definitions always involve a degree of private economic freedom mixed with a degree of government regulation of markets. The relative strength or weakness of each component in the national economy can vary.

As an economic ideal, mixed economies are supported by people of various political persuasions, typically centre-left and centre-right.

Recent Changes

Since 1991, the Government of India has introduced new policies arrived at bringing about a qualitative change in the economy by effecting structural adjustments in the economy. Some of the features are:

- A market-oriented economy (see endnote 1 and 2 for an explanation of 'market' and 'characteristics of market') is emerging with increase in competition as a result of doing away with regulations, contracts and government restriction that had checked the growth of private sector in the past. Liberalization of economy has largely released imports and exports from government imposed restrictions.
- Reductions in custom duty rates and encouragement to foreign investment have placed Indian economy in live with those of other countries.
- While planning has not been discarded, it has become more indicative than before setting directions for economy rather than rigid targets forms the basic root of planning now. State intervention is more market-oriented.

Having said this let us now go back to what we said in earlier part, Part I of this presentation. The rules are set by developed states and globalization and liberalization has not succeeded in alienating poverty. Instead it has resulted in producing a small thin layer of ultra-rich elites—thereby increasing the gap between rich and poor. This gap is at two levels—one within the nation and second among nations.

Farmer Losses and Government Action

Perturbed over the unabated suicides in the country side the Punjab Government according to affidavit filed in Punjab and Haryana High Court informed that Department of Agriculture has requisitioned the services of 44 trained medical persons and 20 psychiatrists from state health department to council farmers and help them in stemming their suicidal tendencies (*Times of India*, 25 May 2009, p. 1).

Certain relief checks disbursed by the state government however remained un-encashed (Checks in Panipat) since no money was there in the government coffers. Follow of action by the government of Haryana helped assuage the situation to some extent (*Times of India*, 20 June 2007). Earlier 100 farmers of Adiyana, Sera and Kavi villages (under Mata Ulda Block) who were given checks to the tune of 37 lakhs in April 2007 failed to encash their checks distributed by Mata Ulda Naib Tehsildar as the Punjab National Bank did not hold enough money.

Agro-Tech Fair 2006

The government has tried to support small farmers under contract farming in the 11th Plan. At the Agro-Tech Fair, 2006 foreign investors showed interest in Indian Agro Industries. Pakistani farmers indicated a tremendous opportunity for Indian Agro Service in Pakistan. Netherlands envoy in India stressing on the state of art cargo facilities focused on the fact that Netherlands is the third largest investor in India. Netherlands ambassador, Eric F. Chic Niehe said (*Hindustan Times*, 3 December 2006) that they needed the support of India which has a huge market as well as export products that can be exported to Netherlands. He also called for co-operation in food processing sector.

Plight of Farmers: Help Forthcoming

In times of farmer's suicides some respite seems to be in the offing. BJP Kisan Morcha (see end note 3) has sought separate budget for agri sector. (Viney Sharma, *The Economic Times*, 25 April 2011, p. 3). This is necessary as the farmer on one front is battling natural calamities, while at the other front he is a victim of poor adminstration. Heavy debts on farmers are due to high input cost and low returns coupled by anti-farmer policies. In such a scenario separate budget for agri sector holds a special significance.

Besides this there are commercial ventures like Bharti-Walmart who are beginning to think along lines that could bring respite to the hapless farmers. The strategic vision of Bharti-Walmart has led to an investment of 30 million dollars in Punjab in Amritsar, Zirakpur, Jalandhar and now Ludhiana. Referring to Punjab as a model state in execution of Direct Farm Programme the Bharti-Walmart wants to replicate its experience across the country. To strengthen its supply chain they aim at roping in more than 4000 farmers in Punjab in the next five years. Nationwide Bharti-Walmart intends to rope in 35000 farmers by 2015 (Viney Sharma, *The Economic Times*, 6 May 2011, p. 2).

Summing Up

If on the one hand, we have crossed trillion $ economy mark, we yet face the painful reality of farmer suicides throughout the country. I will give statistics of the state of Punjab. The voluntary Health Association of Punjab in collaboration with Human Rights Law Network with the help of 8 major farmer organizations in seven districts of Punjab (2006) reveals that the average number of suicides per village is 11 and the range extends from 5 to 74 (Kalka village in Sangrur district has the highest number of suicide cases).

Of the analyzed cases 21.48% were committed in 1990-95, 33.14% in 1996-2000 and 45.38% in 2001-06 showing a consistently rising trend, which is alarming.

Largest no. of suicides were repeated in

Sangrur	1010, followed by
Bhatinda	540
Moga	434
Ferozepur	68
Muktsar	58
Faridkot	25

There are several villages where 2 or more members of the same family have committed suicides.

In 2/3rd cases main earning member has committed suicide—then widows need that financial help and loan waiver.

Empirical studies have shown that as compared to rest of the households, the suicide households have:

(a) a much higher level of total debt.

(b) a much higher dependence on traders and money lenders. and

(c) a higher proportion of debt for non-productive purposes such as social ceremonies, marriages, illness, etc.

In this context, the relevance of Gandhian approach, as an alternative is evident as being neither euphoric but nor does it lead to suicide also. Its goals are peace and self-realization. State governments are beginning to start programmes that help assuage the condition of the hapless farmer. In this connection it may be mentioned that the Punjab Government is considering to introduce pension scheme for the farmers across the state. The scheme is based on the lines of the National Pension Scheme where a fixed amount could be paid by the farmers and an equal amount contributed by the state government.

END NOTES

1. Market
   The market is an important ingredient of the civil society. The classical economists are of the view that a mature civil society depicts three features: individualism, property and the market. These three features of the civil society are also the fundamental principles of any liberal society. Adam Smith (1723-90), a classical economist, after analyzing commercial society's class structure, concludes that the market is the only institution in the society, which can balance various conflicting and competing interests, and also develop cooperation and interdependence among various individuals. According to Smith, the market should be almost, absolutely free to function in the society (Chandhoke, 1979:103, 105). According to C.B. Macpherson, "Human society is essentially a series of market relations." So Macpherson also confirms, that the market is a universal and comprehensive phenomenon (Macpherson, 1962:270). Market is an economic institution which promotes exchange of commodities among the participants *vis-à-vis* balances the market forces: demand and supply to fulfil the needs of human beings. But the liberal's argument, regarding the market, based on philosophical considerations as the market, allocates rewards and resources among the participants without taking into account their personal connections. It provide benefits in proportion to one's contribution in the market. So market is the ultimate dispenser of justice, as Adam Smith observes that the state acts as a representative of private interests. State's intervention also damages the creativity of economic actors. When an individual contributes to the society, he also has the right over the product of his creativity.
   Market is a social mechanism to promote exchange among the economic actors, where they interact with each other on the basis of liberty and equality. These economic actors are stranger to each other before entering

or interacting in the market (Chandhoke, 1979: 87, 102-04). The market treats all human possessions such as land, capital and human being's energies, as commodities and products in the market. The prices of these possessions and products are set by the competition, between 'the buyers' and 'the sellers' in the market (Macpherson, 1962:54). Market sets the prices of the commodities, as is projected by P. Bardhan's observation "Markets are run on price based transactions" (Bardhan 2000:50). People enter in the market with an aim to sell something. The motive behind selling is that it will enable them to buy things which they intent to. By selling, they also get rid of things, which they don't need. 'Reason', works behind people's choice to buy and sell. Market is a place, for people, who have something to sell such as labour power, means of subsistence, etc. (Chandhoke, 1979:104). In the market, there is contract among the economic actors. These economic actors are equal partners in transactions and they have resources for exchange. In other words, contracts are among the people, who have property. It means that they are owner of tools of trade, means of production, such as land, capital, technology, and also controls labour (*Ibid.*, 101). Adam Smith, was in favour of self-regulating market and was against the constraints, upon economic activity. According to him, 'invisible hand' which is the self-interest of economic actor or seller, leads to the benefits of others also (Heywood, 2005 : 333). Each person enters in the market for power. Everyone in the market is to offer some power as a supplier or to acquire some power as a demander. Man's value is determined by the market because market determine the value of things. Market determines the prices of those things, which are offered and wanted. (Macpherson, 1962 39) For the successful operating of the market system, incentives are must for economic actors who contributes in market. Individual or economic actors in the market get incentives in accordance to his effort or contribution in the market. Market gives the right of unlimited individual appropriation for contributing in the market system according to contributor's worth. This right makes the man to do more effort for getting more appropriation and these efforts also leads to or results in more efficient productivity. The work force get wages and has to work on the terms set by the market. The work force is also provided aid from time to time to prevent resentment among them. The emergence of welfare state system, and organized labour, has improved the conditions of labour-force or work-force to great extent. The farmers, manufacturers and the merchants or traders have also the right of unlimited appropriation. The incentives provided by market are for contributing in the market. Therefore, market does not permit any other criteria for the man that the market is to give him according to his worth. But the critics of the market system criticize it, because market does not compensate the economic actors, who get fail in the market. This system also results in alienation according to critics of the market. (Macpherson, 1975:28- 29).

2. *Characteristics of Market* : The market is an economic institution, which can be characterized as follows (Chandhoke, 1979: 106, 105). 1. Market is based on individualism and let individual to pursue his own interest

through competition. 2. There is exchange of the commodities among the economic agents in the market. 3. The individual gets proportionally, what is accrued to him according to his worth or contribution in the market. 4. Social cooperation develops in the market through reciprocal exchange among the economic agents in the market. 5. 'Specialization' and 'division of labour' in the market, facilitates productivity and economic efficiency. 6. The Market creates self-discipline and awareness among the rational economic agents about the needs of others. Therefore, there is competition in the market and individuals excel through the competition with other individuals. There is equality of opportunity to compete in the market, under the equal rules the market to everybody. This competition leads to good quality, optimum pricing and encouragement to work, because everybody gets what he deserves, what talent he has and what he has contributed to the market. Therefore, Market is the ultimate dispenser of justice. This is the area, where contracts among individuals promotes social bonds. Therefore, it is very important institution in the civil society, because it promote 'private gains' as well as 'social harmony'.

3. William Nanda Bissell in 'Making India Work' argues that poverty in India is a result of the government's criminally inept management. It is not inevitable. It is a tragedy that is simply due to failure of leadership. (p. xvi)

References

Sharma, Viney; Punjab to Introduce Pension Scheme for Farmers, *The Economic Times*, 18 May 2012, p. 3.

Rehabilitation Package in Suicide Prone Framers, *EPW*, 29 January 2011, p. 10.

Singh, Ajit (2011), India and the Punjab Economy, Book Review, *EPW*, Vol. XLV1, No. 5, p. 31.

Babu, Kaushik, 2011: India's Food Grain Policy: An Economic Theory Perspective, *EPW*, 29 January, pp. 37-45.

Sharma,Viney; BJP Kisan Morcha seeks Separate Budget for Agri Sector, *The Economic Times*, 25 April 2011, p. 3.

Sharma, Viney; Bharti Walmart to Replicate Punjab Model at Other Stores, *The Economic Times*, 6 May 2011, p. 2.

Farmer's Suicide and The Agrarian Crisis, *EPW*, September 23-29, 2006, p. 4009.

Trends in Agricultural Wages: 1964-65 to 1999-2000, *EPW*, September 2006, p. 4022.

Srivastava, Ravi and Richa Singh; Rural Wages During the 1990's: A Re-estimation, Vol. XLI, No. 38, 23 September 2006, p. 4053.

Farm Suicides Jolt Harvard Students, *The Times of India*, New Delhi, Chandigarh, 2 July 2009, p. 4.

Farm Suicides Not Linked To Caste Religion, Survey, *The Hindustan Times*, p. 6.

National Contract Farming Mission Mooted, *The Hindustan Times*, 3 December 2006, p. 4.

Indian Agro industries Can Make Inroads Into Pakistan, Agro-Tech Fair, 2006, *The Hindustan Times*, 3 December, p. 4.

Netherlands Envoy Invites Indian Companies, Agro-Tech Fair, 2006.
Bissell William Nanda (2009), Making India Work,_Viking, Penguin Books, New Delhi, Toronto, London.
Farmer Losses and Government Action, *The Times of India*, 29 June 2007, p. 1.
Punjab Government Attempts to Bail Out Indebted Peasantry, The Times of India, 2009, p. 9.
Government of India (2005), Economic Survey.
Government of Punjab (2002), Agricultural Production Pattern Adjustment Program for Productivity Growth: A Report.
Government of Punjab (2008), Statistical Abstract of Punjab.
Kaldor, Nicholas (1967), Strategic Factors in Economic Development, Cornell University Press, Ithaca, New York.
Singh, Lakhwinder, Inderjit Singh and Ranjit Singh Ghuman (2007) Changing Character of Rural Economy and Migrant Labour in Punjab, MRPA Paper No. 6420, pp. 1-16.
Ghuman, Ranjit Singh (2001), WTO and Indian Agriculture: Crisis and Challenges, A case Study of Punjab, *Man and Development*, Vol. 23, Number 2, pp. 67-98.
Bardhan, P. (2000), *Development and Change*, Delhi : Oxford University Press.
Basu, D.D. (2003), *Introduction to the Constitution of India*, LexisNexis Butterworths Wadhwa.
Chandoke, Neera (1979), *State and Civil Society: Explorations in Political Theory*, New Delhi: Sage Publications.
Gandhi, M.K., "Theory of Trusteeship", *Harijan*, 16 December 1939.
Gandhi, M.K., "Equal Distribution", *Harijan*, 25 August 1940.
Macpherson, C.B. (1962), *The Political Theory of Possessive Individualism. Hobbes to Locke*, UK : Oxford University Press.
Macpherson, C.B. (1975), *Democratic Theory: Essays in Retrieval*, Oxford : Clarendon Press.
Mckinlay, R.D. and Little, R. (1986), *Global Problems and World Order*, London: Francis Pinter.
Munshi, K.M. (1960), *Reconstruction of Society Through Trusteeship*.
Nayak, Pulin B. (1996), "The State and the Market", *Economic and Political Weekly*, Vol. XXXI, No. 4, January 6.
Oommen, M.A. (1996), "Searching for New Development Strategies : More Basic Issues Involved?", *Economic and Political Weekly*, Vol. XXXI, No. 1, January 6.
Paton, G.W. (2007), *A Textbook of Jurisprudence*, Oxford University Press, UK.
Sabine, G.H. and Thorson (1973), *A History of Political Theory*, Oxford and IBH Publications.
Schumpeter, J.A. (1966), *Capitalism, Socialism and Democracy*, London : George Allen and Unwin Ltd.
Sikdar, Sournyen (2004), *Contemporary Issues in Globalization : An Introduction to Theory and Policy in India*, New Delhi: Oxford University Press.
Thomas, Paul (1980), *Karl Marx and the Anarchists*, London: Routledge and Kegan Paul.

3

Fear and Hope

Gandhi's Cultural Response to Globalization

PREM ANAND MISHRA

No culture can live, if it attempts to be exclusive.
—(Gandhi, Harijan: 09-05-1936).

I think that nobody else can protect our culture for us. We have to protect it ourselves and can destroy it by our folly.
—(Gandhi, Harijan: 25-5-1947).

It [Indian culture] stands for synthesis of the different cultures..... This synthesis will naturally be of the Swadeshi type, where each culture is assured its legitimate place, and not of the American pattern, where one dominant culture absorbs the rest, and where the aim is not towards harmony, but towards an artificial and forced unity.
—(Gandhi, Young India: 17-11- 1920).

These three excerpts of Gandhi do *not* show his cultural response to globalization as we understand it today. The present form of globalization is a post-Gandhi phenomenon; nevertheless these extracts indicate how Gandhi would have, in some way, responded to this dominant discourse and phenomenon of our time. These excerpts, expressing both fear and hope, suggest three important themes; first, Gandhi negates the exclusiveness of Indian culture; second, he gives the notion of 'to protect culture ourselves'; and third, he warns us against any such 'artificial and forced unity' as produced by 'American pattern'. Furthermore, Gandhi vehemently suggests a synthesis of different cultures 'where each culture is assured its legitimate place'.

Attempting to present a thematic exploration on Gandhi's cultural response to globalization, this paper mainly focuses on two seemingly different but interrelated themes. As mentioned above, globalization, in its present form, is post-Gandhi phenomenon; we are left only to speculate what could be the Gandhian response to it or how Gandhi would have responded to it. Thus, first of all, the paper attempts to articulate Gandhi's response to globalization by juxtaposing key features of globalization with Gandhi's key ideas. Second, as Gandhi seriously condemned modern civilization as 'disease', 'satanic', and 'irreligious' and valorized Indian civilization throughout his life for its spiritual orientation, thus, it might be argued that Gandhi's view on Indian cultural identity and his response to the process of modernization may be one important key to unlock the contours of Gandhi's response to globalization, as globalization is also seen as the extended process of modernization that affects local culture.

Structurally, this article is divided into four sections. First section attempts to contextualize the study examining the discourse of globalization, while second section explores the contradictory position of scholars who tries to represent Gandhi either as 'product of globalization' or 'Gandhi against globalization'. Third section is juxtaposing exercise mentioned above and fourth and final section attempts to read Gandhi's Swadeshi as local site of promise and hope against the fear of globalization.

I

To articulate Gandhi's cultural response to Globalization, first of all, it is essential to examine the discourse of globalization. Globalization is generally seen as a process and phenomenon whereby individual lives and local communities are affected by economic and cultural forces that operate worldwide. Anthony Giddens (1990) defines globalization as "the intensification of worldwide social relations, which link distant localities in such a way that local happenings are shaped by events occurring many miles away and *vice-versa*".[1] Giddens views globalization as the spread of modernity and discusses time-space distanciation. He refers to the way in which instantaneous electronic communication erodes the constraints of distance and time on social organization and interaction. Some scholars, such as Robertson (1992), talk of a global culture and 'global consciousnesses'.[2] Martin Albrow (1990) moves further, and argues that globalization results in a 'world society'. He defines globalization as "all those processes by which the peoples of the world are incorporated into a single world society, global society".[3] This notion of a single global society implies homogenization, which has led to the debate about whether globalization results in homogenization or heterogenization.

Thus, globalization suggests a new kind of phenomenon; however, this newness is not something scholars always welcome. As Appadurai argues the main threat posed by the discourse of globalization is the possibility of phenomena of too large, too quick, and too all-encompassing to succumb to our gaze.[4] He suggests that globalization produces an 'anxiety' as it has much to do with powerful interests that routinely use it—banks, multinational corporations, free-marketeers, and aid agencies are among these—and the media echo chamber dutifully endorses the sense that we are now living in a new world of proximity, speed, and interaction. However, especially for those who live in poor societies or in the poorer parts or margins of rich societies, the idea of globalization is cause for alarm.[5]

The 'cause for alarm' that Appadurai observes has several dimensions: economic, social and cultural. For the purpose of this study, I wish to focus on the cultural implications of globalization. It should be clear at very outset that the cultural implication of globalization involves not the simple enforced distribution of a particular western-liberal, secular, possessive-individualist, capitalist-consumerist-lifestyle, but a more complicated dissemination of the entire range of institutional features of cultural modernity. Modernity may be seen here as Giddens (1990) argues; 'it is the abstraction of social and cultural practices from contexts of local particularity, and their institutionalization and regulation across time and space'.[6]

The discourse of globalization has attracted host of Gandhian scholars to interpret Gandhi in its context. Before we proceed to Gandhi's cultural response to globalization locating the key features of globalization and juxtaposing it with Gandhi's view, it seems plausible to briefly mention what kind of arguments are generally advanced on the issue at hand.

II

Gandhian scholars seem divided into two camps in their analysis, with regard to Gandhi and his cultural response to globalization in India. First camp generally sees Gandhi as the 'product of globalization', thus, they argue that Gandhi would have accepted the cultural changes brought out by globalization although with some limitations. Generally such arguments begin with quoting Gandhi who wrote, "I do not want my house to be walled in on all sides and my windows to be stuffed. I want the cultures of all lands to be blown about my house as freely as possible. But I refuse to be blown-off my feet by any".[7]

Gandhi's this famous quote has been interpreted in many ways and will continue to be interpreted in future. On its face value, on the one hand it shows Gandhi's inclusive attitude towards other cultures, on the other, it shows his attitude of firmly rooted in his own culture.

However, 'Gandhi as the product of globalization' camp is best represented by Mukherjee, and I would like to quote him at length as authors summarize almost all major ideas of this camp. In author's view:

> "It seems ironic that worldwide anti-globalization movements often portray Gandhi as someone who shared the same side of the ideological spectrum, when Gandhi himself was clearly a product of globalization. He was educated in London, started his political activities in South Africa before he even joined the political arena in India and was greatly influenced by western figures such as Jesus, Tolstoy, Thoreau and Ruskin".[8]

Author goes on argue that "Gandhi himself was a product of globalization. Hence, he did understand the advantages and disadvantages of globalization. He opined that globalization was not evil but to believe that everything western was superior was not the correct stand to take. He did not perceive any threat to our culture due to globalization but he did believe that it would lead to environmental hazards and consumerism—both of which have proved correct".[9]

This kind of argument seems misleading for two reasons. First, the discourse of globalization is not as simple as presented by the author. In fact, there is wide difference between pre-industrial revolution globalization and post-industrial revolution globalization. Author seems preoccupied with pre-industrial revolution globalization and attempts to locate Gandhi from that perspective. Second, she confuses Gandhi's understanding of advantages of globalization with what Matin Green says 'other west influence on Gandhi' and argues that Gandhi was product of globalization. In fact, Gandhi's universalistic vision is generally confused with globalization. But as Baudrillard suggests, globalization and universality are not equivalent terms; in fact they could be considered to mutually exclusive.[10] Globalization pertains to techniques, the market, tourism, information. Universality pertains to values, human rights, freedoms, culture, and democracy.[11]

In response to Mukherjee's argument discussed above, rather than presenting my own view, I would like to quote Gandhi:

> "Of myself, whilst I have freely acknowledged my debt to Western culture, I can say that whatever service I have been able to render to the nation has been due entirely to the retention by me of Eastern culture to the extent it has been possible. I should have been thoroughly useless to the masses as an anglicized, denationalized being, knowing little of, caring less for and perhaps even despising their ways, habits, thoughts and aspirations".[12]

Gandhi's this argument is enough to explain his own position in this regard.

Contrary to the first camp, some Gandhian scholars argue in more questioning ways as to 'How Gandhi's Ideas can Help to Combat Globalization-related Threats'.[13] This threat is not only economic but also social and cultural. The background of this cultural threat logic is: the process of globalization is not at all a natural process; it is something intentional, dependent on the will, desires and projects of human beings. Further, the interchange of objects, people and ideas creates a situation of general confusion in which people experience the loss of their traditional references, i.e., the loss of what they call their cultural identity. Many critics further argue that the dominance of American culture influencing the entire world will ultimately result in the end of cultural diversity. Finally, it may reach to a point which is called cultural homogenization which O'Connor defines as "the process by which local cultures are transformed or absorbed by a dominant outside culture".[14]

In the backdrop of these arguments, Gandhi's ideas are interpreted by quoting how Gandhi was against the foreign control (both economic and cultural) and favoured local. One of the oft-quoted of Gandhi's statement is, "It is difficult to measure the harm that Manchester has done to us. It is due to Manchester that Indian handicraft has all but disappeared. But I make a mistake. How can Manchester be blamed? We wore Manchester cloth and this is why Manchester wove it".[15]

The argument is: Gandhi sees capitalism as the dynamic force behind colonial imperialism (arguably, he might be read here as against the capitalism's new form, i.e., globalization, as globalization has also been seen as a new form of imperialism) and he relates it with modern civilization. Like Lenin and Marx, Gandhi connects capitalism to colonialism and goes ahead relating it with modern civilization (read globalization).

This kind of arguments gets strength when we find Gandhi observing:

> "India cannot live for Lancashire or any other country before she is able to live for herself. And she can live for herself only if she produces and is helped to produce everything for her requirements within her own border. She needs not be, she ought not be, drawn into vortex of mad and ruinous competition which breeds fratricide, jealousy and many other evils".[16]

These discussions lead us to think 'Gandhi against globalization' at all level with positive solution to it. It is not unsurprising that Gandhi had become a major figure in anti-globalization movement today. With this discussion, one may proceed to juxtapose the key features of globalization with Gandhi's idea.

III

Although there are several features of globalization at different levels, however, at cultural level, its most important feature is Time/Space Compression.[17] While globalization can still remain a vague term even in social science discussions, a great deal of social theory has focused on globalization as a distinct shift in the spatial and temporal dimensions of social and cultural life. More specifically, social and cultural theorists argue that the speed of social life over the past few decades has increased so greatly that social space has become "compressed" or even annihilated. Digital technologies like the Internet, for example, have allowed us to communicate virtually with anyone in the world at any time. Giddens provocatively argues that globalization has led to the creation of a "global risk society".[18] In

Tomlinson's formulation this time/space compression is "a sense of the shrinking of distances through the dramatic reduction in the time taken, either physically (for instance via air travel) or representational (via the transmission of electronically mediated information and images), to cross them".[19]

What would have been Gandhi's response to this time–space compression? For Gandhi, "I wholeheartedly detest this mad desire to destroy *distance and time*, to increase animal appetites, and go to the ends of the earth in search of their satisfaction. If modern civilization stands for all this, and I have understood it to do so, I call it *satanic*".[20]

If Giddens calls globalized world a 'global risk society', Gandhi would have called it as getting more 'satanic'. Gandhi's this 'satanic' is more vocal in his seminal text *Hind Swaraj* that I think throws specific light in this connection. In 1939, Gandhi wrote about his own text *Hind Swaraj*, 'it is an attempt to see beauty in voluntary simplicity [voluntary] poverty and slowness'.[21] He claimed that the increase of speed was covering every field of life in the West. He suggested that life was being lived 'on high speed bases regardless of whether the results in their sum total were beneficial'. Gandhi argues that the power of modern civilization lie in the greater 'speed' and this greater speed is more than the limits of nature hence not only dangerous but 'self -destructive'. Baudrillard seems echoing the same sentiments when he says, "Globalization creates the conditions for its own destruction".[22]

Thus, Gandhi gives a cultural logic of the problem of speed and argues modern civilization (thus also the globalization as extended modernity) expresses the tendency to high and unruly speed directed to worldly affairs, and in this process, it is going to be self-destructive

Gandhi, Globalization and Psychology of Global Consumer Culture

While globalization is the dominant hegemony of the present age, consumerism has become the basis of its wealth. The current practice of consumerism fosters certain forms of identity where fantasies of the self can be articulated in virtual realms.

Bauman (1999) a known critical theorist of cultural globalization, contends that society no longer 'interpellates' its members primarily as producers but first of all as consumers.[23] No more is work the key to identity, social recognition, community, and solidarity. Instead, the model of consumption spreads, say, to politics, meaning that *there is nothing outside of the market*. Such consumption works not by domination or ideological mobilization but through seduction. And such consumption has quickened, as fashions turn over at great speed and new desires are created, making ours a period of extreme transience, shallow attachments, and intense individualization.

Tracing the historical root of modernity and psychology of consumption, Bauman in his conception of liquid modernity that highlights the global consumption psychology says that consumption is conjugated to desire and, later, to the wish that modernity and globalization offers. Bauman describes this evolution from desire to the wish as the freeing of consumption from solid obstacles to new heights of pleasure.[24] The 'need', considered by nineteenth-century thinkers as solid, inflexible, permanently limited and finite– was discarded and replaced for a time by 'desire', which was much more 'fluid' and expanded than need. The reason was: desires had half-illicit connection with changeable and artificial dreams of the authenticity of an 'inner self' waiting to be expressed. Now it is desire's turn to be discarded. It has outlived its usefulness: having brought consumer addiction to its present state, it can no more set the pace. A more powerful and above all more versatile stimulant seems needed to keep consumer demand on a level with the consumer offer. The 'wish' is that much needed replacement: it completes the liberation of the pleasure principle, purging and disposing of the last residues of the 'reality principle' obstacle. Bauman argues that it is the liquidity of signs and images that generates seemingly limitless new objects to which consumers respond as their prerogative to choose and to fulfil their wishes. In other words, consumption abetted by globalization introduces a new type of irrationality. Consumers are so obsessed on the objects of their consumption that they become unaware of their own dilemma.

At material level, globalization has increasingly knitted together the world created unity out of great diversity. Jean (2002) noted that Coca Cola, Disney and McDonald symbolize the process along with Sony, Shell oil and IBM to influence global consumer's taste.[25] These are known and consumed all over the world. In addition, they are powerful companies that drive globalization forward, creating new laws, new business process, new ways to eat and drink new hopes and dreams. The problem is these goods spread the cultural goods. As Mackay (2000) puts, "Cultural goods flow to the rest of the world, inculcating US or Western values in those in recipient nations. This process prepares the ground for the import of other Western goods".[26]

Gandhi raises questions about the logic of modern civilization and it's both symbolic and material aspects, in which 'body welfare' is understood as 'object of life'. According to Gandhi the 'true test' of modern (globalized) 'civilization' lies in the fact that 'people living in it make bodily welfare the object of life'.[27] Gandhi proposes in *Hind Swaraj*, modern civilization is also irrational as civilization sought to increase bodily comforts, and it failed miserably even in doing so. Moreover, this was a new form of enslavement as 'formerly, men were made slave under physical compulsion. Now they are enslaved by temptation of money and of the luxuries that money can buy'.[28] Gandhi went on to say, "Money renders a man helpless. The other thing which is equally harmful is sexual vice. Both are poison. A snake bite is lesser poison than these two, because the former merely destroys the body but the latter destroy the body, mind and soul".[29]

Hence, it was consumption that became essence of every act. Nearly close to Bauman arguments, Gandhi argued, "Consumption does not produce apparent hurt—it even produces a seductive colour ... so as to induce the belief that *all is well*.'[30]

Perhaps this seductive colour is what globalization offers and what Gandhi warns us against. This seduction is at many levels and one may find it in the forms of advertisements-an agency that spreads the message of globalization in all corners of the world.

More important, Gandhi claimed modern civilization that is body centric and increases consumption is deceptive in it psychological effect too. 'There is no end of the victim destroyed in the fire of civilization. Its deadly effect is that people come under its scorching flames *believing it to be all good*'.[31] Further, 'civilization is like mouse gnawing while it is soothing us'.[32]

'All is well' and 'believing it to be all good' is what Gandhi finds in consumption philosophy of modern civilization is in more deadly form in the cultural logic of globalization. It is not a personal case of thinking 'all is well' but it is a political one as it never allows anyone to raise question on the system or the philosophy of system, thus, giving hand to the system to work as it desires. It creates a kind of silence in society, and finally an unquestioned acceptance of market and consumer culture is what globalization teaches us.

Gandhi counters such discourses by highlighting the Indian ancestor's wisdom of limiting desires and keeping low speed in worldly affairs who fully understood the irrationality of consumption abetted by modern civilization. Gandhi argues that our ancestor knew that "mind is a restless bird; the more it gets the more it wants, and still remains unsatisfied. The more we indulge our passions the more unbridled they become".[33]

Gandhi's acceptance of Indian cultural arguments of low consumption might be seen in the light of Bauman's analysis of relationship between globalization and psychology of consumption. Bauman writes people who "live from attraction to attraction, from temptation to temptation, from sniffing out one titbit to searching for another, from swallowing one bait to fishing around for another. As needs turn into desires and then into wishes, so the compulsion to consume runs into the dead-end of never wilting excitation".[34]

Gandhi, Globalization and Global Economy

Globalization involves the opening up of economics and knowledge to the global market and its forces. Friday (2002) contends that it is required that whatever the nature of their economics, knowledge, their level of the development and whatever their location in the global economy, all countries must pursue a common set of economic policies.[35] Of particular importance, they must permit free and discriminate operation of transnational corporation in their economies, open their economies freely and indiscriminately to import and concentrate on exporting.

Although during Gandhi's time there was no such question of location of global economy or common set of economic policies as widespread today, yet, he was able to see the phenomenon that had begun with industrialization. Gandhi's view of industrialization presupposes a kind of cultural change attached to it and he argues,

The fact is that this industrial civilization is a disease because it is all evil. Let us not be deceived by catchwords and phrases. I have no quarrel with steamships or telegraphs. They may stay, if they can, without the support of industrialism and all it connotes. They are not an end. We must not suffer exploitation for the sake of steamships and telegraphs. They are in no way indispensable for the permanent welfare of the human race. . . . India has withstood the onslaughts of other civilizations because she has stood firm on her own ground. Not that she has not made changes. But the changes she has made have promoted her growth. To change to industrialism is to court disaster. . . . Our concern is, therefore, to destroy industrialism at any cost. The present distress is undoubtedly insufferable. Pauperism must go. But industrialism is no remedy. . . .[36]

On the issue of industrialization (and he must had responded to globalization in the same way), Gandhi saw it as a menace to the basic moral ideals of human society. He saw it an endless tangle of moral evils.

Gandhi's view against the industrialization has an important social and cultural logic. Gandhi found that the growth of big industries in some Indian cities attracted the villagers to crowded cities (it can be read in present context as flow of labour and capital across the globe, especially labour from third world countries to developed countries). Ultimately whole process of industrial growth (growth of centred global economy) appeared (must have) to Gandhi as monstrous process of mechanization (high technology and communication), dehumanization and demoralization, by which course individuals could never develop and realize best in them.

Related to this is his idea of machines (in globalization era, high and sophisticated technology). His argument is machine (technology) has its place; it has come to stay. But it must not be allowed to displace necessary human labour. His objection to machinery (high and sophisticated technology) may be summed up as follows:

- The introduction of machinery (high technology that globalization offers) would create more unemployment.
- Exploitation of the poor laborers by rich capitalist (multinationals and transnational companies) will increase and one country (especially third world countries) by another (so called developed world) also.
- The moral evils are attached with machinery (high and sophisticated technology).

However, Gandhi visualized for free India the limited manufacture of machine in nationalized or State controlled factories. In fact, Gandhi favoured self-sufficient decentralized and autonomous village community. He saw them natural with healthy surroundings that help people to live simply, develop more of social sense, cooperative works, and intimate neighbouring love, and the virtues that follow there from.

Gandhi gives a call; perhaps best summarizes his position in this regard. In his words:

> "India's destiny lies not along the bloody way of the West, of which she shows signs of tiredness, but along the bloodless way of peace that comes from a simple and godly life. India is in

danger of losing her soul. She cannot lose it and live. She must not therefore lazily and helplessly say, 'I cannot escape the onrush from the West.' She must be strong enough to resist it for her own sake and that of the world".[37]

IV

Gandhi's *hope* that 'India's destiny lies not along the bloody way of the West', and 'She must be strong enough to resist it for her own sake and that of the world', are based on his reading of the cultural markers of India's antiquity. He wrote, "It is my firm opinion that no culture has treasures so rich as ours has. We have not known it, we have been made even to deprecate its study and depreciate its value. We have almost ceased to live it". [38]

Gandhi's valorization of Indian culture as 'no culture has treasurer so rich as ours', our ignorance and to 'depreciate its study and value' and moreover 'ceasing to live to it' shows his deep engagement to develop an Indian cultural identity. As a matter of fact, the formation of Indian cultural identity through the cultural marker of Indian identity can be traced back to 1909 when he wrote *Hind Swaraj*. In Gandhi's civilization discourse as proposed in *Hind Swaraj*, one may find a strong desire to convince Indians to understand the discourse and narratives of modern civilization and get rid of their illusion. Further one may observe the tendency to forge the collective Indian identity by constructing the hard conceptual boundaries in the text. The simple categorization of Indian and Western civilization respectively as 'moral' and 'immoral', 'soul force' and 'brute force', presents a wholesale indictment of modernity (and globalization as extended modernity), a polarization into an attitude of 'us' against 'them'.[39]

Gandhi's view on Indian cultural identity and process of modernization may be one important key to unlock the problem of Gandhi's response to globalization, as globalization may be seen as extended process of modernization. In other words, globalization is really the globalization of modernity. In fact, Gandhi was able to see the inner logic between the modernization process (also extended globalization process) and the institutionalized construction of Indian identity. Gandhi seems more worried about the construction of Indian identity in terms of process of Westernization/ modernization and globalization and his fears appear in the discussion on this issue.

He wrote in 1931 in *Young India:*

"European Civilization is no doubt suited for the Europeans but it will mean ruin for India, if we endeavour to copy it". [40] Moreover, "My resistance to Western civilization is really a resistance to its indiscriminate and thoughtless imitation based on the assumption that Asiatics are fit only to copy everything that comes from the West".[41]

Thus, Gandhi's objection to modernity and its propagator Western civilization is that it attempts to institutionalize and regulate cultural practices of India. This theme may be applied in present discussion as globalization too attempts to produce a mimic of Western intuitions and cultural practices in India and other third world countries through cultural production.

This cultural production is the prominence and power of the so-called 'cultural industries' generated by Multinational Companies (MNCs)—agencies of globalization. The cultural industries are usually seen as Hesmondhalgh argues "those institutions ... which are most directly involved in the production of social meaning', including advertising and marketing, broadcasting, film, print and electronic publishing, music industries, video and computer games, and other more 'borderline' cases such as fashion, sports, and software".[42]

In this regard, it has been argued by many scholars that the "crucial feature of contemporary cultural globalization is the diffusion by Western cultural industries of the most vacuous and destructive Western ideas and practices out-wards, leading to the involuntary demise of other cultures. A form of imperialism, then, is the most visible process attached to today's globalization in the sphere of culture".[43]

This idea echoes Gandhi's fear what he considered 'indiscriminate and thoughtless imitation based on the assumption that Asiatics are fit only to copy everything that comes from the West', discussed above. It suggests that Gandhi could smell the cultural imperialism through the rhetorical strategy and processes of modern civilization, and logically by the current globalization. It is worth mentioning here that the discourse around cultural imperialism began after Gandhi, especially in 1960s and became popular in the 1970s and 1980s.[44] At present, this notion is captured by terms such as 'Disneyfication', 'Coca-colonization', and 'Westoxification'. These terms convey what Gandhi feared that cultural power is not at all evenly distributed but is largely held by the West, or more narrowly, by America. The result of such more voluminous global cultural flows, then, as Tomlinson argues will be cultural homogenization, a 'world-widé standardization of lifestyles'.[45]

Yet, Gandhi gives *hope* against this cultural imperialism of globalization. Perhaps, it is Gandhi's emphasis of culture of Swadeshi which seems vehemently challenging the cultural globalization discourse. Gandhi's Swadeshi is the local site of promise that represents social-psychology of attachment to locality. As Parikh writes, "this is not an isolated localism of the 'deserted village', that Goldsmith romanticized, or the degradation of caste oppression that Ambedkar revolted against, but rather the local neighbourhood community, the village as the node in a network of oceanic circles that over-lapped and spread out in its ever widening embrace. It is this commitment of the individual to his '*desh*' that was Gandhi's Indian alternative..."[46]

In fact, the village Gandhi idealized was not just a geographic place, or a statistic, or a social class, but it was an event, a dream, a happening, a culture. It indicates Gandhi's three basic themes: self-respect, self-realization and self-reliance. Moreover, Gandhi's village signifies different possible modes of expressions and different consequent suggestions for people's logic of self and of existential well-being. And these differences are all relative to cultural context.

Moreover for Gandhi, Swadeshi is a spirit. In his own definition,

> "Swadeshi is that spirit in us which restricts us to the use and service of our immediate surroundings to the exclusion of the more remote. Thus, as for religion, in order to satisfy the requirements of the definition, I must restrict myself to my ancestral religion. That is, the use of my immediate religious surrounding. If I find it defective, I should serve it by purging it of its defects. In the domain of politics, I should make use of the indigenous institutions and serve them by curing them of their proved defects. In that of economics I should use only things that are produced by my immediate neighbours and serve those industries by making them efficient and complete where they might be found wanting. It is suggested that such Swadeshi, if reduced to practice, will lead to the millennium....".[47]

Gandhi's definition of Swadeshi leads us to think of local culture and institution against the homogenization and cultural imperialism of globalization. This definition further emphasizes on local traditions. One might focus here on this aspect of Swadeshi which has found little space in Gandhian academic circle, although it strongly prescribes how cultural globalization can be challenged by indigenous traditions. In Gandhi's view, which seems philosophical at first glance, each tradition speaks to the moral cooperative nature of men and women and challenges the self interests that are lodged in every person and any society. Each tradition evolves from common origin but each speaks in its own language. Thus, Gandhi seems suggesting, there is no such 'best' tradition and rejects the idea that there can be a universal tradition. He wants individuals work with their own tradition to realize their cultural tradition. Although Gandhi prizes every tradition, he refuses to make it invincible or infallible, thus, it can never be exempt from moral scrutiny. He finds that a tradition is sound when it celebrates the dignity of all persons and provides the moral materials for the good life and good community.

Gandhi sees tradition as resources. To challenge domination, inequality Gandhi finds that one should not leave his own tradition but use it as resource. For this, Gandhi repeatedly insists that it must be actively incorporated into the everyday lives of men and women. Thus, Gandhi finds his tradition not only in texts but also in the country side where people live in true Swaraj. Finally, Gandhi does not see autonomous agent apart from community where he expects them to be active participants concerned with not only their own autonomy but also the autonomy of each other. This prominence of autonomy can be seen in his programme of Swaraj. In the face of cultural imperialism of globalization, Gandhi has hope in a reformed tradition to stand, erectly and resolutely to confront it. For Gandhi, modernity and globalization *as* extended modernity come with heavy and often hidden costs. Gandhi would have seen globalization as addressing a person's interests or *arth* (wealth) and *Kama* (desire), but ignoring questions about a person's *dharma* (responsibility in the wider world). Further, globalization operating as meta-narrative rejects other modes of thinking and moral point of reference, such as those found in religion and tradition.

Notes and References

1. Giddens, Anthony, Consequences of Modernity, Cambridge: Polity Press, 1990, p. 64.
2. Robertson, R., Globalization: Social Theory and Global Culture. London: Sage, 1992, p. 8.

3. Albrow, Martin, Globalization, Knowledge and Society, London: Sage, 1990, p. 9.
4. www.scribd.com/.../Appadurai-1997-Discussion-Fieldwork-in-the-Era-of/Appadurai
5. *Ibid.*
6. *Op. cit.*, Giddens, p. 6.
7. *Young India*, 01-06-1921
8. www.mkgandhi.org/articles/globalisation.htm
9. *Ibid.*
10. Baudrillard, Jean, The Global and the Universal, www.egs.edu/faculty/jean-baudrillard/.../the-global-and-the-universal/ý
11. *Ibid.*
12. *Young India*, 5-7-1928.
13. How Gandhi's Ideas can Help to Combat Globalisation-related Threats, www.mainstreamweekly.net › 2008 › October 4, 2008ý.
14. O'Connor, David E., Encyclopedia of the Global Economy: A Guide for Students and Researchers, Academic Foundation, p. 391.
15. Gandhi, M.K., Hind Swaraj or Indian Home Rule, Ahmedabad: Navajivan, 2008. p. 81.
16. Gandhi, M.K., India of My Dream, Ahmedabad: Navajivan Publishing House, 2011, p. 123.
17. Hardy, David, The condition of post-modernity, UK: Blackwell Publishers, 1990, p. 212.
18. See, Ulrich Beck, Risk Society, Towards a New Modernity. London: Sage Publications, 1992, p. 260.
19. Tomlinson, J., Globalization and Culture, Cambridge: Polity Press, 1999, p. 3.
20. *Young India*, 17-3-1927.
21. *CWMG*, Vol. 70, p. 242.
22. www.ubishops.ca/baudrillardstudies/spiegel.htm
23. Bauman, Z., Globalization: The Human Consequences. Cambridge: Polity, 1999, p. 126.
24. Bauman, Z., Liquid Modernity. Cambridge: Polity Press, 2000, pp. 75-76.
25. Jean, T., The hidden dimension of globalization: What is at stake geoculturally? Global Policy Forum, New York, ATTAC, 2002, May 29.
26. Mackay, H., 'The Globalization of Culture?, in D. Held (ed.), A Globalizing World? Culture, Economics, Politics, London: Rutledge, 2000, p. 48.
27. *Op. cit.*, *Hind Swaraj*, p. 31.
28. *Ibid.*, 32.
29. *Ibid.*, p.82.
30. *Ibid.*, p. 39.
31. *Ibid.*, p. 37.
32. *Ibid.*, p. 39.
33. *Ibid.*, p. 53.
34. *Op. cit.*, Liquid Modernity. p. 75.
35. Friday, M., The Effect of Globalization on Culture in Africa in the Eye of African Woman, *Echo*, World Council of Churches, 2000.

36. *Young India*, 07-10-1926.
37. *Young India*, 07-10-1926.
38. *Young India*, 01-09-1921.
39. For detail analysis see, Mishra, Prem A., Hind Swaraj: A Deconstructive Reading, New Delhi: Abhijeet Publication, 2012, pp. 184-85.
40. *Young India*: 30-04-31.
41. *Young India*, 11-8-1927.
42. Hesmondhalgh, D., The Culture Industries, London: Sage, 2002, p. 11.
43. Chamsy el-Ojeili and Patrick Hayden, Critical Theories of Globalization, New York: Palgrave Macmillan, 2006, p. 140.
44. *Op. cit.*, Hesmondhalgh, 2002, p. 12.
45. *Op. cit.*, Tomlinson, p. 89.
46. Parekh, Bhikhu, Gandhi's Political Philosophy: A Critical Appreciation, Delhi: Ajanta, 1995, pp. 55-6.
47. *Op. cit.*, India of My Dream, p. 120.

4

Relevance of Gandhian Swadeshi in the Era of Globalization and Liberalization

MANISH SHARMA

The 21st Century is said to be a Century of growth, development, science, race of nuclear armaments and above all the century for the new machine generation. Today, we all are becoming habituals of a particular strategy, which is becoming our master and we are just only the toys in its robotic hands. And India is also not behind in the race of mechanization, i.e., we all are heading towards the era of globalization, where each and every thing is made by someone else but sold under different labels and varieties, under huge profits and after cutting lakhs of hands and making them unemployed and poorer day-by-day. And, we all know that the term 'Globalization' is not a new phenomenon as basically it is an extension of what has been going on for thousands of years in different parts of the world. It has also been observed that the word 'globalization' is used in two ways, which are a source of confusion and a cause of controversy. It is used in a positive sense to describe a process of increasing integration into the world economy: the characterization of this process is by no means uniform. It is used in a normative sense to prescribe a strategy of development based on a rapid integration with the world economy. Some see this as salvation while others see it as damnation. Now Liberalization and

Globalization have become the words of hot discussion all over the world.

In fact, the present scenario of liberalization and globalization in India started with the start of 1991, when the Indian economy was opened up for sale. The same thing had happened more than 200 years ago and as a result we were made slaves by the Britishers for nearly 150 years and the same things are repeated again, and no one knows about the future for how much time, we would be the slaves of others.

Generally, Globalization has been defined as an open economy, which is open to the international processes of capital accumulation and distribution. However, a few describe it as a process of exploitation of poor countries by the companies of the developed world and in a way they designate the same as a refined route of colonialism. Others present it as the process of enhancing collective measures to stop international violence and wars, to save global environment and to eliminate the Third World poverty and economic inequality and numerous other disparities through developed communications, financial investments, trade and financial assistance. In fact, to them globalization means that "bigger is always better" in place of "small is beautiful". The multinational companies argue and claim to provide the consumer goods to the masses at cheaper and at affordable rates and lure the people to provide them the adequate employment also. Though such kind of arrangement has the advantage of deriving some financial gains from the International economic and trade agencies like the International Monetary Fund (IMF) and the World Bank, but it has a negative effect also as these agencies try to thrust upon a series of measures like import, liberalization, reduction of subsidies, reduction of public expenditures, opening of economy to foreign capital and deepen marketization of economy. On the other hand, these agencies, practically, want to guide the domestic policies and programmes of the developing countries like India, Thailand, Myanmar, Pakistan, Bangladesh, Sri Lanka, many parts of African Sub-Continental and so many other Third World countries, facing so many financial difficulties.

By one school of thought Globalization is being presented as the process of enhancing collective measures to stop international violence and wars, to save global environment, and to eliminate Third World Poverty and economic inequality through developed communications, investments, trade, and mutual aid. Globalization implies that "bigger is better."[1] Hence, they are much more attracted to the process of Globalization.

But the central question arises: What caused these problems in the first place? Otherwise we end up with the logic of the tragedies caused by drunk driving, more policing, more fines and punishments. While selling more liquor to the drivers, cannot end drunk driving. On the other hand, the solution lies in going to the root of drunkenness, which is alcoholism! The main reasons for the current global malaise may be mentioned as under, which need our immediate attention and action:

(a) Massive and reckless industrialization, without human face, where man does not matter.
(b) Dehumanization of science, technology, and industry,[2] where material matters.

In this situation if we see the status of the country regarding industrialization and mechanization, India has made a great success in both the matters but with all this, the other foreign firms are also doing brisk business here at the cost of Indian masses and the net profit going to their respective countries and not to India. Though development is there, but at the cost of larger increase in unemployment, and a big decrease in the stock of net profits for India. In the present state of chaos and confusion among unemployed youth, the term "Swadeshi" again has to show us some light to come out of the darkness of the gravity of foreign industrialization and mechanization leading to degradation of our environment and dismantling the ecology in the long-run.

In the era of globalization, we have to remember and examine the Gandhian concept of Swadeshi, which is quite significant and relevant in the present context. Gandhi explains:

> "After much thinking I have arrived at a definition of Swadeshi that, perhaps, best illustrates my meaning. Swadeshi is that spirit in us which restricts us to the use and service of our immediate surroundings to the exclusion of the more remote. Thus, as for religion, in order to satisfy the requirements of the definition, I must restrict myself to my ancestral religion. That is the use of my immediate religious surrounding.... It is suggested that such Swadeshi if reduced to practice, will lead to the millennium. And as we do not abandon our pursuit after the millennium because we do not expect quite to reach it

within our times, so may we not abandon Swadeshi even though it may not be fully attained for generations to come."[3]

However, if we want to see the complete structure of Gandhian Swadeshi i.e., redefined concept of Globlization', we will have to go through the entire gamut of his thought, i.e. social, political, economic and religious because he has used this term in wider sense than its ordinary use. He further says:

> "There is no salvation for us without true Swadeshi, not the Swadeshi which can be conveniently put off. Swadeshi, for me, has a deeper meaning. I would like us to apply it in our religious, political and economic life. It is not, therefore, merely confined to wearing on occasions a Swadeshi cloth. That we have to do for all time, not out of a spirit of jealously or revenge but because it is a duty we owe to our dear country. We commit a breach of the Swadeshi spirit certainly if we wear foreign-made cloth, but we do so also if we adopt the foreign cut. Surely, the style of our dress has some correspondence with our environment. In elegance and tastefulness, it is immeasurably superior to the trousers and the jacket. An Indian wearing a shirt flowing over his pyjamas with a waist-cost on it without a neck-tie and its flaps hanging loose behind, is very graceful spectacle."[4]

In fact, Gandhi while explaining the state of slavery, he mentioned that, basically, India was enslaved for satisfying the greed of the foreign cloth manufacturers. When the East India Company came here, we were able to manufacture all the cloth we needed and more for export. By processes that does not need any description here, India became practically wholly dependent upon foreign manufacture for her clothing. But we ought not to be dependent. On the other hand, India has the ability to manufacture all her cloth, if her children will work for it. Fortunately, India has yet enough weavers to supplement the out-turn of her mills.

Besides, the householder has to revise his or her ideas of fashion and, at least for the time being, suspend the use of fine garments, which are not always worn to cover the body. He should train himself to see art and beauty in the spotlessly white Khaddar and to appreciate its soft unevenness. The householder must learn to use cloth as a miser uses his hoard. This reveals the philosophy and art of living.

Similarly, even when the householders have revised their tastes about dress, somebody will have to spin yarn for the weavers.

Everyone spinning during spare hours either for love or money can only do this.[5] He further clarifies the same with the following explanation:

"We are too much obsessed by the glamour of the West. We forget that what may be perfectly good for certain conditions in the West is not necessarily good for certain other, and often diametrically opposite, conditions in the East. Free trade, which may have been good enough for England, would certainly have ruined Germany. Germany prospered only because her thinkers, instead of slavishly following England, took note of the special conditions of their own land, and devised economies suited to them."[6]

According to Gandhiji, much of the deep poverty of the masses is due to the ruinous departure from Swadeshi in the economic and industrial life. If not an article of commerce had been brought from outside India, she would be today a land flowing with milk and honey.[7] But that was not to be. We were greedy, and so England. The connection between England and India was based clearly upon an error. But she does not remain in India an error. It is her declared policy that India is to be held in trust for her people. If this is true, Lancashire must stand aside. And if Swadeshi doctrine is a sound doctrine, Lancashire can stand aside without hurt, though it may sustain a shock for the time being.[8]

Besides, it argues:

"The last though not be the least important part of the maya still remains to be considered. That is Swadeshi. Had we not abandoned Swadeshi, we need not have been in the present fallen state. If we would get rid of the economic slavery, we must manufacture our own cloth and, at the present moment, only by hand-spinning and hand-weaving."[9]

Regarding Swadeshi and Charkha he has said,

"I claim for the Charkha the honour of being able to solve the problem of economic distress in a most natural, simple, inexpensive and business-like manner. The Charkha, therefore, is not only useless, but it is a useful and indispensable article for every home. It is the symbol of the nation's prosperity and, therefore freedom. It is a symbol not of commercial war, but of commercial peace. It bears not a message of ill-will towards the nations of the earth, but of good-will and self-help. It will not need the protection of navy threatening a world's peace and exploiting its resources, but it needs the religious determination of millions to spin their yarn in their own homes. I may deserve the curse of posterity for many mistakes of omission and commission, but I am confident of earning its blessings for suggesting a revival of the Charkha. I stake my all on it. For, every revolution of the wheel spins peace, goodwill and love. And with all that, inasmuch as the loss of it brought about India's slavery, its voluntary revival with all its implications must mean India's freedom."[10]

Again, Gandhi defines Swadeshi as, "I must not serve my distant neighbour at the expense of the nearest. It is never vindictive or punitive. It is in no sense narrow, for I buy from every part of the world what is needed for my growth. I refuse to buy from anybody anything however nice or beautiful, if it interferes with my growth or injures those whom Nature has made my first care. I buy useful healthy literature from every part of the world. I buy surgical instruments from England, pins and pencils from Austria, and watches from Switzerland. But I will not buy an inch of the finest cotton fabric from England or Japan or any other part of the world, because it has injured and increasingly injuring the millions of the inhabitants of India. I hold it to be sinful for me to refuse to buy the cloth spun and woven by the needy millions of India's paupers, and to buy foreign cloth although it may be superior in quality to the Indian hand-spun. My Swadeshi, therefore, chiefly centres round the hand-spun Khaddar and extend to everything that can be and is produced in India. My nationalism is as broad as my Swadeshi. I want India's rise so that the whole world may benefit. I do not want India to rise on the ruin of other nations."[11] Further, he adds that if India wants to be strong and able, India would send out to the world her treasures of art and health-giving spices, but would refuse to send out opium or intoxicating liquors although the traffic may bring much material benefit to India.[12]

It may be mentioned here that at one time our national economy was that just as we could produce our own cotton, spin it in our homes and wear the clothes woven by our weavers from our own yarn. This first part of the description is still true, while the latter part has almost ceased to hold good. A man generally spends upon his clothing a tenth of what he spends upon his food; hence instead of distributing ten per cent of our income among ourselves, we now send it to England or to our own mills. That means that we lose so much labour, and in the bargain spend money on our clothing and consequently suffer a two-fold loss. The result is that we stint ourselves in the matter of food in order to be able to spend on clothing, and sink into greater and greater misery day by day. We are bound to perish if the twin industries of agriculture and spinning as well as weaving disappear from our homes or our villages.[13]

Similarly, if we see the present context again, we will find that goods produced have to be sold and consumed. Hence the rise of the revolution in transportation and communications. While development in transportation helps move goods and travelers, it also helps in the fast moving of war machines and soldiers to every nook and corner of the world. The mass media of communications—from the printing press to computer chips and satellites—have become the instruments of propaganda, thought control, mindset and brainwashing. The Time Magazine imperialism or CNN neo-colonialism are the latest examples. [14]

The globalized messages of racism, ethnicism, sexism, religionism, dogmatism and jingoism have flourished and thrived through the media imperialism. These narrow-minded messages, which are used to boost huge and massive industrialization, have also caused communal antagonisms and blood baths on national and international levels. The craze of too much liberalization has already started the down-fall of Third World Countries and many examples can be quoted in this respect.

Some argue that science, technology and industrialization are not inherently immoral; it is only their misuse that causes problems. True, the sword by itself does not kill people; people have to use it to kill people. But in the human context, the very purpose for the creation of the sword is to inflict pain or death on human beings. This destructive purpose of the sword will not change until the sword, in Biblical terms, is beaten into ploughshare. When it becomes a ploughshare, then it is not a sword by definition and purpose. Thus, ends and means should be integrated, not dichotomized or distorted.[15] Hence, liberalization and globalization are to be studies and analysed in the light of the facts given above.

The Gandhian view suggests: "The outward freedom that we shall attain will only be in exact proportion to the inward freedom to which we may have grown at a given moment. And if this is correct view of freedom, our chief energy must be concentrated upon achieving reform from within."[16] This important aspect should not be neglected.

However, a true votary of Swadeshi, accordingly, "will never harbour ill-will nor be actuated by antagonism towards anybody on earth... To reject foreign manufactures, merely because they are foreign and to go on wasting national time and money in the promotion in one's country of manufacture for which it is not suited, would be a criminal folly and a negation of Swadeshi spirit."[17] This reflects the practical wisdom and scientific temperament of the Mahatma.

Like Swadeshi, in so many other matters, independent India did not even bother to examine the relevance of the Gandhian approach to solve our day-to-day problems. In most of the cases our concern has been marked by public homage and show-off. India opted to depend upon others and forgot the basic principle of self-reliance. In fact, we based our economy on European and American experience and capitalism. The net result was a systemic crisis of modern civilization and culture. Gandhi very rightly had already anticipated such kind of problems in his work Hind Swaraj, which, now has been recognized as a spiritual classic, in which he had warned against the incoming amoral modernity. However, the collapse of socialism and crises of capitalism did not make India to reflect on the western model, as it has again opted for too much liberalization and globalization–too much dependence on others. The ruling class in India has never tried to understand the complications and implications of its menace. As a matter of fact too much liberalization strikes at the very root of Swadeshi, as it permits almost free entry to Multi-National Corporations and Companies. If these corporations and companies change the ownership pattern in their favour, then the country will lose its control over the economy and therefore its economic sovereignty.[18] Not only this, they are allowed to sell even adulterated soft drinks and other food items having poisonous substances without any check, control and interference.

In the present context, Swadeshi, certainly occupies a prominent place and is very much relevant and necessary for the survival of a nation as it reduces the dependence on other countries and strengthens the confidence and efficacy and enhances the spirit of self-reliance among the people. However, there is a great need to understand Gandhi's approach to Swadeshi and its proper application. Swadeshi is Swa-dharma as well as a way of life. Besides, Swadeshi is a philosophy of life to live and to let others to live. It leads to the process of sustainable development.

In fact, Swadeshi, Swaraj and Satyagraha were main methods employed to oppose British imperialistic domination and gain political independence and mastery within the country and above all to gain India's complete freedom in respects. Swadeshi movement as economic battle was necessary link to Swaraj for the political battle for freedom. Economic freedom, according to Swadeshi, is based on endogenously controlled development. The word Swadeshi has an appeal to sections of Indians and perhaps has appeal to all Indians. Swadeshi to many means, "What we can do, let us do."[19] Swadeshi to me means a set of policies that are good for the economic development of the country, not for some section of Indians, be it labour or capital. Rather, it gives us a sense of pride and no one will be against foreign collaborations in those areas in which we lack the expertise. Unfortunately to many intellectuals it is backwardness, to most in media it is amusement, to almost all industrialists it indicates inefficiency and inferior quality and to economists it is bad economics.

In the present context, from Mahatma Gandhi's Swadeshi to current debate on economic nationalism represents a long journey. Two of Mahatma's essays in *Young India* and *Harijan* make his position clearer. Then, as now, a primary concern was the economy. "The situation today is this. The Britisher is the top-dog and the Indian the under-dog in his own country... It can be said without fear of contradiction and without any exaggeration that he has risen upon the ruin of India's commerce and industries. The cottage industry of India had to perish in order that Lancashire might flourish. The Indian shipping had to perish so that British Shipping might flourish... what is equality of rights between a giant and a dwarf? Before one can think of equality between unequals, the dwarf must be raised to the height of the giant."[20] In fact, according to Gandhi, the true meaning of the Swadeshi is the revival and presentation of village industries which is the lifeline of the rural economy and the mode of sustainability of the poor villages and the villagers which in turn is the heart of the complete national economy. According to him, "What is needed is protection of the village crafts and the workers behind them from the crushing competition of the power driven machinery whether it is worked in India or in foreign lands I claim that this is true, fruitful and cent per cent Swadeshi."[21]

According to Gandhi, one rule of Swadeshi is that in serving people we should give priority to those who live near us. There is also an opposite rule, that we should serve first those who are distant from us and then those who are near us. Near in the first rule means physically near, and distant in the second rule means distant from us mentally. Both may mean the same thing. An enemy may be physically near and distant mentally; we should, despite his being distant, serve his first. The reason behind this rule of Swadeshi is that we can't reach all human beings in this world. If you ignore your neighbour and seek to serve someone living far away, that would be pride on your part. We display good manners, culture and learning in serving first those who are mentally distant from us.[22]

At various places, we have seen that Gandhi had emphasised mainly on Swadeshi, the reason behind that was that he wanted to cultivate fearlessness in the people as in those days Indian people did not have the courage to stand up against the British empire. Gandhi considered it the first and foremost quality to cultivate. Therefore, he gave it a religious connotation and initially emphasized upon the need to cultivate Swadeshi in religion also. In fact, Gandhi's Swadeshi aimed at giving an assurance of providing a minimum standard of living to every individual and to provide meaningful employment to all able-bodied citizens and avoid waste and extravagance in utilizing natural resources. As Gandhi opined, earth provides enough for everybody's need but not for anybody's greed. By this he wanted that India should not depend upon others but should stand on its feet itself and should have that status that it can provide help and other needs to others. For that he has emphasised mainly on the proper utilization of the home resources and mankind. According to him, as noted earlier that Swadeshi is a positive concept because a true votary of Swadeshi will never harbour ill-will towards the foreigner; he will not be actuated by antagonism towards anybody on earth. Swadeshism is not a cult of hatred. It is doctrine of selfless service that has its roots in purest ahimsa, that is, love.[23]

In his life, at many stages, Gandhi has emphasized that he is not totally against the mechanization or adoption of new technology or the new terms of globalization but the emphasis of all these should be on the morality of the human nature, i.e., it should help the mankind to get more and more employment and work so that he can fulfil his basic needs–bread, cloth and shelter without any difficulty.

Gandhi while relating Swaraj to Swadeshi and Swadeshi to Swaraj to the ground reality of India, he goes to the basic: the individual being the basic unit if society; and village as the basic unit of human habitation. He always argued that inner change within the individual ought to be the starting point of outer change in society that only self-ruling individuals can usher in true Swaraj. And as individuals mostly live in villages, only self-reliant villagers practicing Swadeshi could become the building blocks of a truly independent state.[24]

When we make comparison between Gandhi and the teachings of the Gita, we find that Gandhi's conception of Swadeshi was very identical to that of Swadharma in the Gita. This Swadharma depends upon Swabhava, one's fundamental nature. People must follow in life such avocations as would not do violence to this nature. The Gita says: "One's own dharma though imperfect is better than the dharma of another well performed. The dharma of another is fraught with fear." Gandhi says of this: "Interpreted in terms of one's physical environment, this gives us the law of Swadeshi, for Swadeshi is Swadharma applied to one's immediate environment."[25]

It has been seen that Gandhi's conception of Swadeshi was both ethical and economic. As a matter of fact, Gandhi made no difference between ethics and economics. He says: "I must confess that I do not draw a sharp line or any distinction between economics and ethics. Economics that hurt the moral well-being of an individual or a nation are immoral and, therefore, sinful. Thus the economics that permits one country to prey upon another are immoral."[26] "It is sinful to eat American wheat and let my neighbour the grain dealer starves for want of custom. Similarly, it is sinful for me to wear the latest finery of Regent Street, when I know that if I had but worn the things woven by the neighbouring spinners and weavers, that would have clothed me, and fed and clothed them."[27] Indian patriots had realized, long before Gandhi, that the poverty of India was principally due to the murder of their industry at the hands of the British. Books were written about this; the most important of these was R.C. Dutta's 'Poverty of India Under British Rule', about which Gandhi said that when he read it, he was so powerfully affected that he began to shed tears. They felt that unless there was a revival of indigenous industry the masses of India, would remain poor. Alongwith the Annual Congress Sessions, therefore, it was customary to call an industrial conference. Resolutions were passed both in the Congress and at the Industrial Conference advising people to use Swadeshi instead of foreign goods.[28]

At another instance, he said: "Duties to self, to the family, to the country and to the world are not independent of one another. One can't do good to the country by injuring himself or his family. Similarly, one can't serve the country by injuring the world at large.

In the final analysis we must die that the family may live, the family must die that the country may live and the country must die that the world may live." "I work for India's freedom because my Swadeshi teaches me that being born in it and having inherited her culture, I am fittest to serve her and she has a prior claim to my service. But my patriotism is not exclusive, it is calculated not to hurt another nation but to benefit all in the true sense of the word."[29]

The neglect of Swadeshi and agriculture which has characterized our Government's economic policies since independence has progressively landed us in the present economic and financial crisis. It had led to our enormous adverse balance of trade with almost every country in Europe and America and with Japan in Asia. It has obliged us to take a deficit financing which has progressively assumed the character of inflation. The effect of this inflation is the rapid rise in prices and the decline in the value of the rupee. It has made the rich richer without in any way improving the real purchasing power of the poor. It has also brought about the devaluation of the rupee.[30]

In the present world, the main contours of development policy after independence thus—aimed at achieving an accelerated pace of industrialisation by building up indigenous production capabilities in the core sector embracing infrastructure, industry and agriculture, particularly its food producing segment. Modernization and certain of a scientific base for technological development of the Indian economy formed a complementary plank of the strategy. A major departure from the past was the institutional framework of policy for giving shape to these objectives. Instead of *ad-hoc* policy measures, a trust to development of the economy was to be imparted within the framework of planning mechanism, coordinated decision-making and through active involvement of the state, not only by formulating policy guidelines but in case of selected key economic activities through direct public sector investments.

Once political independence from British rule had been achieved, surprisingly, one does not find any direct reference to the Swadeshi concepts as it had evolved during the days of the freedom struggle in the policy formulations and planning documents. However, it was there in a modified shape in the garb of the objectives related to achievement of self-sufficiency in crucial sectors, particularly the building up of core sector industries and scientific/ technological capabilities. Moreover, during the initial phase of planning, there was a general reluctance to rely on foreign investments, except in crucial sectors of the economy, primarily those in the capital goods or infrastructure segments where production capabilities could not be built up without recourse to foreign resources, technology and imported inputs. Thus during this phase, although no direct reference was there to the Swadeshi principle, in its essential spirit it was Swadeshi. But it did differ from the historical phase of Gandhian Swadeshi in one very important respect. Its accent, under the influence of leaders and scholars like Nehru and Homi Bhabha, was on development of indigenous technological, scientific capabilities and modernization of the industrial sector whereas Gandhian Swadeshism was by and large wedded not only to the idea of preserving the traditional industries, but preserving them in their old traditional mould and above all providing employments to many hands. Accordingly, it could help many more poor in the country.

However, this does not imply that as a part of planned development traditional industries were to be completely sidetracked. In fact, as generally known, the Karve Committee was appointed to look into their problems and to devise schemes for their enlistment. The setting up of Khadi and Village Industries Board and devising the framework of its responsibilities is something, which owes its origin to 1950s. However, they did not form the kingpin of development programmes, which addressed themselves much more to attempts at modernization and bringing about the necessary structural changes in the economy. Phase II, starting with 1947, more specifically starting with 1951 when the planning mechanism was initiated, can thus be characterized as "Modernised Swadeshi". The gradual transformation towards an increasing range of relaxations contained during the 1980s. a distinct break from "Modern Swadeshi", as we know, came about in 1991 when the policy of liberalization and greater role for the operation of free market forces was adopted. This brought about dismantling of a number of controls including those on foreign exchange, removal or substantial reduction in many of import duties, promotion of foreign investment and free access to foreign technology. Within this framework, the objective of self-sufficiency as a general principle could not find an automatic berth without contradicting the underlying law of comparative advantage and the principles of free market economy. The apparent conflict between the principle of self-sufficiency and theoretical foundations of the law of comparative advantage, as viewed within the framework of neo-classical economics, arises since comparative advantage theory demands that the relative magnitude of domestic production and import of any commodity should be determined by the market mechanism in terms of the degree of comparative advantage that an economy possesses rather than being imposed exogenously through a policy decision. Self-sufficiency can thus be justified only in terms of certain grounds falling outside the realm of neo-classical economics. This should not be taken as an endorsement of superiority of the principle of comparative advantage over the principle of self-sufficiency.

Infact, in the favour of the new economic policy it was suggested that there was no use being out of step with the given socio-economic conditions in India and global developments. It was argued that official policy in India has in past imposed stringent austerity standards. The upper and middle classes in India suffered, in particular more deprivation than middle classes in any other third world country. Liberalisation policy, beginning in mid-seventies and gaining strength in eighties had, therefore, to be developed into a structural adjustment programme, which stipulated that not only by putting pressure on those who had money and means to satisfy their consumption needs in terms of global standards but by satisfying their demands in the market, growth could be stimulated and accelerated. This line of reasoning is followed by the promoters of new economic policy. They also promised that they would find some bypasses to alleviate the conditions of those, the majority of Indian people living at and below the subsistence level.

Here, it is important to appreciate the full implication of the new realities of globalization today. The Nation States have lost a substantial amount of economic, and through that, political sovereignty. They have to accept severe constraints on making their economic policies, expanding money supply, incurring fiscal deficits, determining interest rates or exchange rates, controlling domestic prices, restricting industrial activities besides their reduced ability to control international trade and capital flows. The effectiveness of any policy would depend on what is happening in the world economy and how other countries react. The costs of disregarding such constraints are very large and even the flexibility in taking political actions have become limited. The United States has been trying to crush Cuba for a long time, but with very limited effect, as Cuba managed to utilize the channels of international trade to withstand all the pressure. Iraq is another example. While sanctions largely worked in Rhodesia and South Africa, they do not seem to work today in Iraq. For less resourceful countries, the loss of autonomy may be very severe. The sanctions imposed upon India after the May 11 nuclear test, were not comprehensive and fully enforced. But if they were, and came anywhere near those imposed on Iraq, India would have crumbled. It is good that India does not have the dictatorial regime of Iraq, but as a result, our democratic system is much more vulnerable to economic disruptions and economic disparities.

In the case of the globalization and liberalization, though the benefits are more difficult to measure, because they are largely potential, and they require appropriate policy designs to be translated into the actual practice. Globalization and liberalization expends the opportunities for a country to realize more output, more employment, more social development, or in short higher levels of social welfare from the given resources in the country's command. But expansion of opportunities does not mean that they would be automatically materialized or realized. They would be the need for the state action, in policy design, planning and coordination of activities. There may be increased constraints on the state's autonomy but there will be no decline in the importance of the state's functions.

With the adoption of the Swadeshi approach, Gandhi involved the most common Indian in the economic growth of the country. Not only he raised the self-esteem of the poorest of the poor by providing him employment and a means of livelihood, but also he aspired to make the whole country self-reliant in the long-run. He had realised that unless the people themselves were involved there could not be true economic prosperity in India. He was fully aware that government imposed development schemes didn't bring permanent solution to age-old problems. Therefore, he insisted on people's involvement and participation. This idea is still relevant today. To make India self-reliant what is necessary is making the people a party to all development projects. The people should get involved in deciding what they need and what methods are necessary to achieve their goals. This would bring us to the adoption of the rural self-government and the enrichment of the village life. By this way we can again go back to the villages as still our India lives in villages. As Gandhi too thought that real India lived in her lakhs of villages. He believed that the ancient institutions of Panchayats provided opportunity to the local people to solve their own day-to-day problems. The same approach and practice can be followed today also. For this, it is important that the villages should be made basic units of administration because without the improvement of villages there can't be any progress in the country as India is a country of villages. The rural leadership should be strengthened and made powerful. It should not be restricted to only a few rural people, rather it should be enlarged enough to include all rural mass—the people of all strata and both sex. To make India self-sufficient, self-reliant and India of Gandhi's dream, it is essential to make its villages self-sufficient and self-reliant.[31]

In 1936 in a discussion with the Polish engineer, Maurice Frydman, who did not appreciate the wisdom of Gandhi's technological choice, Gandhi explained how urban industrialism was bound to lead to exploitation of the rural people and could not give them sufficient employment and that what was needed was "production for use", as he put it, localization of production, employment and consuming power on the basis of largely localized, mutually-advantageous exchange of goods and services. Let us quote his words: "Industrialisation on a mass scale will necessarily lead to passive or active exploitation of the villagers as the problems of competition and marketing come in. therefore, we have to concentrate on the village being self-contained, manufacturing mainly for use. Provided this character of the village industry is maintained, there would be no objection to the villagers using even modern machines and tools that they can make and can afford to use. Only they should not be used as a means of exploitation of others."[32] Gandhi was not a reactionary machine-hater who sought a release of the human spirit in primitivism. He was in favour of capital-saving techniques, to begin with. He wanted the rural folk to make modern tools and machines to be used in rural industries. He did not want machinery to be a means to the exploitation of the masses of the population, but as a means to the exploitation of the masses of the population, but as a means to more and better employment accompanied by as little exploitation as possible.

In 1931 when Gandhi was in Europe in connection with the Round-Table Conference he had a chance of discussing with an American journalist the advantages of localization of production and consumption, rather than their increasing centralisation under a system of mass production. Gandhi argued that besides squarely facing the problem of mass unemployment in a poor country, such a system of decentralized production was a way out of the economic travails of even Western countries. He stated: "When production and consumption both become localized, the temptation to speed up production indefinitely and at any price, disappears. The endless difficulties and problems that our present-day economic system presents would then come to an end"[33]. Referring to USA, Gandhi said: "She has reached the acme of mass production, and yet she has not been able to abolish unemployment or want. There are still thousands, perhaps millions of people who live in misery, in spite of the phenomenal riches of the few."[34] Gandhi's context was the great depression with its paradox of "poverty in the midst of plenty". The interviewer suggested that the fault lay in distribution. If distribution could be equalized, mass production could be "sterilized of all its evils". Whereas Gandhi's answer was forthright: "No, the evil is inherent in the system. Distribution can be equalized when production is localized, in other words, when the distribution is simultaneous with production. Distribution will never be equal so long as you want to tap other markets of the world to dispose of your goods."[35] Gandhi was thinking of non-exploitative production and exchange both within the country and across international frontiers. He said that "the Western nations have to use their skill for the good of those who do not have the skill" in order to generate production and employment where they are needed most. He used the same argument on behalf of the vast masses of the unemployed in India.

As we all know that Gandhi was a great enthusiast for hand-spinning, he understood that rural unemployment could not be tackled because of the following reasons:

(a) Without a whole range of village industries supplementing one another, and
(b) A proper cooperative organisation.

Again in 1934, he said that "I discovered that, without the revival of other industries, Khadi could not make further progress. For villagers to be able to occupy their spare time profitably, the village life must be touched at all points."[36] There was a tendency to encourage Khadi as a ritual or sacrament. But there was a contradiction in people's attitude. As Gandhi said: "While people used Khadi exclusively, they were using other things, irrespective of how and where they were made. Khadi was thus becoming a lifeless symbol. There were multitudes with spare time on their hands. Their involuntary and voluntary idleness made them a perpetual prey of exploiters."[37] What was therefore, needed was corporate effort to generate concurrent development of rural industries.

Therefore, liberalization and globalization are not the panacea for the contemporary world crises rather these are deepening these crises. In this respect, Gandhi's approach to Swadeshi (self-reliance) seems to be quite relevant and very significant as he has been a great advocate and supporter of the use of local indigenous industry or small-scale (industries which are primarily built upon the principle of national self-reliance and self-sufficiency, Swadeshi and Swavlamban), minimum surpluses, which will lead to devolution and decentralization of economic productivity and distribution. And such productivity will certainly reduce science-technology to the level suitable to small-scale industries and will reduce the need for raw materials, energy and pollution, and will reduce colonialization, militarization and massive wars.

As a matter of fact, Swadeshi is one of the most important principles of Gandhi's economic thought, as there exists a relationship between this doctrine and others, which are fundamental doctrines of Gandhian economics. However, to understand Gandhi's view of Swadeshi, one has to go through the entire gamut of his thought—social, political, economic and religious. Etimologically, the term may mean 'of one's own country', however, country's component is not its connotation but a sub-characteristics called 'uplakshan' in Hindi. Accordingly, Swadeshi includes all indigenous things—both abstract and concrete, namely, native language, wisdom, culture, dress and other products also. The core of the concept, however, is 'self-reliance' and 'self-governance' which reduce the extent of dependence on others to the minimum.

Although Gandhi did not coin the term 'Swadeshi', yet he contributed a lot in this respect by infusing new meanings to it. His understanding and approach to Swadeshi seems to be very dynamic, scientific, and more convincing. In the field of economics, the principle of Swadeshi means that a person basically uses those things, which are produced, in his immediate neighbourhood and serves those industries by making them efficient and meaningful. In other words, we can say that Swadeshi was the lifeblood of a Gandhian village. By giving the best illustration, Gandhi explains:

> "Swadeshi is that spirit in us which restricts us to the use and service of our immediate surroundings to the exclusion of the more remote... In the domain of politics, I should make use of the indigenous institutions and serve them by curing them of their proved defects. In that of economics, I should use only things that are produced by my immediate neighbours and serve those industries by making them efficient and complete where they might be found wanting".

Gandhi further clarifies that the neighbour thus served, has in his turn to serve his own neighbour. Accordingly, in practice, it is never exclusive and it recognizes the scientific limitations of human capacity for service. However, the principle of Swadeshi demands that a person must give preference to local manufactures even if they are of inferior quality or more costly than articles of foreign make. It functions with right spirit. There is no place for hatred for the foreign made things also. Therefore, he advises the use of foreign made articles if there is no substitute. He defined a Swadeshi article as any article which "sub-serves the interest of the millions even though the capital and talent are foreign but under effective Indian control" However, Gandhi did insist upon the exclusion of such foreign made commodities whose import was harmful to the indigenous industries. He pleaded strongly for stiff protective duties upon foreign goods in order to nurture national industries. The principle of Swadeshi suggested him the universalizing of Khadi or the spinning wheel to enable the crores of our semi-starved countrymen to live.

Further, it may be added that in advocating the complete boycott of foreign cloth, Gandhi had no ill will at all. He said, "To reject foreign manufactures merely because they are foreign, and to go on wasting national time and money to promote manufactures in one's own country for which it is not suited, would be criminal folly and a negation of the Swadeshi spirit."[38] He further added:

> "A true votary of Swadeshi will never harbour ill-will towards the foreigner, he will not be activated by antagonism towards anybody on earth. Swadeshism is not a cult of hatred. It is a doctrine of selfless service, that has its roots in the purest Ahimsa, i.e., love."[39]

Thus, Gandhi's concept of Swadeshi is wider one and has wider connotation also. Regarding the exclusion everything foreign, Gandhi does not leave any room for doubt when he says:

> "I have never considered the exclusion of everything foreign under every conceivable circumstances as a part of Swadeshi. The broad definition of Swadeshi is the use of all homemade things to the exclusion of foreign things, in so far as such use is necessary for the protection of home industry, more especially those industries without which India will become pauperized. In my opinion, therefore, Swadeshi which excludes the use of everything foreign, no matter how beneficent it may be, and irrespective of the fact that it impoverishes nobody, is a narrow interpretation of Swadeshi."[40]

Secondly, Gandhi is clear that his insistence on priority for the immediate neighbour will not mean injury to or unconcern for the interest of those who are not in the neighbourhood. However, each has to give priority to his or her neighbour, or bases his action on concern for his or her neighbour, there can be contradiction or conflict, and no unconcern or injury.[41] In this respect Gandhi fully believed that a man could serve his neighbours and humanity at the same time, the condition being that the service of the neighbour was in no way selfish or exclusive, i.e., did not in any way involved the exploitation of any other human being. Thus, considered, it would spread like the proverbial snowball gathering strength in geometrical progression encircling the whole earth. It followed that Swadeshi was that spirit which dictated man to serve his next-door neighbour to the exclusion of any other as already mentioned. Accordingly, Swadeshi is never exclusive. Regarding the third question of an element of hatred or chauvinism for the foreigner it may be added here that Gandhi's arguments in this case were as under:

> "I have never been an advocate of prohibition of all foreign things because they are foreign. My economic creed is a complete taboo in respect of all foreign commodities whose importation is likely to prove harmful to our indigenous interest. This means that we may not in any circumstance import a commodity that can be adequately supplied from our own country. For instance, I would regard it a sin to import Australian wheat on the score of its better quality, but I would not have the slightest hesitation in importing oatmeal from Scotland, if an absolute necessity for it is made out, because we do not grow oats in India. In other words, I would not countenance the boycott of a single foreign article out of ill-will or feeling of hatred".[42]

On the contrary, he pointed out that India produced a sufficient quantity of leather and "it is my duty, therefore, to wear shoes made out of Indian leather only, even if it is comparatively dearer and of an inferior quality, in preference to cheaper and superior quality foreign leather shoes. Similarly, I would condemn the introduction of foreign molasses or sugar, if enough of it is produced in India for our needs. It will be thus clear from the above that it is hardly possible for me to give an exhaustive catalogue of foreign articles whose importation in India ought to be prohibited.

I have simply inculcated the general principle by which we can be guided in all such cases. And this principle will hold good in future, too, so long as the conditions of production in our country remain as they are today".[43]

Similarly, in the economic field, our activities are oriented towards the production and consumption of goods and services for the satisfaction of our wants. Let us see how Gandhi's philosophy applies to both these fields. In production, one will have to give priority to the utilization or employment of local resources in material sand manpower in consumption too one will have to give priority to what is manufactured locally. In both cases, the arguments that are put forward against according priority to the neighbour or local manpower and resources, and in the field of consumption, to local employee is incompetent, he is inadequately equipped in skills his technology is inferior, and therefore, the quality of his products cannot be compared with the quality of the goods produced elsewhere, generally in other countries. The second argument is that indigenous products are costlier, more expensive. If we follow these arguments and switch to or prefer goods manufactured in other countries, we will put our neighbour out of employment and contribute to a money drain that will benefit other countries at the cost of our nation.[44] As a result the spirit of Swadeshi would certainly demand that one should work for the improvement of our skills, improve our technology and improve the quality and excellence of our goods, and put up with poorer quality till such time as we improve the quality of our goods. In reality the spirit of Swadeshi thus acts as an incentive to improve our technology. And, there is nothing in the philosophy of Swadeshi that asks us to be content with archaic or ineffective technology or to abjure the up gradation of technology.

The above discussion shows that to Gandhian Swadeshi is both a principle of evolution or construction, a creative principle, as well as an instrument of struggle for the economic regeneration of the masses. Swadeshi is equally valid in all spheres of human activity and all spheres in which man is capable of evolution. The stream of culture demands that we should not uproot ourselves from our heritage, which has taken its shape and texture from the thoughts and efforts of those who are, and who were proximate to us. To be ignorant of this heritage or to repudiate it is inconsistent with the spirit of Swadeshi as it is the base on which one builds. Therefore, one should contribute to its improvement or enrichment. This needs a lot of introspection and one must be able to detect and remove deficiencies and whatever is untenable. Besides, one should not fear any exposure to other cultural heritage. Rather, one should absorb whatever one finds it better. However, one should not allow one's roots to wither away or be eroded. Gandhi has very beautifully presented his ideas in the following words:

> "I do not want my house to be walled in on all sides, and my windows to be stuffed. I want the cultures of all lands to be blown about my house as freely as possible. But I refuse to be blown off my feet by any. I refuse to live in other people's houses as an interloper, a beggar or a slave...Mine is not a religion of the prison house"[45].

Thus, Swadeshi is the doctrine consistent with the law of humanity and love as envisaged by Gandhi. This involves love and service of motherland and mankind as a whole. This means that we can do the best to those who are immediately known to us and our neighbour and our countrymen must be the first to receive our service. This, in fact, is nothing but humanism or love of mankind. So, Swadeshi is a dynamic concept in Gandhian thought and spirit.

Keeping in view this question, it is important to examine the results of the policies and decisions implemented since the dawn of Independence. It has been seen that even after more than fifty years of our Independence, it is very sad and distressing to experience that India, the so-called largest democracy in the world, still continues to be one of the foremost poorest countries in the world.[46] It is the tragedy of the first magnitude that crores of Indians, representing more than 40 per cent (figures vary) of the population, are living below the poverty line. Similarly, the numbers of unemployed and under-employed are on the increase. At present there are several crore job-seekers (including professionals like engineers, doctors, etc.) on the live registers of the various employment exchanges in the country. We are becoming bankrupt as a government with a huge amount of debt (external and internal) resulting, we occupy the unenviable position of ranking fourth in foreign indebtedness among the countries of the world.

After the entry of the multinationals in India, the situation has not improved at all. Rather, India has been dubbed as a land of bootleggers, smugglers and black-marketeers. Firstly, the thirst for power, pelf and position of the political bigwigs remains unquenched and sound democratic practices are thrown to the winds. The fundamental rights guaranteed by the original first Constitution are no longer fundamental now. The increasing statism, the denigration of the judiciary, the criminalization of politics, the politicization of criminals and sedulous promotion of personality cult are complete negation of democratic principles. At present politics has become the most paying profession. Rank political opportunism has become the rule of the day. Corruption is being institutionalized and it has also been said that now India has become a land of whiners, corrupt, gamblers and faultfinders.

In such an economic-political set-up, with booming population and meager capital, what is the way out? The need of the hour is to reverse the country's economic policy with a view to redistributing income to attain economic freedom, to fulfil basic material needs of every citizen and to develop a self-reliant economy. Our political freedom is incomplete without economic independence. The deepening economic crisis should open our eyes. We should not ape alien models of economic progress. We should evolve an indigenous model based on our culture, our past traditions, present requirements and aspiration for the future. We must devise an economic system based on materialistic management and humanistic economics (integral humanism) and create an infrastructure in which and by which the inherent potentialities of man may find their highest fulfilment.[47] The man—the integral man (and his happiness) must be the centre of this system. Swadeshi may provide an alternative.

In fact, without Swadeshi, where is the solution? Swadeshi, through decentralized rural industry and village arts and crafts, can provide employment and steady income and can also help in reducing the poverty of the millions. Trained in the Western way, we often forget that 'Small is Beautiful'. We should aim at gross village product (GVP) instead of GNP. Rightly did Gandhi declare in the forties, "Cut down your wants and at once all your economic problems will be solved." The theory of non-possession has a deep rooted meaning in economy.

However, in spite of the logic in the above contentions, people are still doubtful about the concept of Swadeshi, which they ridicule as old-fashioned, out dated and reactionary. The craze for foreign articles among the country's elite and middle class people has no limit. Moreover, their possession has become a status symbol. Such an attitude is not a healthy one as it will hamper the country's progress and development. We may lose our individuality and become slaves once again. Therefore, we must revive the spirit of Swadeshi and encourage the use of Indian goods, Indian resources and modernise indigenous technology wherever necessary. Swadeshi in consumption is essential for evolving a self-reliant economy. The positive content of Swadeshi should be used as the cornerstone for the reconstruction and promotion of our economy.

Further, where industrialisation is a must, it must not be in blind imitation of the West. Nature is to be milked and not misused or abused. There should be integrated thinking in ecology, economics and ethics. Emphasis should be laid on labour intensive rather than capital-intensive industries under the present grim situation. The problem of unemployment and under employment must be handled on war footing. Economic and industrial policies be aimed at maximising employment so as to enable the people to have more purchasing power having our focus on the needs of the poor masses.

As a matter of fact, Gandhi developed Swadeshi movement during our struggle for freedom as a weapon to cut the roots of colonial economic interests and exploitation as well as to utilized our own local resources and manpower to the maximum. Now the time has come to rebuild the same spirit of Swadeshi and self-reliance to defeat the evil design of neo-imperialistic economic vested interests of multi-nationals and economically advanced nations. Sometimes, one has to face the music of too much liberalization as the side effects prove to be very dangerous and fatal ones. Our multi-crore security scams and other scandals are the best illustrations in this respect.[48] Undoubtedly, India needs rapid economic development, however, it is not possible without inculcating the spirit of Swadeshi, self-reliance and self-confidence. For this purpose there is an immediate need to understand the meaning of true Swadeshi which means lesser dependence on foreign goods and maximum use of our own resources keeping in view the basic needs of our immediate surroundings without neglecting the universal human element and Swadeshi is the way to solve the problem of exploitation and inequality. Accordingly, there is an urgent need to examine and re-examine the growing impact and merits and demerits of liberalization and globalization.

Notes and References

1. Naidu, M.V., "Globalization: Threat or Promise?" in *Gandhi Marg* (New Delhi: Gandhi Peace Foundation), Vol. 21, No. 1, April-June 1999, p. 21.

2. *Ibid.*
3. Ahluwalia, B.K. (ed.), M.K. Gandhi—Selected Speeches (New Delhi: Sagar Publications), October 2, 1969, p. 30.
4. Gandhi, M.K., Collected Works of Mahatma Gandhi (New Delhi: Publication Bureau, Government of India), November 1964, January 1915-October 1917, Vol. No. 13, p. 261.
5. Gandhi, M.K., *Young India* (Ahmedabad: Navajivan Publishing House), 1981, Jan. 19, 1921, Vol. No. III, p. 20. (Herein after to be cited as *Young India*).
6. *Ibid.*, May 12, 1927, Vol. No. IX, p. 150.
7. Hingorani, Anand T. (ed.), Gandhi For 21st Century (Mumbai: Bharatiya Vidya Bhavan), 1998, Vol. No. 22, p. 4.
8. *Ibid.*
9. Tendulkar, D.G., Mahatma (New Delhi: The Publications Division, Ministry of Information and Broadcasting), Vol. II (1920-29), New Edition (Revised), March 1961, p. 21.
10. *Young India*, Dec. 8, 1921, Vol. No. III, p. 406.
11. *Young India*, March 12, 1925, Vol. No. VII, p. 88.
    "I work for India's freedom because my Swadeshi teaches me that being born in it and having inherited her culture, I am fittest to serve her and she has a prior claim to my service. But my patriotism is not exclusive; it is calculated not only not to hurt any other nation, but to benefit all in the true sense of the word. India's freedom, as conceived by me, can never be a menace to the world."—*Young India*, April 3, 1924, Vol. VI, p. 109.
12. *Young India*, March 12, 1925, Vol. No. VII, p. 88.
13. *Young India*, January 8, 1925, Vol. No. VII, p. 11.
14. The Developed World controls 60% of the World's Newspapers, 65% of the World's Radios and 65% of the Books published in the World. See Sean McBride *et al.*, Many Voices, One World (London: UNESCO and Kogan Press), 1980, p. 125.
    See also: Naidu, M.V., "Globalization: Threat or Promise?" in *Gandhi Marg*, Vol. 21, No. 1, April-June 1999, p. 22.
15. *Ibid.*, pp. 22-24.
16. The Selected Works of Mahatma Gandhi (Ahmedabad: Navajivan Trust), Vol. VI, The Voice of Truth 1968, p. 441.
17. Ibid. p. 339.
18. Menon, M.S.N., "Swadeshi Spells Success" in The Tribune, Chandigarh, March 10, 2002, Spectrum, p. 1.
19. Tandon, B.B., "Swadeshi Today—Issues Before Us" in Arya, P.P. and Tandon, B.B., *Multinationals Versus Swadeshi Today—A Policy Framework for Economic Nationalism* (New Delhi: Deep & Deep Publications Pvt. Ltd.), 1999, p. 4.
20. CWMG, *op. cit.*, 1971, December 1930-April 1931, Vol. No. 45, p. 342.
21. Hingorani, Anand T. (ed.), The Gospel of Swadeshi (Bombay: Bharatiya Vidya Bhavan), 1967, Vol. No. 16, p. 93.
22. Hingorani, Anand T. (ed.), Service Before Self (Bombay: Bharatiya Vidya Bhavan), 1998 Edition, Vol. No. 22, p. 53.

23. Gandhi, M.K., From Yeravda Mandir (Ahmedabad: Navajivan Publishing House), December 1999, p. 38.
24. Gill, S.S., Gandhi A Sublime Failure (New Delhi: Rupa & Co.), 2001, p. 133.
25. Kripalani, J.B., "The Meaning of Swadeshi" in *Gandhi Marg*, *op. cit.*, July 1967, Vol. 11, No. 3, p. 284.
26. *Ibid.*
27. *Ibid.*
28. *Ibid.*, pp. 284-85.
29. *Ibid.*, p. 287.
30. *Ibid.*, p. 289.
31. Panda, A.N., "Swadeshi: The Gandhian Approach to Self-reliance" in Mishra, Anil Dutta (ed.), *Challenges of 21st Century—Gandhian Alternatives* (New Delhi: Mittal Publications), 2003, p. 189.
32. Quoted by Ganguli, B.N., Gandhi's Social Philosophy—Perspective And Relevance (New Delhi: National Gandhi Museum), 2000, pp. 299-300.
33. *Ibid.*
34. *Ibid.*
35. *Ibid.*
36. *Ibid.*, p. 301.
37. *Ibid.*
38. Gandhi, M.K., From Yeravda Mandir, *Op. cit.*, p. 38.
39. *Ibid.*
40. *Young India*, 17-2-1929, p. 218.
41. Varma, Ravindra, "Gandhi's Philosophy of Swadeshi" in Gangrade, K.D. and Radhakrishnan, N. (eds.), Gandhi and The Changing Facets of India (New Delhi: Gandhi Smriti and Darshan Samiti), 1998, p. 26.
42. *Young India*, 15-11-1928.
43. *Ibid.*
44. Varma, Ravindra, "Gandhi's Philosophy of Swadeshi", *op. cit.*, pp. 27-28
45. *Young India*, June 1, 1921, pp. 170-71.
46. Manohar Lal Sharma, "Globalization And Swadeshi: A Gandhian Perspective" in *Social Sciences Research Journal*, (Chandigarh: Panjab University), Volume 7, Nos. 1 and 2, 1999, p. 132.
47. *Ibid.*, p. 133.
48. *Ibid.*, p. 134.

5

Reversing Globalization

An Indian Experience

PRAVIN KUMAR

The year 1991 denotes a turning point in Indian Economic History. A new economic principle was formulated due to growing international pressure and internal economic compulsions whereby self-contented, internalized, introvert, state-controlled slow moving Indian Economy were transformed into an open, liberalized, ever-expanding dynamic one under a process popularly termed as *Globalizing Indian Economy*. This was not an easy process. Through a combination of economic, technological, administrative, cultural and constitutional initiatives, the closed doors of Indian Economy was opened (albeit forcefully) and gradually integrated into Global Economic Highway through different generations of Reform. Opening of Indian trade for international traders and institutions, attracting global Investment for internal reconstruction and regeneration of productive bases, facilitating capital flow across the national boundaries, making disinvestment to encourage private sector and to dilute the steel grip of public sector over economy, forcing bureaucracy to decontrol its command over different sectors of economy, etc. were some of the steps which were taken to integrate Indian economy with that of World Economic Order. Computerization and modernization of Information Technology played a crucial role in the process. At the heart of the process lied the deepening trend of privatization whereby Indian Government gradually put herself outside the business of the state. Competition at the Marketplace than the Governmental management of the economic affair became keyword of economic organization. An altogether a new dynamics of Economic Process was tried to be created after 1991 primarily to make Indian Economy subservient to the needs of Western Multinational Companies once again in less than 50 years of its decolonization. Though Indian Economists and Administrators on their part try to use this situation in the best of the Indian interests to force Indian Growth story to enter into a new realm altogether. Thus, Indian Experience of Globalization put before us a dialectical reality with regard to differing interests of global business interest *vis-à-vis* their Indian counterpart which needs to be decoded while evaluating the performance of the new economic regime.

Globalizing Indian economy from 1991 to 2013 therefore raises two sets of questions. Whether forced opening of otherwise closed doors of Indian economy did result into making Indian economy subservient to the needs and requirements of the western world and the Multinational Companies therein. Did they succeed in converting India into their vast market for the consumption of goods and services which was vital for their long term sustenance? In other words, whether western economies through the International Institutions like IMF and World Bank did succeed in reversing the process of decolonization of 1950's or 60's and converting countries like India into their neo-colonies. If not, then is it due to the internal resilience of the native economies like that of Indians or because of the internal weaknesses of the western countries that crept into their economic system in 1970's, or because of both. Was it proved detrimental to their sucking abilities of native resource base as was the English case in the last two centuries with respect to her Indian colony, once regarded as the brightest jewel of English Crown? What made economies like India competitive even in newly-globalised liberal regime? Was it because of growing solidity of system as a result of post-colonial consolidation under Jawahar Lal Nehru and Indira Gandhi? Or, was it because of a new vision of Governance of Rajiv Gandhi, youngest of the Indian prime ministers with child like innocent charm, and the subsequent Computer Revolution which was in fact the most important contribution to India by him. Are we in position to give credit for the resurrection of India after 1991 to the policies of Narsimha Rao and Manmohan Singh who made India withstand to the recent onslaught of western penetration? What kind of role did ever expanding young Indian Middle Class play in this extraordinary about turn of the native economy in the First decade of the twenty-first century? Whether the second decade of 21st century is witnessing some sort of reverse globalization and if yes, then how and why? Before we attempt to answer these questions, let us dwell in short on the history of globalization in the West and also in India as it will provide us the proper plateform to go deep into these issues.

GLOBALIZATION IN THE WEST

Before the beginning of Modern Era with Renaissance, the history of the West is best characterized in terms of prevailing feudal tendencies which meant, apart from other things, localization of productive processes resulting into self-sufficient local economies where production was aimed, at best, for local consumption than the distant market. Inter-geographical connections through distant and overseas trade was therefore more or less irrelevant, though the existing feudal economy did create demand of luxurious goods for few of the feudal elites of the society but the volume of such demand was too limited to foster the growth of regular inter-regional links. Urbanization, monetization, opening of economies, etc. were hardly required in such societies. Things however started changing with the beginning of Geographical Discoveries. Renaissance and Reformation Movements in the different parts of Europe which helped in the process by creating necessary sociological environment for the growth of inter regional trade and therefore integration of markets in Europe and across it. Thus began an era which is identified as an era of *Proto-globalization* by the eminent historians such as *Chirstopher Baily* and *A.G. Hopkins*[1]. Colonization, creation of Colonial Empires, formation of Regulating and Charters Companies such as British East India Company and French East India Companies among the others, Bullionism, Mercantalism, etc. were some of the feathers of the era from 1600 to 1800.[2] The resultant European expansion and consequent hegemony proved detrimental to the big economies of the East such as that of Ottoman Empire or Chinese or Mughal Empire which were forced to the brink of virtual slavery and bankruptcy. Slave trade, Thirty Year Wars, English Civil War, etc. were some of the ugliest chapters of the change from the womb of which gradually came into existence what we proudly refer to as the beginning of Modernity and Capitalism, along with growing tendencies of revolt, insurgency, resistance to change among the popular sections of society globally as its byproduct.

With Industrialization, growth of Capitalism, Communication Revolution through steam engines, rails, canals, ships, post or cables and democratization of European polity, the form of proto-globalization process started transforming into fully grown globalization of modern type which, unlike earlier stage, was not limited to only Europe and European Colonial and semi-colonial Empires but it started engulfing into it virtually all the regions of the globe. The process expressed itself through some of the most inhuman and unequal exchange of men, material, crops and diseases. The world became more unequal and more uneven.[3] It was due to the necessity of searching raw materials for European and American Industries, creating markets in Asia, Africa, Australia and Latin America for European and American Industrial productions and services, outlets for the Investments and maintaining the mega profiteering tendencies of Western Capitalism. Not only that the developed economies of Europe and America started specializing and monopolizing in the productive processes. For example, Developed European economies started over emphasizing on the production of staple industries like those of coal, ship-building or steel. Similarly, United States concentrated on the production for consumer markets with special attention on motor-vehicle industries. Eastern European countries and U.S. also started monopolizing the Agrarian trade World over. If one goes back to the first half of the 20th century, the only financier world over were the Americans. These were some of the factors that started globalizing the world economy. That is why the politicians from the different parts of the world agreed in the Bretton Woods Conference (1944) to lay down the framework of International monetary policies with regard to trade, commerce, investment and finance. The ongoing world recession due to 2nd World War conditionality, with regards to fiscal and balance of payment situation and oil payment related problems forcing the countries to opt protectionist devices to safeguard their respective national interests, compelled the economists and decision-makers of liberal school to take immediate initiative in the right direction to thwart the possible protectionist direction of the world economy. Therefore, Charter of the *International Monetary Fund* and the *World Bank* were drafted and signed in this very Conference. Two years later from the formation of these two International Economic Organizations, USA put forwarded a draft for the creation of another international organization known as International Trade Organization as the third pillar of the globalizing economy. The attempt however didn't succeed as US Congress was in no mood to support the initiative. But in 1947, 23 countries which included India finally agreed to sign the General Agreement on Tariffs and Trade which acquired a definite organized shape next year in 1948 during Havana Conference. World economy started integrating due to the eight rounds of negotiations amongst the member states from 1947 to 1993. The Table 1[4], drawn below, could give us a brief idea about the related developments, in between:

TABLE I

Year	*Rounds*	*Place*	*Subjects Negotiated*	*Number of participating states*
1947	First	Geneva	Reduction in trade and tariff barriers (t&t)	23
1949	Second	Annecy	147 sets of bilateral negotiations on t&t	13
1951	Third	Torquay	Widening of membership than any reform	38
1956	Fourth	Geneva	Countries including China withdrew from it	26
1960-61	Fifth	Geneva (Dillon Round)	Tariffs relating measures	26
1964-67	Sixth	Geneva (Kennedy Round)	Tariffs and Anti-Dumping Measures	62
1973-79	Seventh	Geneva (Tokyo Round)	Tariffs, Non-tariff Measures and "Framework" Agreements	102
1986-93	Eighth	Geneva (Uruguay Round)	Tariffs, Non-tariff Measures, rules Services, Intellectual Property Rights, Dispute Settlements, Establishment of WTO, etc.	123

Despite definite progress towards globalization under GATT, the world economic community felt an urgent need of an International body to further the cause of free global trade during the Uruguay Round itself and as a result of this realization; *World Trade Organization (WTO)* came into existence in January 1, 1995. Apart from raising standards of living and income, ensuring full employment, expanding production and trade and optimisingly using the world resources, WTO also aimed at promoting the idea of "sustainable growth" and decentralizing the profit of globalization to the developing and under-developed countries through enlarging their share in the international trade. To ensure them, WTO accepted the responsibility to administer and implement the multilateral and plurilateral trade agreements, act as a forum for multilateral trade organization, resolve trade disputes, oversee national trade policies and co-operate with other international institutions involved in global policy making. WTO with membership more than 148 (more and more willing to join), unlike GATT, is empowered to enforce rules of global commerce through the coercive tools of economic sanction and other measures with regards to food and environmental standard, regulation of services such as insurance and transport, use of tax dollars, copyright and patent laws, farm policy, etc. Thus emerged an institution with its dispute settlement organ intact emerged strongly on the world platform to enforce globalization through:

1. Reduction of trade barriers to permit free flow of goods and services among the different countries;
2. Creation of economic and moral environment in which free flow of capital could take place across the globe;
3. Making of environment friendly development through free flow of technology between developed and developing economies; and
4. Encouragement of an environment of reciprocity in which developed countries of the world need to be encouraged and, if necessary, be forced to permit the free movement of labour from the developing and under-developed countries of the world.

Obviously Globalization refers to a process of internationalized liberalization fostering "closer integration of the countries and peoples of the world which has been brought about by the enormous reduction of costs of transportation and communications, and breaking down of artificial barriers to the flow of goods and services, capital, knowledge, and (to a lesser extent) people across borders."[5]

GLOBALIZATION IN INDIA

India witnessed two distinct kinds of globalization. One with the beginning of modernity in the 18th and 19th century and another by the end of 20th century, precisely from 1991, when the closed doors of Indian economy was forced to be opened for the world capitalism. First dose of globalization was somewhat distorted one. Before the battle of Plassey in 1757, when the fortune of the state for future was virtually sealed in favour of the business interest of the East India Company, the Indian economy was fairly integrated with the world economy and according to one estimate, 25% of the world trade at that time was actually Indian export trade to the markets of the western world. In the first phase of colonization of Indian economy, the EIC actually tried to monopolize the Indian export trade so as to make it the most successful English company dealing with the commerce of Orient or otherwise.[6] The distortion though began in the second phase of colonialism when the bases of Indian handicraft Industry was destroyed and dismantled in the most clinical fashion with the Introduction of the so-called policy of 'free trade' with the introduction of the Charter Act of 1813.[7] Through this policy of (partial) free trade, the Indian export market was cleverly dismantled to make it reserve for neo-emerging industrial economy of the Great Britain; the flow of the British industrial and capital goods to Indian market was made smooth with absolutely no friction in the form of any protective tariff and finally Indian economy was transformed gradually into a supplier of the raw material to British Industries. In a way, Indian Economy was made subservient to the needs of British Capitalism. The constitutionalist national fighters of freedom known as the Moderates created successfully a strong public opinion amongst the Indian masses against this ruining, drain and destruction of Indian economy by the British Colonial political and economic structure.[8]

It was this background that forced the decision-makers in India after Independence in 1947 to opt for a policy of protected growth against the policy of globalization which had already started in taking a definite shape in the other side of the World about which we have discussed in the previous section. Again the economic destruction and subsequent crisis forced the Indians not to take the route of the globalization, though India definitely needed western capital and technology to rebuilt and reconstruct otherwise tottering Indian economy. The strategy of planned development within protected market with over-emphasis on Public Sector at the cost of Private

Sector based on the notion of competitive excellence gradually resulted in bureaucratic red-tapism, sluggish growth and what is known as the License-Quota-Permit Raj.[9] The overall result of the strategy of planned growth in the protected market could be sensed from the Table 2[10]:

TABLE 2

Sl. No.	*Plan*	*Plan-Period*	*Target*	*Actual*
1.	First Plan	1951-56	2.1% per Annum	3.6% per Annum
2.	Second Plan	1956-61	4.5% per Annum	4.1% per Annum
3.	Third Plan	1961-66	5.6% per Annum	2.8% per Annum
4.	Fourth Plan	1969-74	5.7% per Annum	3.3% per Annum
5.	Fifth Plan	1974-79	4.4% per Annum	4.8% per Annum
6.	Sixth Plan	1980-85	5.2% per Annum	5.7% per Annum
7.	Seventh Plan	1985-90	5.0% per Annum	6.0% per Annum

The statistics, mentioned above, put us in a strange situation. It is clear that Fifth to Seventh plan period between 1974 and 1990 showed impressive performance as the actual growth rate remained on higher side than the projected ones. Fifth Plan period performed with growth rate of 4.8% than the project rate of 4.4%, whereas in Sixth Plan period, the actual growth rate was 5.7% against the projected rate of 5.2%. Same was the case with Seventh Plan where actual growth rate achieved was 6.0% than the projected rate of 5.0%. It was hard then to grasp the fact the most severe political (decline of Congress regime and Janta Party experiment) and economic crisis that India was forced to face occurred in this period only. In the beginning of the last decade of 20th century, Indian Economy was facing the problems of high fiscal deficit, high current account deficit, growing burden of external debt, etc. She had been finding difficult to handle the situation of oil crisis which had nothing to do with internal dynamics of Indian Economy. With growing burden of foreign debt which amounted to about 84 billion dollars in 1990-91 and rocketing inflation rate of 16.7% in the same period, Indian economy started crumbling with its own weight.[11] Experts and Common People both started losing faith in the strategy of planned development in the protected market. Thus emerged the background in which opening of Indian economy to the world forces was planned by the Indian economists or forced upon us by the external agencies after exploiting the crisis situation at our hand.

Whatever the case might be, doors of Indian market were forcefully opened and the process of globalization began. A new strategy of growth came into existence under the leadership of Narasimha Rao and Manmohan Singh. This time, it was strategy of *planned development in the open market.*

INDIAN ECONOMY: OPEN AND GLOBALIZED

With economic reforms of 1991, India experienced a paradigm shift in her growth strategy. The philosophy of planned development remained intact but it was synchronized with the requirements of a truly globalized economy but not in one go but through generations of reform. New refreshing wind was unleashed that transformed otherwise self contented, introvert, slow and highly regulated and regimented economic structure into one that was transparent, competitive, open and growth stimulating. Though beginning was made to tackle the foreign exchange liquidity crisis due to Gulf War and flight of capital, but very soon the problem of fiscal crisis took the centre stage. The experts provided us two pronged strategy for tiding over the immediate and the long term crisis. The first of the steps were taken at the level of macroeconomic stabilization to overcome the problem of fiscal and balance of payment deficits. Another set of reforms were initiated to correct long term ailments relating to the policies of trade and industry through a definite and strong dose of liberalization, both through deregularization and decontrol over domestic and foreign investment as well as through opening of trade policies to enable the entry of foreign business elements. This ended the old era of License Permit Raj and created an environment of competition. Eighth, Ninth, Tenth and Eleventh Plan had tried to flee on a new growth trajectory on this very idea. Even, with the introduction of the Twelfth Plan, we do not expect any substantial change in this growth strategy.

When fiscal reform[12] was initiated, the aim was to simplify the existing structure, to make it efficient and logical which was thought necessary for widening of the tax base and therefore for augmenting the Financial foundation of the country. Without resorting to this step, it was impossible for the Government to control the ever increasing Budget deficit over the years and to bring back the economy on the right path. Similarly reform was initiated for the Financial Sector[13] as well whereby restrictions pertaining to administered interest rate, credit flow, high reserve requirements under Cash-Reserve Ratio and pre-emption of significant proportion of lendable resources for the priority Sectors, etc. were removed to make this sector vibrant and dynamic. Like banking sector, the doors of the Insurance Sector were also opened for private participation.[14] The Government announced a new Industrial Policy in July 1991which introduced radical changes to unshackle the Indian economy from the cobwebs of unnecessary bureaucratic control and MRTP was empowered to initiate investigation suo moto or on complaints received from Individual consumers or classes of consumers about monopolistic, restrictive and unfair trade practices. Momentum to the process was given by simplifying custom duties, removing quantative restriction on Imports, establishing new exchange rate policies and making Indian currency fully convertible. Thus gradually emerged an economic system based on privatization, decontrol, liberalization and thus on Globalization that provided wings to the Indian growth story. The sense could be decoded when one compares the 1.4% growth rate of 1991-92 when India was trapped in crisis with that of the average growth rate of 5.8% in the period between 1992-03 to 2002-03 or with amazing growth rate of 8.5% that India experienced between 2002-03 to 2010-11.[15] The overall performance of the Indian Economy in this period could be understood with the help of Table 3:[16]

TABLE 3

Sl. No.	*Economic Indicators*	*1951-52*	*1990-91*	*2007-08*	*2010-11*
1.	GDP at Current Price Factor (In Crore)	9719	515032	4582086	7157412
2.	Gross Domestic Saving (% of GDP)	8.6	22.8	36.8	32.3
3.	Agricultural Prod. Index (Base-1981-82)	46.2	148.4	207.1	215.3
4.	Industrial Prod. Index (Base: 2004-05 = 100)	7.9	91.6	141.7	165.5
5.	Export (In Crore)	606	32553	1374436	1142649
6.	Import (In Crore)	608	43198	1012312	1683467
7.	Foreign Exchange Reserve (In Rs. Crore)	911	4388	1196023	1225999

What clearly emerges from the table that Indian economy expanded at surprising rate in the era of globalization if one compares it with the performance in pre-globalization era. Rate of gross domestic saving which was only 8.6% of GDP in 1950-51 reached to its peak of 36.8% in 2007-08. It shows that India at that time had capacity and potential to take a quantum jump towards its economic expansion and growth. Same trend was visible if one compares the data relating to agricultural and Industrial production. Indian economy was on the verge of transforming into one of the most developed economies of the world. But careful examination of the data also establishes the fact that economic acceleration started slowing down after 2007-08. A sense of economic fatigue was clearly visible in overall performance of Indian economy. That was quite an alarming signal for the decision makers in Indian Government. Whether it was a result of gradually emerging global economic crisis or a result of prevailing attitude in the bureaucracy, which had been being explained these days with the phrase of 'policy paralysis' in the Government Working, or of both, needs to be examined carefully. The experts also need to ascertain whether failure on the part of the government to introduce timely the next generations of reform had any role in the growing slow down effect. It might be because of gradual strengthening of the Western economy, especially that of US and others.

Whatever the case might be, the result of this policy-stagnation and inability on the part of Government Agencies to enhance and introduce the new generations of reform has been proving detrimental to the economic stability of the developing countries like India. Even the Report of the World Commission on the Social Dimension of the Globalization (WCSDG)[17] supports the varied impact of globalization over varying regions and economies. Though we have to accept the fact that during the period from 1990-2003, Indian trade grew at the impressive rate of 9.1%,[18] whereas the rate of growth for the same of China and Mexico was much faster which grew at the rate of 16.2% and 11.4% respectively in the same period. But even this moderate momentum of growth with respect to Chine standard failed to continue in the later part of globalization period. Same is the case with the service sector which expanded with the rate of 17.5% in the same period[19] which was better than that of Chinese rate. There is also no denying of the fact that with the process of Globalization, the size of Foreign Direct Investment increased considerably over time, especially in the high priority areas such as energy, tele-communications, electrical elements, computer software, transportation and metallurgical industries through the slow pace of the approval and clearance of some of the projects based on FDI remained the cause of concern. But the negative aspect of this globalization is the fact that import grew at faster rate than the export[20] resulting into negative balance of trade and [21] payment and therefore rising pressure over the Indian which was responsible for its gradual devaluation with respect to dollar and other major world currencies. These were the inherent weaknesses of Indian process of globalization that made Indian economy vulnerable to the current crisis in the World economy. We are now experiencing negative growth rate in our Industrial production, the exchange rate of Indian currencies has been witnessing considerable devaluation and experts fear that it may soon touch to Rs. 65 with respect to US dollar. The overall growth rate has declined to less than 5% resulting into serious social and economic crisis. In other words, we are very close to the end of the glorious chapter of globalization which began in 1990.

The social consequence of the globalization is significant while evaluating the durability and continuation possibility of the process of liberalization and Globalization. It is strange but interesting to note that even in the period between 1990 and 2003 which was one of the better periods of the Globalization, the open unemployment increased world over and the situation was more severe in Latin America, the Caribbean and the South-East Asia. In India, for example, the growth rate of employment declined to 0.98% in 1994 to 2000 period which was 2.04% in the period from 1983 to 1994 as per Table 4.[22]

TABLE 4
Growth Rate of Employment

Sl. No.	*Sectors*	*1983-94*	*1994-2000*
1.	Agriculture	1.51	-0.34
2.	Mining and Quarrying	4.16	-2.85
3.	Manufacturing	2.14	2.05
4.	Electricity, Gas and Water Supply	4.50	-0.88
5.	Construction	5.32	7.09
6.	Trade	3.57	5.05
7.	Transport, Storage and Communication	3.24	6.04
8.	Financial Services	7.18	6.20
9.	Community and Personal Services	2.90	0.55
	Total	2.04	0.98

It is clear from the above Table that employment generation capability in the period of the most dynamic period of Globalization remained restricted to manufacturing, construction, trade, transport, storage and communication; rest of the sectors showed negative growth rate in the same period. Due to global slowdown and the so called policy paralysis in the bureaucratic decision making, situation even in these sectors look depressing. There is no denying of the fact that this employment growth in certain sectors was responsible for the expansion of the Great Indian Middle Class who provided the desired leadership in creating the famed Indian growth story of the last and first decade of the 20th and 21st century. But the same Indian Middle Class looked very nervous with the emerging economic Indicators in the recent times, especially with those of growing fiscal and current account deficit, decelerating manufacturing sector, declining foreign direct investment to the country, rocketing oil bill and rate of inflation and depreciating Indian currency. The other sections of Indian Society hardly gained anything substantial from this globalizing Indian economy. Rising cost of living further created economic pressure on them. The situation could be understood in terms of Human Resource Development Index where India stood on the 134th ladder of the pyramid in 2011 whereas the small state like Sri Lanka holds the 97th position, and Singapore, Korea and Japan hold the 26th, 15th and 12th position respectively.[23] The differing social indicators with regards to Indian economy over a period of time would further de-complicate the issue which could be sensed from the Table 5.[24] What is though clear from it is that despite all the

TABLE 5

Selected Indicators for Indian Society

Sl. No.	*Social/Other Indicators*	*1990-91*	*2007-8*	*2010-11*
1.	Population (In Crore)	83.9	113.8	121.0
2.	Birth Rate (per 1000)	29.5	23.5	22.1
3.	Death Rate (per 1000)	9.8	7.4	7.2
4.	Male Literacy Rate in %	64.1	—	—
5.	Female Literacy Rate in %	39.3	—	—
6.	Total Literacy Rate in %	52.2	—	74.0
7.	RMP per 10000	4.7	—	—
8.	No. of Universities/Deemed Univ.	—	—	436
9.	No. of Professional colleges	—	—	25938
10.	No. of Polytechnic Colleges	—	—	1914

brave talks of Shining India or that of spectacular growth story, the social infrastructure is so bad that the slightest fluctuation in economic performance had potential to create a sense of uneasiness and at times even some sort of social insurgency in the already unstable Indian society. One such example was the event of 2012 when people and leaders related to more than 60 popular movements decided to hold a cooperative parliament at Jantar Mantar at New Delhi. All these things suggest that Indian economy in globalizing state has now reached to a crossroad when a major decision or diversion is definitely required if the decision makers are in the mood to answer some of the challenges which have been put before us in the most threatening manner.

Is Reversing Globalization only Alternative to the Emerging Problems?

By the middle of 2013, It has become almost clear that the kind of Globalization India had carefully developed over the last 25 years in its current form lacks potential to serve panacea for her all the economic ills. Even other participating countries in the process, and some of them who are outsiders, have witnessed the growing dischantment against the policy of free trade, liberalization and globalization on various counts. One, the process of globalization has started reducing the role of nation states in favour of International agencies such as World Bank, WTO, International Courts, NGOs, global philanthropic groups, etc. Once globalizing economics starts faltering on performance, the opposition to it was bound to emerge as is the case in India now a days. Even arguments such as globalization being responsible for spread of diseases as diseases are transcending national boundaries due to it, are being articulated by the critics everywhere. Spread of AIDS/HIV, tuberculosis, small pox, chagas disease, etc. are attributed to this process. Environmentalists have their own concern against this process. For example, according to one of the reports, "the world's ecological capacity is simply insufficient to satisfy the ambitions of China, Japan, India, Europe and the United States as well as the aspirations of the rest of the world in a sustainable way",[25] and if China and India were to consume as much resources as those US or Japan by 2030, a full planet of earth would be required to meet their aspirations.[26] But economic experiences in India after independence emphatically shows that protectionist policies that India followed from 1950 to 1990 resulted in sluggish growth and license-permit-quota raj, whereas the policy of liberalization, decontrol, completion and free trade under Globalization made India one of the most promising economies world over. Due to policy shift in 1991, about 300 million people which are equivalent to the entire population of the US have successfully crossed the poverty line, a wonderful achievement which is attributed to this policy. There is no denying of the fact that this policy has resulted in emergence of very powerful and vibrant Indian Middle Class which has created a huge market not only for the Indian consumer Industries but the consumer industries of the whole world. In other world, the positive potentialities of this policy could not be simply put aside.

However, growth strategy needs to be redefined so that a more equitable development trajectory could be achieved. Not only that, we are also required to make certain subtle changes in our policies and performance to distress our economic system of unproductive burdens which are reasons for growing politics of subsidies such as plan of MGNREGA or food security which has already bleeded or has potential to bleed the economic system in most uneconomic ways. We are not at all suggesting overturning the policy of Inclusive development or what the experts these days insists upon, i.e., development with human face. What we are suggesting to make the strategy of equitable development more productive, efficient and self-sufficient that the state is not required financing it through subsidies and other unproductive tools. Once this aim is achieved, on which India needs to concentrate in this juncture, a reverse Globalization is bound to start where FDI would automatically start flowing to our side provided we are ready to remove all the resisting elements from our system through next generations of reform. Balance of payment is bound to become positive and in our favour in opposition to the colonial reality when integration of Indian market to world capitalism resulted in ruin and drain of our economy. The ailment of fiscal and current account deficit is bound to wipe out from our economy to make it productive and efficient.

The most important question before us is as to how Indian economy is going to achieve the above stated aim to start a reverse kind of globalization where integration with the world market result in inflow of resources to our side. In our opinion, we are now in a position to adopt again the old strategy of mixed economy as our growth strategy but with a difference. We have to recognize the fact that India is run on two different kinds of economies. One is that of highly vibrant, lubricated and efficient kind of economy, mostly visible in big and metropolitan cities, which is termed now-a-days as the actual India. Another of them is slow moving, fund and resource hungry and inefficient rural India, described in media and expert's discourse as Bharat. The first one is now strong enough to sustain itself on its own provided the bureaucracy and Indian decision makers agree to allow it. To do exactly that the government is actually required following the policies of disinvestment vigorously, to hand over handles of the urban economy in the private hands. It will create huge resources for the Government and also free it from all the financial liabilities. The government will also be able to collect resources from tax collection from ever expanding arm of this economy. The domain of rural economy will have to be made the responsibility of the public sector where reconstruction and rebuilding of infrastructure is urgently needed. With huge resources at its hand, the government through its public sectors could initiate major reconstruction projects with aim to industrialize and modernize rural Indian economy. The Government is also required to encourage the progressive elements of rural society to re orient their economic direction to make it competitive not only with its urban counterpart but with anyone in the World. Once India decides to move in this direction, we are sure that very soon we shall be able to reach the stage of reverse globalization where we can use the world resources to our advantage.

Notes and References

1. Globalization in World History, A.G. Hopkins (ed.), New York, 2003.
2. For further details, please refer to Europe In Transition by Arvind Sinha, Manohar, New Delhi, 2010 or Rise of the Modern West by Meenaxi Phukan, Macmillan India Limited, New Delhi, 1998.
3. To have the proper understanding of the process, please refer to the books by E.J. Hobbesbawm such as Age of Revolution, Age of Capital and Age of Empires, etc.
4. World Trade Organization, P.K. Vasudeva, Pearson Education, Singapore, 2005' p. 13.
5. Employment, Social Institute and Societal Well-being, Joseph, E. Stiglitz, *International Labour Review*, 2002, Vol. 141, Nos. 1-2, p. 9.
6. Mode of Production Debate, Bipan Chandra and others, Gyan Publishing House, Delhi.
7. Essays in Indian History: Towards a Marxist Perception, Irfan Habib, Tulika, 1995.
8. See, Rise and Growth of Economic Nationalism in India, Bipan Chandra, Macmillan India, Delhi.

9. See, Samaveshi Vikash: Vaikalpik Aarthik Sudharon ke Naye Daur ki Jarurat, Dr. Pravin Kumar, in the forthcoming issue of Lok Prashashan in 2013.
10. Planning Commission, Ninth Five Year Plan (1997-2002).
11. *Ibid.*, Dr. Pravin Kumar.
12. Please refer to Raja Chillaia Committee Report, 1991.
13. Please refer to Narsimham Committee Report, 1991.
14. Please refer to Malhotra Committee Report, 1995.
15. This calculation of the growth rate is credited to Arvind Panagaria on the basis of CSO data. India's Reforms, How they produced Inclusive Growth, Jagadish Bhagavati and Arvind Panagaria (Edt.), OUP, 2011.
16. See Economic Survey, 2011-12, OUP, Govt. of India.
17. WCSDG Report, 2004, p. 25.
18. See Economic Survey, 2011-12, *Ibid.*
19. *Ibid.*
20. *Ibid.*
21. See, WCSDG Report, 2004, p. 41.
22. Report of the Task Force on Employment Opportunities, 2001.
23. See Asia Pacific Human Development Report, 2012.
24. See Economic Survey, 2011-12, *Ibid.*
25. State of the World Report, 2006.
26. Booming Nations 'Threaten Earth', *BBC News*, 12 January, 2006.

6

Globalization Effects on Women

D. Venkateswara Rao

Within the past two and half decades, globalization has created a tremendous impact on the lives of women in developing nations. Globalization can be defined as "a complex economic, political, cultural, and geographic process in which the mobility of capital, organizations, ideas, discourses, and peoples has taken a global or transnational form"[1]. With the establishment of international free trade policies, such as North America Free Trade Agreement (NAFTA) and GATT, transnational corporations are using the profit motive to guide their factories toward developing nations in search of "cheap" female labor. Corporations prefer female labor over male labor because women are considered to be "docile" workers, who are willing to obey production demands at any price. In developing nations, certain types of work, such as garment, agricultural labour, aqua processing units, are considered to be an extension of female household roles. Therefore, cultural influences in developing nations also impacts employment stratification. Bringing a high demand of employment opportunities for women in developing nations creates an instantaneous change within the social structure of these societies. Although the demand for female employment brings about an array of opportunities and a sense of independence, the glass ceiling continues to exist with the "feminization of poverty"[2]. Researchers in the fields of Sociology, Anthropology, and Economics have collected empirical data that shows the consequences of globalization on the lives of women and their families in developing nations. Given these circumstances and the empirical evidence collected in the various studies, does globalization have an overall positive or negative impact on the live of women in developing nations?

The phenomenon of globalization is difficult to define neatly or precisely because it is not a uniform, coherent process in which all aspects of political, economic and social life change in one direction. Rather, it is a complex process that consists of many facets, proceeds at a different pace in various parts of the world, affects different groups of people differently, and often has contradictory consequences. A fundamental component of globalization on which there is wide-spread agreement is that it consists of unchecked spread and intensification of commercialized relations across the world as western multinational corporations and funding agencies increasingly integrate national and regional economies into a world capitalist market. This process brings with it disregard for human needs of an impersonal marketplace, uneven development and fragmentation of humanity into the poor and the rich, and exacerbates divisions—economic, political, educational, and social—between women and men. However, at the same time that globalization creates exploitation and marginalization of many women workers, it also opens up spaces for the empowerment of women.

Another aspect of globalization of which we are all increasingly made aware is that the world is becoming a smaller place as computer and satellite technology and advances in transportation bring people closer together. While this has the potential for developing networks and alliances across differences of culture and nationality, the technology is too frequently used as a medium for imposing North American and Western European ideas and lifestyles on the rest of the world. Rather than becoming a vehicle for indigenous and local expression, the mass media too often present a homogenized, unidimensional view, as, for example, of western feminism. On the other hand, modern technology can be, and has been used by regional and local groups, including women's groups, in their efforts to resist the forces of global homogenization.

WOMEN IN INDIA

It's true that we are in the midst of a great revolution in the history of women. We see the evidence everywhere; the voice of women is increasingly heard in Parliament, courts and in the streets. While women in the West had to fight for over a century to get some of their basic rights, like the right to vote, the Constitution of India gave women equal rights with men from the beginning. Unfortunately, women in this country are mostly unaware of their rights because of illiteracy and the oppressive tradition. Names like Kalpana Chawla: The Indian born, who fought her way up into NASA and was the first women in space, and Indira Gandhi: The Iron Woman of India was the Prime Minister of the Nation, Beauty Queens like Aishwarya Rai and Susmita Sen, and Mother Teresa are not representative of the condition of Indian women.

The Constitution of India guarantees equality of sexes and in fact grants special favors to women. These can be found in three articles [Article 14 , Article 15(3) and Articles 15(A)(e)]. All these are fundamental rights. Therefore, a woman can go to the court if one is subjected to any discrimination. The most important issues stand as those pertaining to marriage, children, abortion, crimes against women, and inheritance. Crimes like rape, kidnapping, eve teasing and indecent exposure can be grouped as crimes against women.

India today, a country where women are becoming more prominent, yet increasing numbers, women are fighting long-standing prejudices. Women still faces enormous pressure to conform to social mores—conforming to traditional roles within families poses as much of a barrier to businesswomen in India as the still-too-thick glass ceiling at companies. Though women have made great strides in the corporate world in the last three decades, women from all income classes are still too often discouraged by family members from having careers that infringe too much on family life.

WOMEN'S CONTRIBUTION TO THE ECONOMY

Although most women in India work and contribute to the economy in one form or another, much of their work is not documented or accounted for in official statistics. Women plough fields and harvest crops while working on farms, women weave and make handicrafts while working in household industries, women sell food and gather wood while working in the informal sector. Additionally, women are traditionally responsible for the daily household chores (e.g., cooking, fetching water, and looking after children). Since Indian culture hinders women's access to jobs in stores, factories and the public sector, the informal sector is particularly important for women. There are estimates that over 90 percent of workingwomen are involved in the informal sector.

The informal sector includes jobs such as domestic servant, small trader, artisan, or field laborer on a family farm. Most of these jobs are unskilled and low paying and do not provide benefits to the worker. More importantly, however, cultural practices vary from region to region. Though it is a broad generalization, North India tends to be more patriarchal and feudal than South India. Women in northern India have more restrictions placed on their behavior, thereby restricting their access to work. Southern India tends to be more egalitarian, women have relatively more freedom, and women have a more prominent presence in society. Cultural restrictions however are changing, and women are freer to participate in the formal economy, though the shortage of jobs throughout the country contributes to low female employment. But in the recent years, conditions of working women in India have improved considerably. More and more women find themselves in positions of respect and prestige; more and more workplaces are now populated with women who work on equal terms as men. Working is no longer an adjustment, a mere necessity; but a means to self worth and growth.

Women have now not only found their place in work places but are also wants their part in governance. In recent years there have been explicit moves to increase women's political participation. Women have been given representation in the Panchayati Raj system as a sign of political empowerment. There are many elected women representatives at the village council level. At the central and state levels too women are progressively making a difference. Today we have woman as Speaker of Parliament of India and few women Chief Ministers in large states of India. The women's reservation policy bill is slated to further strengthen political participation.

GLOBALIZATION

Globalization has also meant the imposition of western liberal democracy as the only desirable model of government and political ideology. "Democratization" is widely perceived today as a movement toward multiparty systems of government and free elections. However, because political democracy is typically confounded with economic liberalization, the shift toward capitalist market economies is seen as part of the global democratization movement. Many assume that as new political systems give more people a "voice," the simultaneous introduction of market economies provides them with greater "choice" as producers and consumers.

Although academics and economists differ on the definition of globalization, globalization can generally be defined as the integration of world economies by removing barriers to trade and encouraging the free flow of foreign investment, private portfolio capital and labor across national boundaries. The main principles upon which the entire theory of globalization is based are as follows:

- Sustained economic growth, as measured by gross national product, is the path to human progress;
- Free markets i.e., markets that are free from government intervention, generally result in the most efficient and socially optimal allocation of resources;
- Economic globalization, is achieved by removing barriers to the free flow of goods and money anywhere in the world, which in turn fosters competition, creates jobs, increases economic efficiencies, lowers consumer prices, increases consumer's choice and is generally beneficial to everyone by increasing overall economic growth; and
- Privatization, which transfers functions and assets from government to the private sector, improves efficiency.

Despite this optimistic outlook towards globalization, globalization has a dark side and has the power to create highly undesirable adverse effects. In particular, globalization has the potential to lead to exploitation of the female workforce and even to jeopardize their safety. It is in this context that the following examination of the concept of globalization and its impact on the working women is necessary.

ECONOMIC GLOBALIZATION

The world economic market depends on the flow of imports and exports between developed and developing nations. Throughout history, developing nations are faced with the lack of capital for the internal development of their country. Deficient funds also puts limitations on the amount of imports transferred from developed to developing nations. In order to stabilize the flow of international capital, the World Bank and International Monetary Fund (IMF) enforce structural adjustment loans (SALs) in developing nations. The amount of power and influence over the World Bank and IMF depends on the amount of capital being invested into the World Bank. The United States has an extremely large amount of capital invested into the World Bank, and is therefore a major instrument in determining the actions and procedures taken by the IMF and World Bank.

The IMF creates "one-sided structural adjustment[s] involving the destruction of real economic activity as well as attempts to construct new forms of production bit without a corresponding destruction of financial capital and without a reconstruction of international financial flows"[3]. Structural adjustments are mainly the privatization of exports in developing nations. Privatization, which causes a dependence on imports from developed nations because the loans from the World Bank, is used to support export factories and can not be distributed to support local firms that don't have an international affiliation. Capitalism motivates corporations towards countries that provide the most labor or resources at the cheapest cost. Corporations have changed the employment structure in developing nations. Prior to development, men and women relied on agricultural production as their main source of occupation. Upon entering these nations, corporations have created a sectoral shift in the labor force from the agricultural sector, to working in other production industries. Females are attracted to assembly production because of the lack of opportunities for female employment in other informal sector. The main reason for this lack of employment is gender employment segregation, which subjects women to inferior employment positions than those held by men. Corporations are reinforcing women's subordinate economic position in society by offering them inferior employment positions and wages that sustain this position.

Globalization has opened up broader communication lines and brought more companies as well as different worldwide organizations into India. This provides opportunities for not only workingmen, but also women, who are becoming a larger part of the workforce. With new jobs for women, there are opportunities for higher pay, which raises self-confidence and brings about independence. This, in turn, can promote equality between the sexes, something that Indian women have been struggling with their entire lives. Globalization has the power to uproot the traditional views towards women so they can take an equal stance in society.

Globalization has had negative implications for Indian women. Their plights are similar to those of women in other developing regions such as Africa and Asia. Globalization has made many international corporations richer by the billions. However, what most people are not aware of is that women in these developing countries are suffering enormously due to this expansion of corporate empires. According to estimates from World Development Indicators, "Women work two-thirds of the world's working hours, produce half of the world's food, but earn only ten percent of the world's income, and own less than one percent of the world's property". According to Vandana Shiva, and Indian eco-feminist and scholar, globalization along with the support of organizations such as the World Bank and the International Monetary Fund, have created slave wages. These wages are not necessarily the result of "unjust" societies, but of the fact that global trade devalues the worth of people's lives and work. While globalization has brought jobs to rural, developing areas such as India where there was previously no employment, these jobs seem to be wolves in sheep's clothing. The work available to women is almost always poorly paid, mentally and physically unhealthy, demeaning, or insecure.

Women are suffering two fold. As women in developing countries move into the work force, their domestic responsibilities are not alleviated. Women work two full time jobs. One in a factory, where they are paid next to nothing, the second is in the home where they are paid nothing. According to Merlin A. Taber and Sushma Batra, editors of the book Social Strains of Globalization in India, development for poor women has meant the migration of men to cities, higher prices for commodities, poorer job opportunities. "The mixture of corporate capitalism and Western culture models is dissolving family and community social controls as witnessed by higher rates of family violence, rape, divorce, and family breakdown."

THE IMPACT OF GLOBALIZATION ON WOMEN IN INFORMAL SECTORS

The emergence of a global market, with its associated policies of privatization, "stabilization", and liberalization, has led to the setting up of smaller new industries with highly flexible organization and simple infrastructure in developing countries. Closely related to this "in formalization" of work is the feminization of work. Labor-intensive industries move to developing countries where women are the preferred labor force, because they can be hired at a low wage. Jobs become available for women, but only as unorganized laborers with no right to form unions or fight for their basic rights: the situation of women working in the garment industry is a case in point. Low-skilled jobs with low wages, long hours of work and lack of job security are typical of the feminization of labor in unorganized sectors. The state generally supports the management and ignores any violation of the labor laws. It is clear that the women are being exploited, but they may not raise their voices—not even against the sexual harassment they may face in the work place.

THE IMPACT OF GLOBALIZATION ON WOMEN IN AGRICULTURE

"Agriculture contributes just over 30 per cent of GNP and accounts for 60 per cent of employment. Nearly 63 per cent of all economically active men are engaged in agriculture, compared to 78 per cent of women. In the three rice-growing states of Andhra Pradesh, Kerala, Tamil Nadu and West Bengal, women provide more than 2/3 of the inputs including transplanting, weeding, manuring and fertilizing, harvesting, threshing, winnowing, drying, stacking and carrying produce. In the tribal economy of Orissa, women spent 105.4 hours per year on shifting cultivation compared with 50.11 by the men. In the Himalayas, a research study found that where a pair of bullocks works 1,064 hours and a man for 1,212 hours a year, a woman works 3,485 hours a year on a one-hectare farm. A woman on an average works for 640 hours for agricultural operations like weeding, 384 hours for irrigation, 650 hours for transporting manure, 557 hours for sowing, 984 hours for threshing and harvesting."[4] Women's double burden—working long hours in the field as well as attending to household chores like cooking and collecting water and fuel for the day—is often taken for granted. The technology used in agriculture is making women to cope with the technology.

Another development has been the attempt by major corporate groups to go into agricultural production directly, like the recent attempt by the Reliance group in Gujarat to set-up its own organic farming units involving setting up SEZs by taking over peasants' lands. At best, this will, given the pre-existing patriarchy in Indian agriculture, mean that the compensation in the form of cash will go to males. It is the experience of the present author, that when compensation is paid, whether in the Narmada eviction cases in Western India (since the 1970s) or in Singur in West Bengal (2006), most often the money is given singly to a male "head of household". In the case of the Narmada displacements, that "head of household" has even been as young as a thirteen year old boy. One result of the displacements due to the building of the Bargi Dam on the Narmada was the influx of rural women into prostitution in nearby Jabbalpur city. Even when that does not happen, the shift from an agricultural to a non-agricultural economy is traumatic, and women lose much of their voice in family level decision-making as men control the money.[5]

CULTURAL GLOBALIZATION

The culture of female employment in developing nations is based on "formal labor, housework, and informal-sector production"[6]. Only a small proportion of women work in export factories compared to the entire female population. Most work in agriculture, perform housework, or are employed in the informal sector. Females in these nations are limited in society by patriarchal control. These societies claim that female labor is an extension of their household chores. This ideology is "interwoven in the capitalist economy to justify women's subordination on the global assembly line, in the home and informal sector".[7] Regardless of which sector of employment women are working in, they are given limited access to resources and authority over their work. Employment opportunities within the informal sector are also stratified according to gender. Like the formal sector, males hold supervisory positions, while females are simply sub-contracted workers. Women perform informal assembly work in their homes or factories as methods of survival. Working in the home allows women "to care for their children and to retain control over the profits of their labor. These women cannot seek formal sector employment due to their family responsibilities within the household. Informal/domestic jobs also provide a survival strategy for women dealing with husbands who don't want to contribute enough of their wages to provide for the families. Although women may feel a sense of empowerment, their wages are substantially low in comparison to their male counterparts.

Another problem that exists among women in developing nations is that "unpaid domestic tasks are private rather than social and because they are both unpaid and private, there is no social system of incentives, of rewards and penalties, to encourage change"[8]. Women whose daily lives are centered around housework are solely dependent on their husbands for financial support. They do not have access to the public sector that will enable them to enter the market. The lack of assistance towards women who perform housework, places them in a vulnerable position in relation to their husbands. They might feel obligated to their husbands for financial needs and possibly withstand cases of abuse in order to provide for their families. Corporations target young female workers without thinking about the cultural changes that they create within developing societies. Based on the literature, it appears that these females live a "westernized fantasy" by working in export factories. Corporations are imposing ethnocentric values (independence—both financial and socially) upon factory workers, without consideration for the implications that result from these value adjustments. The fact that female workers who leave the factories are forced to look for husbands in order to survive in society, makes it seem as though the efforts of these women to gain their independence were merely a waste of time. Corporations might be using the independence factor to lure young women into their factories. Nevertheless, females are still subjected to a subordinate status in society once they leave the export factories.

POLITICAL GLOBALIZATION

Women in various communities throughout developing nations have created self-help groups that "might provide a springboard to transformation if...[women] were redirected toward women's strategic gender needs as well as toward their practical gender needs"[9]. As mentioned earlier, the SALs require cuts in public expenditure. Therefore, poor women and children are unable to gain adequate access to the resources mentioned above. Women and children are suffering from the results of this inequality, as well as the effects of economic globalization.

While the goal of gender equality has been lauded in many international agreements, including the Millennium Development Goals, many governments lack meaningful female participation. Increased female representation in governmental institutions and decision-making bodies is crucial for the overall empowerment of women, especially their inclusion in decisions about all issues—not just those that are traditionally known as "women's issues," such as child and elder care and reproductive health. 1995 Fourth World Beijing Conference on Women recommended that the international community and civil society (including non-governmental organizations and the private sector) take strategic action in order to reduce inequality between men and women in power-sharing and decision-making.

Many of the seats in various countries legislative bodies are attributed to political measures such as quotas that were adopted on a voluntary basis. There are 77 countries that have set quotas for women's political participation[10]. By the end of January 2012, women accounted for 19.7 percent of parliamentarians worldwide. This is almost a 75 percent increase since 1995, when women held 11.3 per cent of seats worldwide, and a 44 percent increase over the 2000 level[11]. However, there are more dimensions to increasing women's representation than simply seats available to them.

Starting at the local level is important for women in developing nations because it enables more workers to join forces and create an awareness of women's needs throughout their country. These women share common backgrounds such as: abuse, poverty, and lack of adequate wages and resources. Creating support groups unites women towards a common goal in achieving more rights. The governments within developing nations should become aware that while males are being given more rights, wages, and access to resources, they are using these rights frivolously. Women are responsible for most of the household necessities and should be compensated in order to meet these needs. The NGOs have a significant impact of the lives of women in developing nations and offer women a form of support and protection against unfair conditions.[12] With the rise of non-governmental organizations in the 21st century, various organizations have been founded and created to defend the rights of women around the world and to further their advancement. NGOs have been a prime actor in educating women and, as a result, produce some of the greatest political leaders in our global society today.

WOMEN AND POLITICAL DEMOCRACIES

Along with the curtailment of social services all over the world, many countries have also increasingly promoted traditional familial ideologies which have provided the rationale for the weakening of the welfare state. These developments paradoxically have gone hand-in-hand with the rhetoric of the new political liberalism that formally encourages "freedom" and "democracy."

What these developments have meant in practice, however, is the exclusion of women from full participation in these so-called democracies. In most countries that have recently undergone a change toward a liberal democratic form of government and capitalist market economy, women's political representation has decreased or remained low and their economic unemployment and underemployment typically has increased.

The popular notion of democracy and democratization that is exported by the West confounds liberal democratic ideology and capitalism, assuming that freedom is synonymous with the "free market" and "minimal state." Moreover, it reduces the notion of democracy to political representation in governing bodies and to electoral procedures. With the fall of socialism in Central-Eastern Europe, there has been a declining support for the traditional formulas of socialist democracy (i.e., responsibility for overseeing social solidarity), even among social democratic parties. And direct, participatory democracy tends to be dismissed as a utopian, unattainable dream.

Because of the increasing homogenization of the concept of democracy, much of the local, community-based or grassroots political work in which women are involved, which typically creates opportunities for greater participation, and thus contributes to democratization, goes unrecognized.[13] Moreover, the cuts in social programs and government spending, done in the name of democratization, are threatening the existence of many women's community-based organizations. In countries as different as Tanzania, Singapore, El Salvador, Ireland and Canada, women are struggling to hold onto consensus-based organizations that work to meet the needs of women and families in their communities.

Ironically, however, globalization has increased connections and communication between people, countries, and organizations around the world, and has also led to the growth and visibility of women's local, community-based activities through the international women's movement. This trend is linked to the work of international agencies such as the United Nations as well as many voluntary agencies and non-governmental organizations. For instance, the four United Nations conferences on women, the Environment conference in Rio de Janeiro in 1992 and the Population conference in Cairo in 1994, became important forums for grassroots organizations and other NGOs from all over the world to debate issues of women's equality. These gatherings also became vehicles for women to speak out, network with one another, and influence the platforms adopted by the participating countries. This contributed to the growth and strengthening of the transnational women's movement as well as the influence of local women's groups at the level of international institutions, influence which is crucial in an era of globalization, given the power of these institutions to shape policies and to carry them out.

MAHATMA GANDHI AND GLOBALIZATION

It seems ironic that world-wide anti-globalization movements often portray Gandhiji as someone who shared the same side of the ideological spectrum, when Gandhiji himself was clearly a product of globalization. He was educated in London, started his political activities in South Africa before he even joined the political arena in India and was greatly influenced by western figures such as Jesus, Tolstoy, Thoreau and Ruskin. Gandhi himself identifies globalization as an ancient phenomenon, whereby he claimed that it was not a bigger threat to India as various races starting from the Greeks and Huns to the British had invaded India but ended up being a part of the nation.[14] He believed that the mingling of cultures in India would not be a threat to India's own customs and culture. However, he did identify that the establishment of a global society would carry certain dangers for the sovereign nations such as colonialism, both cultural and political, industrialization and commercialization of the economy leading to class antagonism and environmental hazards. Today, we see many of those problems emerge clearly in our lives and hence, Gandhi's relationship with globalization remains extremely important and his ideas valid even today. In this context we should recollect the Gandhiji's words: "I do not want my house to be walled in on all sides and my windows to be stuffed. I want the cultures of all lands to be blown about my house as freely as possible. But I refuse to be blown off my feet by any."[15]

However, many of Gandhiji's principles remain valid even today and applied worldwide, the most notable being the principle of Satyagraha. He brought forward practical issues facing the globalization process today that of environmental concerns, equality of rights for all, rural development and evils of violence. However, it is appropriate to say that Gandhian attitudes towards globalization as it stands today, it seems apt to conclude by quoting Kaviguru Ravindranath Tagore—"We have for over a century been dragged by the prosperous West behind its chariot, choked by the dust, deafened by the noise, humbled by our own helplessness and overwhelmed by the speed. We agreed to acknowledge that this chariot-drive was progress, and the progress was civilization. If we ever ventured to ask, 'progress towards what, and progress for whom', it was considered to be peculiarly and ridiculously oriental to entertain such ideas about the absoluteness of progress. Of late, a voice (Gandhi) has come to us to take count not only of the scientific perfection of the chariot but of the depth of the ditches lying in its path."[16]

What is significant here is Gandhiji's image of woman and his hope for her, so radically different from that of any earlier reformer. He was not the first to address women's issues in India; the great cultural renaissance, as also the ferment of political agitations for freedom had already reached a high peak in the late nineteenth century. Before the advent of Gandhi on the scene, the attitude to women, though sympathetic, was patronising; leaders and social reform groups thought in language that made women look helpless. They wanted to protect, uplift, bring relief to women. No doubt there was value in all of it. Yet, with Gandhi a new, unique element emerged. Woman to him was neither man's plaything, nor his competitor, struggling to be like him.[17] What she needed most was education, the recognition of her birthright to be free and equal, to steer her own destiny side by side with man. It is noteworthy that present day conferences on women's issues insist similarly on women's own leadership, initiative, and self-help. For instance, Ela Bhatt, General Secretary of SEWA (Self-Employed Women's Association) and winner of the prestigious Magsaysay Award for her work with women in India, speaks up against the still persistent attitude of superiority among men. Social workers around the world encounter the same attitude.

Any tribute to Mahatma Gandhi, the Great Soul, would be an empty one, if we take no cue for our own guidance from his words and from his life; for him ideas and ideals had no value if they were not translated into action. He saw men and women as equals, complementing each other. And he saw himself not as a visionary, but as a practical idealist. If then, men and women work together selflessly and sincerely as equals with a faith like Gandhi's, they may indeed realise Ram Rajya, the perfect state.[18] Traditionally, woman has been called abala. In Sanskrit and many other Indian languages *bala* means strength. *Abala* means one without strength. If by strength we do not mean brutish strength, but strength of character, steadfastness, endurance, she should be called sabala, strong.

CONCLUSION

At presently scenario is changed, L.P.G. (Liberalization, Privatization and Globalization) and new economic policies were laid by Indian Government in 1992. In that process it's made free trade among the countries of the world. It's based on the principle that on account of several factors some countries could specialize in the production of certain goods in most expensive way. Technological flows of market in different countries in terms of production of goods or services are dependent on each other. If you see the history of globalization, we will find that from Bill Gates to Aziz Premji, the market's big celebrities are the results of globalization. The difference between rich and poor has also increased around the world during last five decades. The rich people's income increased 7 times. During 1960 to 1991, 70 to 85% income has risen for 20% population of the people. The gap between rich and poor is growing on and on. 43% people of India are directly or indirectly dependent on agriculture for a livelihood. But export earnings from agriculture are only 0.6%. In the process of Globalization and economic liberalization since last two– three decades all different issues of developing countries at different scales by World Bank, W.T.O. and multinational companies to protect the interests of several other U.S. systems. These policies affect the poor, disadvantaged rural farm workers and women workers. Most of the third world countries economy is based on agriculture. Agriculture is a major part of our country's economy. The means of livelihood of 65 percent people are based on agriculture. Structural adjustment under the terms of the loan and first five year plans were loaded with policy issues which affected the farmers and women worker of the country's agricultural sector. Today the World Bank is saying that because of its structural adjustment programme, the human development will be taken care. Government claims of poverty alleviation are proved as false at the time when we look at the high price rates. Reality is that, economic policies have adversely affected the poor class, farmer and women workers. This sad position is clearly reflected when we see poverty, malnutrition, access to health services and unemployment figures. The arrival of certain new policies made to cut the spending on rural development and agriculture.

Globalization has had various impacts on the lives of the people ranging from rich to poor, black to white, man to woman, rural to urban, etc. Though, in the global village, there's no difference between man and woman, but due to women's deprivation from resources and other opportunities, they are more affected by globalization and deeply experiencing its effects. The impacts of globalization on women are more prevalent and more complicated. Highlighting the positive aspects of globalization, a number of economists believe that women have mainly acquired noticeable benefits from economic reforms. One of the opportunities that globalization has provided for women is the increase in employment.

By expanding mass communication Medias, globalization has also boosted women's awareness level so that they have better chance to prove themselves and have more chances for selection as well.

Using internet, which demonstrates globalization, has created chances for e-commerce. For instance, in India more than 60000 rural women have been able to deliver their goods to the market through marketing by using digital photos. Such process of direct delivery of goods to the market with no need of vehicles has enabled women to earn more profit from their sales. Women's employment helps boost their income level and therefore women have more access to human development indicators such as training, health, free access to information and communication, participation in social and political life. In addition, women's employment is impactful in their social choices since most young women have their own income or in some cases, they have more income and more job opportunity compared to men. Through this, they can develop to be independent in choice. They will have freedom in choosing to marry whomever they please or they can choose to remain single as they will.

References

1. Moghadam, Valentine M., 1999, "Gender and Globalization: Female Labor and Women's Mobilization." *Journal of World Systems Research* 2: 367-88.
2. *Ibid.*, p. 372.
3. Elson, Diane, 1992. "From Survival Strategies to Transformation Strategies: Women's Needs and Structural Adjustments." pp. 26-48 in *Unequal Burden: Economic Crises, Persistent Poverty and Women's Work,* Lourdes Beneria and Shelley Feldman, editors. Boulder, CO: West view Press.
4. Dr. Harjoth Kaur and Gurupreet Kaur, The Impact of Globalization on Women in India, 2010.
5. Soma Marik, Globalisation in India and Women, 2009.
6. Ward, Katharine, 1990. *Women Workers and Global Restructuring,* New York: Cornell University Press. (Introductory chapter)
7. *Ibid.*
8. Elson, Diane, 1992. "From Survival Strategies to Transformation Strategies: Women's Needs and Structural Adjustments." pp. 26-48 in *Unequal Burden: Economic Crises, Persistent Poverty and Women's Work,* Lourdes Beneria and Shelley Feldman, editors, Boulder, CO: West view Press.
9. *Ibid.*
10. Women in National Parliaments, Inter-Parliamentary Union, 2012, Retrieved from http://www.ipu.org/wmne/arc/classif300906.htm.
11. Wall, T. (2012). Retrieved from United Nations website:http://

mdgs.un.org/unsd/ mdg/ Resources/Static/Products/Progress2012/ English2012.pdf.

12. Nazreen Bacchus, The Effects of Globalization on Women in Developing Nations, Pace University, 2005, http://digitalcommons.pace.edu/ honorscollege theses/2.
13. Bystydzienski, Jill M. and Joti Sekhon (eds.), 1999. *Democratization and Women's Grassroots Movements.* Bloomington: Indiana University Press.
14. Nelson Mandela: Long Walk to Freedom: An Autobiography (London: Abacus, 2003).
15. Mohandas Karamchand Gandhi: Hind Swaraj and Other Writings (Cambridge: Cambridge University Press, 1997).
16. Quoted in R. Sudarshan, Globalization and Gandhi at the Dawn of the New Millennium.
17. Sita Kapadia, "A Tribute To Mahatma Gandhi : His Views on Women And Social Changes", Director of the Self-Enhancement Learning Forum in Houston, Texas, was earlier Associate Professor of English at the City University of New York.
18. *Ibid.*

7

Khadi and Village Industries in Global Perspective

SADHAṄA THAKUR

After the collapse of socialistic system in the Soviet Union and Eastern Europe, US-led capitalistic philosophy began to stretch its feet in the Global world. In accordance with this, Narasimha Rao government introduced, "Structural Adjustment Programme", which laid down the foundation of globalization in the name of Economic Reforms, The NDA government led by Atal Bihari Vijapayee did not only follow the some path but implemented all contents of the globalization at very fast speed. Under this Policy several public sector units which played a major role in high national-building and being destroyed systematically. Out of them some home been closed and some home been privatized. Subsidy on the farmers and weaker one drastically cut. Small scale and tiny section on the various commodities have plummeted due to cheaper imports. Neither the producer nor the consumers are benefited, but trades make super profit. Thousand of the employed pesos have been done out of Jobs. Present paper the research when attempts to study the Khadi and Village Industries in the Global perspective to solve the problem of consumers and producer from Gandhian ideology for employment, economic empowerment of the poor and self-dependence of the rural economy.

Globalization is presented as the process of enhancing collective measure to stop economic inequality and increasing economic integration through developed communications, investments, trade and aid. It aims at softening economic and trade barriers across countries so as to facilitate a free interflow of capital, technology, goods and services.

Under this policy, the government opens up its economy for foreign firms and investment and trade agreements which are fair to all. Thus, the idea of globalization is a world order that benefits all.

From this it would be clear that globalization aims at establishing one world market or world economy instead of national or regional markets or economies. This idea of globalization has many advantage as well as disadvantages. These are trade agreements fair to all. Efforts for proper harnessing of resources, development of under developed regions, growth of Indian exports, quantum jump in foreign exchange earnings, induces competitiveness and forces industries to improve quality.

From this we can say that globalization brings fairness in economics practices resulting in competitiveness and development of under-developed regions. Now the disadvantage of globalization are competiveness through lowering of real wages, increased hours of work, reduced job security, location of hazardous industries in under-developed countries, losing control by local market forces and local government, smaller enterprises with lesser financial strength may be marginalized if they don't become competitive in the global market.

But disadvantages can be there only in the beginning stages of globalization till things stabilize and a "level playing field for all" comes into being. Now, if we consider the Khadi and Village Industries in a global perspective, first we will need to see what Bapu had to say regarding the issue of globalization and the world becoming "One big village".

> "I do not want my house to be walled in on all sides and my windows to be stuffed. I want the cultures of all lands to be blown about my house as freely as possible. But I refuse to be blown-off my feet by any."
>
> —*M.K. Gandhi*

Gandhi was himself a product of Globalization. He was educated in London. Started his political career in South Africa before even becoming active in his won country. He was greatly influenced by Jesus, Tolstoy, Thoreau and Ruskin. This clearly shows that Gandhiji was never against interaction of cultures. Societies and economics, rather he himself was a product of globalization. Gandhiji was very open to the idea of the world community.

GANDHIJI DIDN'T SUBSCRIBE TO THE FAMOUS LINES OF KIPLING

"East is East and West is West and Never the twin shall meet."

He was closer to Tennyson who talked of "Union between East and West" in this poeam 'vision'. Gandhiji believed that the distinctions between the western and Indian civilization was melting away, giving place to a modern civilization, which is purely material. Gandhiji said globalization is an ancient phenomena' and it can never pose any threat to India as various races starting from the Greeks and Hoons to the British had invaded India but ended up being a part of the nation. Gandhiji was not against economic globalization also. Rather, he held a very dualistic view of economic globalization in which countries would be self sufficient on most accounts but mutually dependent on some counts.

Thus, it would clear that Gandhiji also advocated a union between the east and the west. He had realized that the barriers between various cultures. Civilizations and societies were breaking down. He had forseen that with the development of faster communication systems and transport, people living across seven seas also would come together one day resulting in a new civilization and a new economic order.

Our country India is a great nation with a rich cultural heritage, a golden past and a promising future. This great nation of ours nurses and promotes a wide socio-economic, cultural and lingual diversity in its lap. Perhaps, this is the only country on the face of the earth, where prople of different backgrounds, religions, languages and through co-exist together with respect for each other. In this great nation, the rich and the poor, the haves and have-nots, educated and the uneducated, the strong and the weak all co-exist together, and lend a helping hand to each other through various socio-economic mechanisms and bondages. These human bondages are the strength of our country.

Although our country gave the concepts of "People's Welfare State" and "democracy" during the ancient times, but from time-to-time, the country had to face the onslaught of various invaders right from the Hoons to the British and had to suffer the insult of subjugation for long periods. But every time some charismatic personality, emerged to unite the whole nation and fight against subjugation. Mahatma Gandhi was that charismatic personality and Khadi was the rallying point and the symbol of hope which enabled us to fight against the British and attain independence.

Khadi had basically emerged as a socio-economic tool for socially uniting the nation and for economic empowerment the poor so as to give them strength against the political subjugation and economic onslaught of the British, Khadi emerged as a symbol of independence–the symbol with which every citizen of the nation could related to or identity with, khadi aimed at the economic self-dependence of the smallest unit of our country i.e., the village. He, father of our nation, said about the underlying philosophy of the Khadi movement.

"If poverty stricken India were to be free from the clutches of miseries, then each hand in the rural India must take up productive work based on local resources, local technology and local market. Each village needs to develop a rural economy based on the principal of self-sufficiency so that it is not prone to exploitation by anybody".

"India must learn to look upon the spinning wheel and hand spun yarn as the symbol not only of freedom but also of its bread and butter. There could be no better means than Khadi and rural industries to provide full employment to the two-thirds of India which lives in villages and also to fulfill their socio-economic needs with honour and dignity."

We can sum up Khadi Philosophy following manner that the lack of capital, use of indigenous technology, availability of huge manpower in rural areas and use of indigenous locally available resources for ful-filling the needs of the village in the village itself, and thus attaining self-dependence were the guiding factors for this Khadi movement. Our great Mahatma sums up the Khadi philosophy beautifully in the following lines :

> ''हमें कम पैसे में अधिक लोगों के रोजगार देने और गाँवों को आर्थिक रूप में स्वावलंबी बनाने की बात सोचनी चाहिए, जिससे हमारे गाँव मजबूत हो सकेंगे तभी हमारा देश आर्थिक रूप से उन्नति कर सकेगा।''

Means hand-spun and hand-woven clothes, provides employment to millions of people in millions of tiny rural or cottage industries in every village household. Insures security to poor and helpless rural men and women. Promises social and economic equality of all is a eco-friendly product. The herbal unit which not only "Hearls" but also 'Feeds'. Doesn't destroy all machinery. It regulates its use. Doesn't promote unhealthy competition between villagers and city dwellers. Doesn't create hatred between producers and consumers. Doesn't encourage the concentration of economic and political power rather encourages democratization of society. Does't disturb the existing environmental balance. It encourages pollutions free eco-system. Buying Khadi means service to the nation.

Khadi emerged as a strong socio-economic and political tool in the 21th century in our nation. It is nearly 66 years since we got independence and lot of socio-economic and political changes have taken place not only in our country but also all over the globe. The Khadi and Village Industries sector also has undergone a lot of changes since its emergence and has seen may ups and down. But it would be heartening to note that this sector has been maintaining a steady progress inspire of the various odds. The data which will come later will prove that the sector has emerged as one of the strong pillars of our rural economy.

But as the world is progressing from the concept of various separate nations to the concept of big village socio-economic barriers are being broken everyday. The walls separating people are falling and the new era of economic liberalization and globalization is taking shape the Khadi and Village Industries also faces new challenges.

Khadi philosophy stand in this framework of globalization. For this we will have to seriously look at various tenets of Khadi philosopohy, various strengths and weaknesses of the Khadi and Village Industries sector so as to decide whether the sector has anything common with the philosophy of globalization or whether it is a total antithesis only then we can infer whether the sector can survive and proper in the new era of globalization. The international perspective of the Khadi philosophy can be states as under:

> "Although Khadi was born basically as a tool for attaining self-reliance and fight the onslaught of western trade and economy, but if we think deeply it becomes clear that the basic idea of emergence of Khadi came from the determination to compete with the economies of the western world".

This underlying Philosophy of competitiveness is the SEED

which needs to be carefully planted and nurtured so as to grow into the tree of global perspective of Khadi and Village Industries.

This clearly shows that the basic philosophy of Khadi was competiveness and hence it has this as one important qualification to face of challenges globalization.

If we look at the other qualifications or bench marks which a sector needs to have for surviving and prosperring in the era globalization. We can list out the following seven bench marks for the same.

(1) Quality Standard, (2) Eco-friendliness, (3) Modern Packaging, (4) Durability, (5) Ethnic Tough, (6) Modern Marketing Techniques.

Khadi and Village Industries sector is a major employment provider especially in the rural area and has been progressing steadily as far as production and sales are concerned. This shows that the sector is vibrant and kicking.

Quality improvement at the pre-spinning, spinning, weaving and finished product state.

Machine design development and easy availability of spare parts at the production centers. New design inputs in woven and printed fabrics based on colour forecasts. Introduction of new technical for better fastness properties. Production planning according to market trends. Aggressive marketing strategy, involvement of technically qualified personnel in khadi sector, HRD programme on continuous basis, healthy working conditions at the production centers. Modern packaging project, environment friendly image and brand image.

Now we have ample indication that the Khadi and Village Industries sector has potential to compete in the global market and we have also identified the interventions required in general terms to make the sector completive. But this would not be enough. What perhaps, needs to be done is to get down to the basics and indentify certain specific thrust areas which the sector needs to concentrate to make itself globally competitive. Some of these thrust areas are as under:

For improvement of quality of khadi and quality maintenance, it is essential to have quality norms for different fibres used such as cotton, wool and silk and various yarns and fabrics produced. Proper technical supervision and regular quality checks would help in maintaining the quality.

Design developments based on colour forecasts and market trends would be very useful for value addition and to boost the khadi sales.

Low strength is one of the drawbacks associated with the khadi yarns and fabrics. The strength of khadi yarns can be enhanced by yarn mercerization. This would lead to considerable. Mercerization has several other advantages such as improvement in dye uptake, luster and chemical reactivity. These are most important properties for value addition.

Dyeing is a perennial probem in khadi sector, properties, shade matching and shade variations, etc. Selecting of proper dye class and standardization of dyeing parameters for selected dye class is necessary. There is a revival of natural dyes due to environmental considerations. Khadi being eco-friendly, there would be further value addition if dyed with natural dyes.

One of the major problems associated with khadi garments is wrinkle formation during use and on washing. This adds cost to the maintenance of khadi garments. This problem can be dealt with by imparting wrinkle free finishing to khadi garments. This is a popular concept and would not only give value addition but also boost khadi garment sales.

At present polyvastra yarn (polyester/cotton blend) is used for the manufacture of woven fabric. This yarn can also be used for the production of knitted fabric, which then can be used for product development like T-shirts, which has good market potential.

KVIC will need to work as facilitator in developing modern eco-friendly attractive package for the products of this sector and mount a massive global compaign for development a strong eco-friendly and human brand image. Very fast all over the world and these issues provide a distinct advantage to the Khadi and Village Industries Sector. These concerns will automatically improve the acceptability and demands of the Khadi and Village Industries products in the global market.

SUMMING UP

In this new era of mounting challenges triggered by globalization, the Khadi and Village Industries sector is in a position to face the challenges effectively and successfully mainly due to its inherent strengths of environment friendliness, democratic decentralization of economic power, empowerment of the poor and the women-folk in rural areas, ethnic appeal and the widely growing sensitivities towards these factors in the global market. Technological up-gradation, product diversification, world-wide proactive marketing stategy, credit facilitator and eco-friendly ethnic brand image with unlimited frontiers throughout the globe. It will became a potential opportunity for Khadi and Village Industries and sky would be the limit for them.

References

Gill Stephen; Market Civilization and Disciplinary Moliberalism, Millennium, Vol. 24(3), 1995.

Held, Devid, Global Transformation: Politics, Economics and Culture. Cambridge, 1999

Kapoor, Mastram, Globalization *v.* Social Justice, *Dainik Jagaran*, 2011.

Dr. Agya Ramshakya, Third Concept, Vol. 17, No. 198, August 2003.

Nayyar, D: Globalization : The Past in Our Present, *Indian Economics Jurnal*, 43.

Sen, A. : Global Justice : Beyond International Equity" in I Kaul '(ed.), Global Public Goods, Oxford University Press, New York, for the UNDP.

World Bank (2002; Globalization, Growth and Poverty Building Report, Oxford University Press, New York).

Mehta, J.K., Studies in Advanced Economics Theory, Premier Publishing Co., Delhi, 1950.

Schumakar, E.F., Small is Beautiful—A study of Economics as if People Mattered, Vintage, Random Houses, London, 1993.

Yunus, Muhammad, Building Social Business, The New Kind of Capitalism that serve humanities most pressing needs, Public Affairs, New York.

Hobsbawn, Eric, How to Change the World, Little Brown, London, 2011, Tales of Max and Marxim.

8

Role of Swadeshi in Globalized World

A Gandhian Assessment

MANOHAR LAL SHARMA

Today the world looks to be smaller and shorter in size because of advancement in science and technology. As a result, the world scenario in terms of culture, politics, economics and social activities has been changing with a very high speed. The word 'Globalization' has become quite popular and now dominating the globe of the Universe. Globalization, some think, gives the impression that the days of self-reliance, self-sufficiency, self-governing, etc. for the individual nations are over and they are dependent on foreign aids by World Organizations such as World Bank, International Monetary Fund (IMF), W.T.O. and many world famous multinational corporations and companies.

Some scholars interpret globalization in terms of an open economy, which is open to the international processes of capital accumulation and distribution. A few describe it as a process of exploitation of poor countries by the companies of the developed world and in a way they designate the same as a refined route of colonialism. Others present it as the process of enhancing collective measures to stop international violence and wars, to save global environment and to eliminate the Third World poverty and economic inequality and numerous other disparities through developed communications, financial investments, trade and financial assistance. In fact, to them globalization means that "bigger is always better" in place of "small is beautiful". The multinational companies claim to provide the consumer goods to the masses at cheaper and at affordable rates and lure the people to provide them the adequate employment also. Though such kind of arrangement has the advantage of deriving some financial gains from the International economic and trade agencies like the International Monetary Fund (IMF) and the World Bank. It has a negative effect also at these agencies try to thrust upon a series of hard measures like import, liberalization, reduction of subsidies, reduction of public expenditures, opening of economy to foreign capital and deepen marketization of economy. On the other hand, these agencies, practically, want to guide and control the domestic policies and programmes of the developing countries like India, Thailand, Myanmar, Pakistan, Bangladesh, Sri Lanka and so many other Third World countries.

If we go back to the historical background of this important issue, we may find two root factors responsible for the current global malaise, such as firstly craze for massive and reckless industrialization and secondly dehumanization of science, technology and indigenous industry for more and more material gains and as much profit as possible.

Therefore, it may be mentioned here that "massiveness" means mass production leading to mass surpluses requiring mass consumption through massive technologicalization, capitalization, monopolization and governmentalization. Secondly, dehumanization means complete concentration and centralization of the industries of commercial profit and economic power to a total exclusion of concerns for human health and happiness in terms of physical, intellectual and economic well-being. It is a fact that the process of globalization and massive industrialization necessitates the bulk or huge supplies of raw materials, energy sources, capital, trade along with markets also affects the environment. The amassing of these ingredients is the initial stage of industrialization which creates an exploitative system within the society which may be called a domestic colonialism.[1] As a matter of fact as soon as industrialization becomes more and more massive, it certainly leads to reckless expansion of colonialism abroad.[2] Similarly, informal and *de-facto* colonialism has also been branded as the neo-colonialism. Practically, the oppression of the people in the colonies, in the struggle to maintain, defend or expand colonies, necessitates militarization, inter-colonial wars, besides world wars.[3]

As a result, in the name of globalization, the goods are being produced recklessly on a large scale and the same have to be sold for consumption, which requires a huge open market to serve the purpose. So this process, accordingly, gives rise to the field of transportation and communication. While development in transportation helps more goods and travellers, it also helps in the fast moving of war materials and war machines and soldiers to every nook and corner of the world. And, the mass media of communication–from the printing press to the computer chips, satellites and internet webs have become the instruments of propaganda, thought control and even brain washing. In this respect the examples of the Time Magazine, imperialism of CNN, neo-colonialism are worth quoting.[4] In fact the globalized messages of racism, sexism, religionism, dogmatism, ethnicism and jingoism have been flourishing through the imperialist of media. These narrow-minded messages, which are used to boost industrialization, have also caused communal antagonisms and bloodshed on national and international levels. Thus, its side effects are very much visible.

Besides, it is also a fact that huge industrialization is not possible without globalized colonialism and colonialism is unavoidable for global industries. It is, obvious, on the otherside to argue that globalized poverty and economic disparities and inequalities could be eliminated only by globalized industrialism or neo-colonialism. So far as economic disparities exist on the canvas of this Universe and as long as the rich and the developed nations insist on improving and sustaining their own wealth and well-being, globalization of free trade and investment will never bring about equitable economic benefits to all the nations in the World. Some regions and nationalities, within and outside the state, will always end us as the victims of trade inequalities. Further, the mass production built upon the assembly line and automation makes employees redundant. As a result, unemployed workers create strains and stresses on the economic-political system. The Europe of the eighteenth and nineteenth centuries got rid of its surplus unwanted population by shipping them out to new countries. These days, millions of descendants of European ancestry are spread all over the World. Such emigration not only reduced tensions within Europe but also created colonies that became the suppliers of raw materials, slaves and cheap labour, captured markets, controlled the huge investments and other profit-making agencies, thus having focus on all available opportunities. Besides, worse than that the colonies provided arms, armies and even battlefields. Such kind of history is not advisable to be repeated to help the industrialization of the Third-World countries. Likewise, the "techno-industrial military complex" also became the powerful vehicle of militarization, world ward and colonization and every technological improvement was quickly translated into more and more destructive weaponry. Accordingly, this has been the legacy of globalization of massive industrialization and now the contemporary advocates of globalization are shouting slogans that what is good for the developed West, is also good for the poor and developing countries. And, the haunting fact remains that the United States, one country out of 185, uses up nearly 40 per cent of the resources of the world itself. The propounders, supporters and advocates of globalization are pushing free trade treaties and Multinational Agreements on Investments (MAI). They have formed free trade zones, NAFTA, ECM, WTO, etc. Free trade and investment are undoubtedly profitable for the developed countries, but its utility or usefulness to the Third World nations is quite doubtful, rather in a way, it is dubious one.[5] The recent economic collapse of Asia's 'minor dragons' betrayed the Asian countries is the manifestation and net result of liberalization and globalization that is being advocated by multinational companies, the IMF and the World Bank as in the recent past the economic troubles of Asia led to a bailout programme by World Bank and International Monetary Fund. In this respect, the most interesting point has been that some of the conditions imposed were the hiring of workers, raising of taxes and interest rates, reduction on social expenditures and so on so forth.[6] Therefore, it is true when someone tries to justify that free trade is the weapon of the strong and protectionism is the shield of the weak.

Moreover, there is another tragic consequence and that is often played down by the advocates of massive industrialization, is the fact that the more technological and industrialized economy creates, and generates more unemployment through trade cycles of booms and bursts through redundancy. Mechanization displaces workers and automation makes worker redundant. Advanced industrialization, whether under capitalism, communism or fascism, becomes dehumanized by focusing on productivity and competitiveness, and on power and profit, through increased automation and rationalization and unemployment. Further, while proclaiming pious platitudes of humanitarianism, the investors and moneylenders from the rich countries work for their own profitability. It is like a banker who lends money but seeks high interest rate and a mortgage on everything one owns- from cuff-links to cars–and is ever ready to confiscate them when one fails to make the payments. Now the question is very simple that should this Shylock Banker, who desires his pound of flesh, claims that he is doing a favour? Globalization of trade, investments, and banking can only mean further dictation, subordination and domination of the developed countries and further indebtedness and impoverishment of the developing countries. This will certainly demand its own big share and will never spare it free. Thus, the answer to globalized militarization and wars, to globalized pollution and ecological disaster and to globalized exploitation, poverty and inequality, is not more globalization, but less of it, and its eventual elimination.

Accordingly, there are some serious side effects of such kind of globalization. The poor masses of the developing countries are impoverished, exploited to the maximum and oppressed by the unholy alliances of monopoly houses, multinational companies and corporations having huge foreign interests. These companies generally try to lure the people to buy their consumer requirements from paste to power and plunder several crores of currency annually from these poor countries. To depend on foreigners for life saving drugs, can be tolerated but not for the daily basic needs which can be produced and distributed locally. The mad race or craze to go in for everything foreign like brush, paste, soap, shaving cream, blade, cosmetics, textiles, and other ordinary domestic gadgets must be curbed. However, the developed countries, in fact, are using the developing countries as guinea pigs to experiment their dangerous banned medicines through M.N.Cs. Accordingly, the deepening economic crisis should open our eyes. And, it has been rightly said that the expanding economy is destroying the beauty of the natural scenery with ugly high buildings, polluting the air and poisoning the rivers and the lakes and global warming.

SWADESHI AS AN ALTERNATIVE

Therefore, liberalization and globalization is not the panacea for the contemporary world crises rather it is deepening these crises. In this respect Gandhi's approach to Swadeshi (self-reliance) seems to be quite relevant and very significant as he has been a great advocate and supporter of the use of local indigenous industry or small-scale (industries which are primarily built upon national self-reliance) and self-sufficiency (Swadeshi and Swavlamban), minimum surpluses, which will lead to devolution and decentralization of economic productivity. And, such productivity will certainly reduce science-technology to the level suitable to small-scale industries, will reduce the need for raw materials, energy and pollution, and will reduce colonialization, militarization and massive wars.

Swadeshi is one of the most important principles of Gandhi's economic thought, as there exists a relationship between this doctrine and others, which are fundamental doctrines of Gandhian economics. In fact, to understand Gandhi's view of Swadeshi, one has to go through the entire gamut of his thought–social, political, economic and religious. Etimologically, the term may mean 'of one's own country', however, country's component is not its connotation but a sub-characteristics called 'uplakshan' in Hindi. Accordingly, Swadeshi includes all indigenous things—both abstract and concrete, namely, native language, wisdom, culture, dress and other products also. The spirit and core of the concept, however, is 'self-reliance' and 'self-governance'.

Although Gandhi did not coin the term 'Swadeshi', yet he contributed a lot in this respect by infusing new meanings to it. His understanding and approach to Swadeshi seems to be very dynamic, scientific and much more convincing. In the field of economics, the principle of Swadeshi means that a person basically uses those things, which are produced in his immediate neighbourhood and serves those industries by making them efficient and meaningful. By giving the best illustration, Gandhi explains:

> "Swadeshi is that spirit in us which restricts us to the use and service of our immediate surroundings to the exclusion of the more remote... In the domain of politics, I should make use of the indigenous institutions and serve them by curing them of their proved defects. In that of economics, I should use only things that are produced by my immediate neighbours and serve those industries by making them efficient and complete where they might be found wanting".[7]

Gandhi further clarifies that the neighbour thus served, has in his turn to serve his own neighbour. Accordingly, in practice it is never exclusive and it recognizes the scientific limitations of human capacity for service. However, the principle of Swadeshi demands that a person must give preference to local manufactures even if they are of inferior quality or more costly than articles of foreign make. It functions with right spirit. There is no place for hatred for the foreign made things also. Therefore, he advises the use of foreign made articles if there is no substitute. He defined a Swadeshi article as any article which "sub-serves the interest of the millions even though the capital and talent are foreign but under effective Indian control".[8] However, Gandhi did insist upon the exclusion of such foreign made commodities whose import was harmful to the indigenous industries. He pleaded strongly for stiff protective duties upon foreign goods in order to nurture national industries. The principle of Swadeshi suggested him the universalizing of Khadi or the spinning wheel to enable the crores of our semi-starved countrymen to live [9]

Furthermore, it may be added that in advocating the complete boycott of foreign cloth, Gandhi had no ill will at all. He said, "To reject foreign manufactures merely because they are foreign, and to go on wasting national time and money to promote manufactures in one's own country for which it is not suited, would be criminal folly and a negation of the Swadeshi spirit."[10] He further added:

> "A true votary of Swadeshi will never harbour ill-will towards the foreigner, he will not be activated by antagonism towards anybody on earth. Swadeshism is not a cult of hatred. It is a doctrine of selfless service, that has its roots in the purest Ahimsa, i.e., love." [11]

Therefore, Gandhi's concept of Swadeshi is wider one and has wider connotation also. Regarding the exclusion of everything foreign, he does not leave any room for doubt when he says:

> "I have never considered the exclusion of everything foreign under every conceivable circumstances as a part of Swadeshi. The broad definition of Swadeshi is the use of all homemade things to the exclusion of foreign things, in so far as such use is necessary for the protection of home industry, more especially those industries without which India will become pauperized. In my opinion, therefore, Swadeshi which excludes the use of everything foreign, no matter how beneficient it may be, and irrespective of the fact that it impoverishes nobody, is a narrow interpretation of Swadeshi."[12]

Secondly, Gandhi is clear that his insistence on priority for the immediate neighbour will not mean injury to or unconcern for the interest of those who are not in the neighbourhood. However, each has to give priority to his or her neighbour, or bases his action on concern for his or her neighbour, there can be contradiction or conflict, and no unconcern or injury.[13] In this respect Gandhi fully believed that a man could serve his neighbours and humanity both at the same time, the condition being that the service of the neighbour was in no way selfish or exclusive, i.e., did not in any way involved the exploitation of any other human being. Thus, considered, it would spread like the proverbial snowball gathering strength in geometrical progression encircling the whole earth. It followed that Swadeshi was that spirit which dictated man to serve his next-door neighbour to the exclusion of any other as already mentioned. Accordingly, Swadeshi is never exclusive. Regarding the third question of an element of hatred or chauvinism for the foreigner it may be added here that Gandhi's arguments in this case were very convincing.

He reiterated, "I have never been an advocate of prohibition of all foreign things because they are foreign. My economic creed is a complete taboo in respect of all foreign commodities whose importation is likely to prove harmful to our indigenous interest. This means that we may not in any circumstance import a commodity that can be adequately supplied from our own country. For instance, I would regard it a sin to import Australian wheat on the score of its better quality, but I would not have the slightest hesitation in importing oatmeal from Scotland, if an absolute necessity for it is made out, because we do not grow oats in India. In other words, I would not countenance the boycott of a single foreign article out of ill-will or feeling of hatred".[14]

On the contrary, he pointed out that India produced a sufficient quantity of leather and "it is my duty, therefore, to wear shoes made out of Indian leather only, even if it is comparatively dearer and of an inferior quality, in preference to cheaper and superior quality foreign leather shoes. Similarly, I would condemn the introduction of foreign molasses or sugar, if enough of it is produced in India for our needs. It will be thus clear from the above that it is hardly possible for me to give an exhaustive catalogue of foreign articles whose importation in India ought to be prohibited. I have simply inculcated the general principle by which we can be guided in all such cases. And this principle will hold good in future, too, so long as the conditions of production in our country remain as they are today".[15]

Similarly, in the economic field, our activities are oriented towards the production and consumption of goods and services for the satisfaction of our wants. Let us see how Gandhi's philosophy applies to both these fields. In production, one will have to give priority to the utilization or employment of local resources in materials and manpower in consumption too one will have to give priority to what is manufactured locally. In both cases, the arguments that are put forward against according priority to the neighbour or local manpower and resources, and in the field of consumption, to local employee is incompetent, he is inadequately equipped in skills his technology is inferior, and therefore, the quality of his products cannot be compared with the quality of the goods produced elsewhere, generally in other countries. The second argument is that indigenous products are costlier, more expensive. If we follow these arguments and switch to or prefer goods manufactured in other countries, we will put our neighbour out of employment and contribute to a money drain that will benefit other countries at the cost of our nation.[16] As a result, the spirit of Swadeshi would certainly demand that one should work for the improvement of our skills, improve our own technology and improve the quality and excellence of our goods, and put up with poorer quality till such time as we improve the quality of our goods. In reality, the spirit of Swadeshi thus acts as an incentive to improve our technology. And, there is nothing in the philosophy of Swadeshi that asks us to be content with archaic or ineffective technology or to abjure the up-gradation of technology.

The above discussion shows that to Gandhi, Swadeshi is both a principle of evolution or construction, a creative principle as well as an instrument of struggle for the economic regeneration of the masses. Besides, Swadeshi is equally valid in all spheres of human activity and all spheres in which man is capable of evolution. The stream of culture demands that we should not uproot ourselves from our heritage, which has taken its shape and texture from the thoughts and efforts of those who are, and who were proximate to us. To be ignorant of this heritage or to repudiate it is inconsistent with the spirit of Swadeshi as it is the base on which one builds. Therefore, one should contribute to its improvement or enrichment. This needs a lot of introspection and one must be able to detect and remove deficiencies and whatever is untenable. Besides, one should not fear any exposed to other cultural heritage. Rather, one should absorb whatever one finds it. However, one should not allow one's roots to wither away or be eroded. Gandhi has very beautifully presented his ideas in the following words:

> "I do not want my house to be walled in on all sides, and my windows to be stuffed. I want the cultures of all lands to blow about my house as freely as possible. But I refuse to be blown off my feet by any. Mine is not a religion of the prison house"[17].

Therefore, Swadeshi is the doctrine consistent with the law of humanity and love as envisaged by Gandhi. This involves love and service of motherland and mankind as a whole. This means that we can do the best to those who are immediately known to us and our neighbour and our countrymen must be the first to receive our service. This, in fact, is nothing but humanism or love of mankind. So, Swadeshi is a dynamic concept in Gandhian thought and spirit.

After the entry of the multinationals in India, the situation has not improved at all. Rather, India has been dubbed as a land of bootleggers, smugglers and black-marketers. Firstly, the thirst for power, pelf and position of the political bigwigs remains unquenched and sound democratic practices are thrown to the winds. The fundamental rights guaranteed by the original Constitution are no longer fundamental now. The increasing statism, the denigration of the judiciary, the criminalization of politics, the politicisation of criminals, nexus among politicians, businessmen, bureaucrats and sedulous promotion of personality cult are complete negation of democratic principles. At present politics has become the most profitable profession. Rank political opportunism has become the rule of the day. Corruption is being institutionalised and it has also been said that now India has become a land of scams, gamblers and criminals.

Further, while industrialisation is a must, it must not be in blind imitation of the West. Nature is to be milked and not misused and abused. There should be integrated thinking in ecology, economics and ethics. Emphasis should be laid on labour-intensive rather than capital-intensive industries. The problem of unemployment and underemployment must be handled on war footings. Economic and industrial policies be aimed at maximising employment so as to enable the people to have more ethical purchasing power.

It must be noted here that Gandhi developed Swadeshi movement during our struggle for freedom as a weapon to cut the roots of colonial economic interests and exploitation as well as to utilized our own local resources and manpower to the maximum. Now the time has come to rebuild the same spirit of Swadeshi and self-reliance to defeat the evil design of neo-imperialistic economic vested interests of multi-nationals and advanced nations. Sometimes, one has to face the music of too much liberalization as the side effects prove to be very dangerous and fatal ones. Our multi-crore security scams and other scandals are the best illustrations in this respect. Undoubtedly, India needs rapid economic development, however, it is not possible without inculcating the spirit of Swadeshi, self-reliance and self-confidence. For this purpose there is an immediate need to understand the meaning of true Swadeshi which means lesser dependence on foreign goods and maximum use of our own resources keeping in view the basic needs of our immediate surroundings without neglecting the universal human element. No doubt Gandhi has indicated his limits to globalization, liberalization and privatization (LPG), yet he does not minimize the importance of what is in the interest of the country.

Notes and References

1. Naidu, M.V., "Development and Peace: An Attempt at Conceptualization of Initial Development", in Naidu, M.V. (ed.), *War, Security, Peace* (Ontario: M.I.T.A. Press), 1996, pp. 415-16.
2. Naidu, M.V., Dimension of Peace (Ontario: M.I.T.A. Press), 1996, pp. 222-23.
3. Wright, Quincy, A Study of War (Chicago: University of Chicago Press), 1965, Second Edition.
4. MacBride, Sean., Many Voices, One World (London: UNESCO and Kogan Press), 1980, p. 125.
5. World Statistics in Brief (New York: United Nations), 1979, pp. 158, 224.
6. WINNING FREE PRESS, January 17, 1998.
7. Gandhi, M.K., *Harijan*, 23-3-1947.
8. Gandhi, M.K., *Harijan*, 25-2-1931.
9. Gandhi, M.K., From Yeravda Mandir (Ahmedabad: Navajivan Publishing House), January 1986, Reprinted, p. 3.
10. Gandhi, M.K., *Young India*, 18-6-1931. See also Gandhi, M.K. From *Yeravda Mandir*, *op. cit.*, p. 38.
11. *Ibid.*
12. Gandhi, M.K., *Young India*, 17-2-1929, p. 218.
13. Varma, Ravindra, "Gandhi's Philosophy of Swadeshi" in Gangrade, K.D. and Radha Krishnan, N. (eds.), *Gandhi and the Changing Facets of India* (New Delhi: Gandhi Smriti and Darshan Samriti), 1998, p. 26.
14. Gandhi, M.K., *Young India*, 15-11-1928.
15. *Ibid.*
16. Varma, Ravindra, "Gandhi's Philosophy of Swadeshi", *op. cit.*, pp. 27-28.
17. Gandhi, M.K., *Young India*, June, 1921.

9

Globalization

A Boon or a Bane for India?

SEEMA THAKUR

Globalization is a process of growing interaction and interdependence between economies, societies and nations across large distances. Though globalization process is not something new, but it became a popular word in late 20th century and has been the main topic of debate for many economists, media and entrainment, politicians, academics and many other sections of the society.

The World Bank defines globalisation as "Freedom and ability of individuals and firms to initiate voluntary economic transactions with residents of other countries".[1] In 1997, World Economic Outlook, the International Monetary Fund (IMF) also defines globalization as "the growing economic interdependence of countries world-wide through increasing volume and variety of cross-border transactions in goods and services, freer international capital flows, and more rapid and widespread diffusion of technology".[2]

Anthony Giddens has described globalisation as the "intensification of worldwide social relations which link distant localities in such a way that local happenings are shaped by events occurring many miles away and *vice versa*. This is a dialectical process because such local happenings may move in an obverse direction from the very distanciated relations that shape them. Local transformation is as much a part of globalisation as the lateral extension of social connections across time and space."[3]

Similarly, Fredric Jameson describes globalization as a phenomenon that "reflects the sense of an immense enlargement of world of communication, as well as of the horizon of a world market, both of which seem far more tangible and immediate than in earlier stages of modernity".[4]

From the various definitions it can be concluded that globalization has powerful economic, political, cultural and social dimensions. In other words, globalization *per se*, may uphold the norm of one worldliness, global intermingling or striving for universalism. It is observed that the process of globalization has been accelerated by modern means of communication and transportation, and gives the image that the world is unified globally. This ideology may also be seen in "Vasudhev Kutumbakum"[5] the theme of the Rig Vedic period in India. Such idealism seems to have been well depicted by the following, "This is mine that is another's, such reckoning are narrow minded. For the noble hearted, the whole world is one family."[6] Thus, it can be said that the 'world has become a global village'.

It may be mentioned here that India's march towards globalization had commenced with the introduction of economic liberalization in July 1991. Before 1991, India was a nation with political independence but there was no economic freedom. The adverse economic situation made the Government of India review the policies followed in the preceding four decades. The country was in deep crisis, when foreign currency reserves had plummeted to almost $1 billion; inflation had reached to an annual rate of 17 per cent; fiscal deficit was very high and had become unsustainable; foreign investors and NRIs had lost confidence in Indian Economy. While presenting the Budget for 1991-92, Dr. Manmohan Singh asserted—"there is no time to lose. Neither the Government nor the economy can live beyond its means year after year. The room for manoeuvre, to live on borrowed money or time does not exist any more. Macro economic stabilisation and fiscal adjustment alone cannot suffice. This must be followed by essential reforms in economic policy and economic management."[7]

Consequent to this, India finally took a historic step on a comprehensive reform of the economy to widen and deepen its integration with the world economy as a part of structural adjustment. However, there has been considerable debate on the contents of the reform package, their sequencing and the pace, their implementation and their impact. The crisis situation led the government in June 1991 to pursue the New Economic Policy (NEP), based on stabalisation and Structural Adjustment Programmes (SAP) in which, in return for loans, the Government of India undertook to reduce its role in the economy through a policy of liberalisation, deregulation, privatisation and globalization.[8]

Globalization refers to economic globalization through trade, foreign direct investment, capital flows, migration, and the spread of technology. Globalization is a phenomenon on over the world, so it affects all countries, all aspects of our daily life, such as society, culture and economics. It is significant to note that the globalization has helped to create wide opportunities for some people, groups and countries. It came to India through the economic reform and it has brought both opportunities and challenges.

GLOBALIZATION : A BOON FOR INDIA

Undoubtedly, the process of liberalization and globalization have brought many benefits for the country in many ways. With 1.2 billion people and the World's fourth largest economy, India's recent growth and development has been one of the most significant achievements of globalised era. Human indicators such as literacy, school enrolment, infant mortality rate, and life expectancy have enormously improved in the last few decades. Life expectancy has increased from 49 years in 1970 to 65 years in 2011, infant mortality of under five per 1000 live births has fallen from 114 in 1990 to 61 in 2011, adult literacy rate have risen from 18.33 per cent (1951) to 74.04 in 2011 and annual growth rate of GDP is also increased in the same period from 3.2 per cent to 8.6 per cent.

The Table 1 clearly depicts the brightest side of globalization. The rate of growth of the Gross Domestic Product of India has been on the increase from 5.6 per cent during 1980-90 to 6.7 per cent in the 1992-97 period. In the last two years, the annual growth rate of the GDP was impressive at 8.0% (2009-10), 8.6% (2010-11). It is observed that only after 1980s the annual growth rates shifted into high gear otherwise till 80s it was stagnant.

Investment has always been an issue for the developing economies such as India. Before 1991 the GDP of India was low. Due to the welcome of FDI's there has been lot of growth in sectors such as IT, banking and financial sector, telecommunication, and infrastructure. Foreign direct investment (FDI) in India has played an

TABLE I
Growth Rate in India Over Successive Plan Periods (1951-2010-11)

Five Year Plan Period		Annual Growth Rate of GDP %	Average Annual Gross Domestic Capital Formation (as % of GDP at Factor Cost)
I	1951-56	3.6	10.3
II	1956-61	4.2	14.4
III	1961-66	2.8	15.6
IV	1969-74	3.3	17.0
V	1974-79	4.8	20.2
VI	1980-85	5.6	21.9
VII	1985-90	6.0	25.2
VIII	1992-97	6.7	25.4
IX	1997-02	5.5	25.9
X	2002-07	7.6	27.5
	2005-06	9.5	34.2
	2006-07	9.6	35.9
	2007-08	9.3	38.0
	2008-09	6.8	35.4
	2009-10	8.0	36.1
	2010-11	8.6	35.8 (QE)

Source : Economic Survey, 2011-12.

important role in the development of the Indian economy during the recession. Foreign Exchange Reserves in India increased to 14760.70 INR Billion in June of 2013 from 14228.40 INR Billion in May of 2013. Historically, from 1990 until 2013, India Foreign Exchange Reserves averaged 4856.84 INR Billion reaching an all time high of 14760.70 INR Billion in June of 2013 and a record low of 23.86 INR Billion in June of 1991. Foreign direct investment is one of the measures of growing economic globalization.

As a matter of fact, India is one of the fastest growing economies in the world today. As of 2010, in respect of market capitalization (which takes into account the market value of a quoted company by multiplying its current share price by the number of shares in issue),

India is in the fourth position with $ 4.06 trillion after the US ($ 14.66 trillion), and China ($10.09 trillion), Japan ($ 4.31 trillion).[9]

India's share of world merchandise exports increased Exports have reached a record figure of US $ 102.7 billions during the financial year 2005-06. India's exports grew by 22.5 per cent in August 2010 to 16 billion US Dollars.

However, reducing poverty is a key element in Indian inclusive growth strategy. According to Planning Commission of India, the number of people below poverty line in 1993-94 was 36.0 per cent and it came down to 27.5 per cent in 2004-05. However, Tendulkar Committee estimated it 45.3 per cent in 1993-94 and 37.2 per cent in 2004-05.

Another benefit of globalization is said to create absolute livelihood opportunities and add to decent employment commensurate with the expectations of growing labour force. It is observed that an insignificant increase in employment between 2004-05 and 2009-10 is seen in the decline in labour supply itself as indicated by sharp decline in Labour Force Participation Rates (LFPR), from 42.85 per cent in 2004-05 to 39.80 in 2009-10, (resulting into an increase only of 11.7 million in labour force in a five year period as compared to over 12 million per year during 1999-2000/ 2004-05.

TABLE 2

Labour Force Participation Rate (LFPR) (% to Population)

	1993-94	*1999-2000*	*2004-05*	*2009-10*
LFPR all age groups				
Male	55.62	54.06	55.94	55.69
Female	28.74	26.01	28.86	22.87
Total	42.68	40.52	42.85	39.80
LFPR for age group (15–24)				
Male	68.55	65.07	64.98	53.70
Female	35.45	30.33	32.55	22.20
Total	52.80	49.06	49.56	38.80

Source : Various Rounds of NSSO Report on 'Employment and Unemployment Situation in India', Ministry of Statistics and Programme Implementation, Government of India.

As a result, in spite of a slow growth in employment, unemployment rates in 2009/10 are estimated to be significantly lower than in 2004-05. Unemployment, in fact, declined in absolute term by 6.3 million.

One of the most powerful effects of globalization is the spread of education. Today, you can move in the search of the best educational facilities in the world, without any hindrance. There is a worldwide market for the companies and for the customers there is a better access to products from different countries. India has 2nd in position as mobile phone user and occupies 16th position in internet users. Cultural intermingling has increased and every nation has tried to know more about the other nations' cultural preferences.

GLOBALISATION : A CURSE

On one hand globalisation is considered to promote global economic growth and social progress, while on the other hand, it is responsible for growing income inequality and environmental degradation, causing social degeneration and difficulty of competition. According to various reports, the gap between countries has widened, even though there has been worldwide surge in economic growth over the past decades, but it has benefited only a handful of countries and most of the countries are in a big loss.

In this respect, the World Bank observes that when looking at total consumption, the wealthiest 20 percent consume 76 per cent of the world's resources, while the world's poorest 80 percent consume just 1.5 percent. Therefore, the distance between the richest and poorest is growing. Though the rate of poverty declined by 25 per cent between 1980 and 2005, but still more than 3 billion people around the world live at or below the poverty line (which today is measured as anyone who makes $2.50/day or less). Further, a full 80 per cent of the world's population lives on less than $10 a day.[10]

While the rich are getting richer, the poor are struggling for a square meal. At the 2011 World Economic Forum in Davos, income inequality and corruption were singled out as the two most serious challenges facing the world. And in a recent keynote address to an OECD policy forum on income inequality, Richard Freeman, professor of economics at Harvard University, noted that "the triumph of globalization and market capitalism has improved living standards for billions while concentrating billions among the few. It has lowered inequality worldwide but raised inequality within most countries."[11] The regional disparities have increased due to globalization. Developed countries are benefited more than the developing countries. Similarly, within the country the richer states would benefit while the poorer states might become poorer. Between 1999 and 2008 the annual growth rates for Gujarat (8.8%), Haryana (8.7%), or Delhi (7.4%) were much higher than for Bihar (5.1%), Uttar Pradesh (4.4%), or Madhya Pradesh (3.5%).

Similarly, India's ranking in the Human Development Index may also be a reflection on the condition of social sector. According to UNDP Human Development Reports, India's progress from 'low to medium' category of human development is accompanied by its 134th ranking in Human Development Index. This gives a negative picture of social sector of India. India's Human Development Index is much lower than the East and South-East Asian countries like China, Indonesia, Republic of Korea, Malaysia, Philippines and Thailand.

Moreover, the Indian economy has been undergoing a process of development and diversification for a long time. This process accelerated after independence when the country recorded a major increase in its growth of GDP and per capita income. India has become the fourth largest economy in the world due to a strong economic growth but still has a low per capita income. India has moved up the ranks, but is still the poorest among the G-20 and the per capita income of India stood at $1,527 in 2011 as noted by World Bank Report. Furthermore, World Bank report on poverty mentioned that "...this is perhaps the most visible challenge. Similarly, India accounts for one-third of the world poor people living on less than USD 1.25 (about Rs. 65) per day. A 2007 Report by the state-run National Commission for Enterprises in the Unorganised Sector (NCEUS) found that 25% of Indians, or 236 million people, lived on less than 20 rupees per day.

Agriculture continues to be the predominant sector in India. Agriculture contributes 17.5% to GDP. More than 52% of India's population depend on agriculture for employment. During the post-reform phase the sectoral distribution of Gross Domestic Product (GDP) in India has seen a consistent declining share of agriculture. Globalization has caused misery and despair among millions of Indian farmers, driving large numbers of them to suicide. Exacerbated by two years of drought in 1965 and 1966, the Indian Government turned to high yielding, genetically modified, "miracle-seeds" provided by the World Bank and the United States. Economic reforms have given farmers access to expensive and promising biotechnology.

Reforms opened Indian farmers to global competition, such as with the United States and UK who receive over $18 billion a year in subsidies. In order to compete, many farmers turned to high-cost seeds, fertilizers and pesticides, believing in easier returns. Forcing farmers into a debt trap are soaring input costs, the plummeting price of produce and a lack of proper credit facilities, which makes farmers turn to private moneylenders who charge exorbitant rates of interest. More than 100,000 farmers have taken their lives since 1997. 86.5 per cent of farmers who took their own lives were financially indebted.

Further, it is observed that due to the new development paradigm, the agrarian sector too is undergoing crisis. Acquisition of agriculture land for setting up SEZs (Special Economic Zones) is adversely affecting the farmers. Workers, interests too are badly affected by SEZs because of no provision to set trade unions in the SEZs and the workers have no right to take actions against any violation of their basic rights. Thus, there have been adverse results against the workers and labourers.

Further, globalization of trade is also manifested in the implementation of the WTO's agreement on Trade Related Aspects of Intellectual Property Rights (TRIPS), which extends patent protection on new drugs for a minimum period of 20 years. As a result of high prices, TRIPS threatens to limit and undermine access to new medicines, especially to poor populations living in the developing world. Consequent to this, the implementation of TRIPS can be seen as exacerbating health risks in India and many other developing countries.

Besides, gender equality is critical to the development process. The globalization has had a mixed impact on women's rights. On the one hand, aspects of globalisation have provided women with increasing opportunities to work in solidarity at regional, national and international levels to demand their rights but at the same time globalisation has had adverse effects on women in India. Women have entered the workforce in large numbers in states that have embraced liberal economic policies. As consumers, women are increasingly facing a consumer culture which reduces them to commodities and as producers, women are exposed to work exploitation and occupational hazards.

Globalisation affected the Indian culture also. It is found that the deeply rooted traditions and values in India are changing. The nuclear family pattern which is gaining importance and acceptance in Indian society can affect more of the dimensions.

Similarly, fast food chains like McDonalds and KFC are spreading fast in the developing world. People are consuming more junk food which has an adverse impact on their health.India alone is responsible for 60% of the global population lacking access to basic sanitation. According to UN Report 2010, it is observed that about half of its 1.2 billion residents are mobile subscribers, but only 366 million people (about one-third of its population) have access to toilets.

CONCLUSION

Thus, globalization has both positive as well as negative impacts on various sectors of Indian Economy. Though globalization has significantly improved the Indian economy, but due to unbalanced and uneven economic growth, the world's social and poverty problems have been magnified. The Human Development Index and Gender Inequality Index are still low. Despite the concerted development in manufacturing and service sectors, despite the remarkable inflow and overflow of foreign reserves, agriculture is still the largest industry providing employment to about 56 per cent of the workforce in the country. The share of agriculture in the GDP is only 17.5%. The number of landless families has increased and farmers are still committing suicide. Our Small Scale Industry Still more than 236 million people of India, lived on less than 20 rupees per day.

There are many positive sides of globalisation too. It can not be denied that India gained highly from the LPG model as its GDP increased from 3.6 per cent in 1951 to 8.6 per cent in 2010-11. In respect of market capitalization, India ranks fourth in the world. It helps in increased access to better and qualitative education for Indians. There has been a tremendous increase in consumerism, for goods and services. Scientific and technological innovations have made life quite comfortable, fast and enjoyable. Greater and faster flow of information (through TV, Internet) between countries and greater cultural interaction has helped to overcome cultural barriers. But seeing both the negative and positive effects of globalization in the country, it can be said that very soon India will overcome these hurdles too and march strongly on its path of development.

NOTES AND REFERENCES

1. As defined by World Bank and quoted in Milanovic, B. (2002), "*True World Income Distribution, 1988 and 1993: First Calculation based on Household Surveys Alone*", *Economic Journal*, 112 (476), pp. 51-92.

2. International Monetary Fund (IMF) (1997), *World Economic Outlook*, Washington, D.C.: IMF.
3. Giddens, Anthony, (1990), *Consequences of Modernity*, Cambridge, UK: Polity Press.
4. Jameson, Fredric (1998), 'Notes on Globalization as a Philosophical Issue'. In the Fredric Jameson and Masao Miyoshi (eds.), *The Cultures of Globalization*, Durham and London: Duke University Press.
5. The whole world is but one Family.
6. http://www.enlightenedleadershipnow.com/Home/power-of-unity-or-oneness/what-is-spiritual-leadership/vasudhaiva-kutumbakam-vasudhaiva-kutumbakam.
7. Budget speech of the Union Finance Minister presenting the Budget for 1991-92 Part A 24-07-1991.
8. Jauhari, B.M. (ed.), (1996), *Economic Liberalisation and Globalisation*, New Delhi: Commonwealth Publishers.
9. WWW.worldbank.org/DATASTATISTICS/Resources/GDP_PPP.pdf
10. http://www.helium.com/items/2351722-the-challenge-of-global-poverty.
11. Richard Freeman, Speech at the OECD Policy Forum on Tackling Inequality, Paris, May 2, 2011.

10

Techniques of Non-Violent Protest

Global Context

Ghanshyam Roy

INTRODUCTION

Nonviolent civic action is often utilized in response to a power imbalance. As reflected in the word "civic", nonviolent civic action is a technique or method that can be utilized by ordinary citizens, including the young, and is often implemented at the grassroots or community level. When individuals or groups of people share a common grievance, or experience an injustice together, they often find support by uniting. When unified, they can more effectively mobilize and challenge their opponents. In order to increase its power, a movement must build a cohesive coalition of organisations, groups, and institutions that is unified around common objective and struggle by nonviolent methods to achieve their goal. Finally, nonviolent civic action requires targeted and skillful action. Like so many other movements around the world, it should not be achieved without a concerted proactive and determined effort. Throughout history, people have used nonviolent civic action, even if it was called by a different name, to achieve political, economic and social advances around the world.

DISCUSSION

When conducted skillfully and strategically, non-violent movements have the potential to topple the most ruthless dictator, force remediation and revise laws or policies that violate rights. Those in power do not typically concede their power voluntarily. Rather, they must be made to feel heightened political and economic cost in maintaining the *status quo*. While strategic nonviolent action has the potential to empower previously disenfranchised, disempowered and marginalized people, there is never a guarantee that a nonviolent movement will succeed. In this pretext some of the non-violent movements adopting different techniques organised during 20th and 21st century globally are analysed and detailed as follows:

1. Fighting to Overcome Authoritarianism

Nepal

In 2001, in response to resist new king Gyanendra's authoritarian direct rule, an alliance of Napalese political parties launched a nationwide movement of protests for three weeks in April 2006 Pro-democracy mobilization, including a general strike, brought the daily activities of Kathmandu to a halt. In defiance of the curfew and their government, hundreds of thousands of citizens rallied in the streets of the capital for a series of major protest demonstrations. Their non-violent action had brutal repercussions. Despite the repression, the leaders of political parties defiantly insisted that they would not stop the social agitation until the king reinstated the Parliament and permitted a refrendum on the Constitution that had given the monarchy control of the military. With most of the country united against the unpopular and repressive king, Gyanendra finally gave in to the movement's demand. Parliament was reconvened and a seven party alliance of the largest political parties began work on a constitutional referendum.

Other nonviolent movements fighting to overcome authoritarianism and military rule include the following :

(i) *Russia* : In 1905, some 15,0,000 workers in St-Petersburg challenged the autocratic rulers. Backlash was severe, and became known as *"Bloody Sunday"*. However the protest spread and led to the country's first elected national parliament.

(ii) *Denmark* : National non-cooperation and acts of sabotage against the Nazi German occupation during World War II saved the lives of most Danish Jews.

(iii) *Chile* : The country-wide "No" campaign ended the dictatorship of Angusto Pinochet in the late 1980s.

(iv) *Georgia* : The youth led Kmara movement brought about the end of the Soviet style presidency of Eduard A. Sherardnatze, resulting in sweeping political reforms in 2003.

(v) *Lebanon* : During the Lebanese "Intifada for Independence" in 2005, one quarter of the country's population gathered in Beirut to protest the assassination of a popular political leader to demand the resignation of the Syrian-controlled government and the removal of Syrian troops.

(2) Fighting for Human Rights and Democratic Freedom

Argentina

The mothers of the Plaza de Mayo is an organization that grew over three decades with a simple demand i.e., to know the fate of some 30,000 "disappeared" daughters and sons, who were abducted by agents of the Argentina government during the "dirty war" (1976-83). During this time the military dictatorship, under the leadership of Jorge Rafael Videla, was responsible for systematic repression of trade unionists, activists, students, and others in what was known the National Reorganization Process. The majority of those who "disappeared" were tortured prior to being executed standing up against a merciless military regime, a group of mothers gathered regularly on a weekly basis in the Plaza de Mayo square, starting in April 1997, demanding to know the fate of their children. The women's actions spurred a human rights movement that would raise the issue of Argentina's political repression to the consciousness of the international community. In quiet acts of bravery, for years the mothers stood together in the face of the ruthless military Junta, which would 'disappear' three of the founders, while many others faced threats and beatings. In December 1981, the mothers held their first Resistance March and have continued the annual tradition ever since. To this day, they still ask to learn the fate of their children, even though their movement has also incorporated other social issues such as national debt, poverty, unemployment, and the release of political prisoners.

Other nonviolent movements advancing human rights and democratic freedoms are following :

(i) *Pakistan* : Known as Pakistani Lawyer's Movement, lawyers across Pakistan in 2007 to demand the restoration of Pakistan's chief justice, along with 60 other judges who were dismissed illegally by the military dictator, General Pervez Musharraf.

(ii) *South Africa* : The anti-apartheid struggle culminated with the release of Nelson Mandela from 27 years of imprisonment and his eventual presidency.

(iii) *Madagascar* : In 2001, a fraudulent election, followed by mass demonstrations, brought the entire country to a stand still for seven weeks until the incumbent president fled the country.

(iv) *Iran* : In 2009, demonstrations were launched to protest the re-election of President Mahmound Ahmedinijad, particularly at the behest of opposition candidate Mir Hossein Mousavi.

(v) *United States* : The U.S. Civil rights movement, whose best known leader was Martin Luther King Jr. brought about major changes in laws and policies upholding racial discrimination against black Americans.

(3) Other Especially Challenging Cases

(i) *Mynmar* : Mynmar is currently under the control of a ruthless military junta, which has suppressed the basic freedoms of the Burmese for the past four decades. A highly co-ordinated pre-democracy movement has surged both internally within Burma's borders, and externally through diaspora populations and sympathizers. Burmese monks have orchestrated a series of protests, demonstrations and marches, most recently in their 2007 Saffron Revolution. However, the junta's iron first has quashed dissident efforts and tortured and killed numerous leaders despite international outcry. Pro-democracy leader Aung San Su Kyi has been under house arrest for over 20 years. Su Kyi has been released and she is continuing here peaceful effort to establish democracy in Mynmar.

(ii) *Zimbabwe* : Despite attempts for free and fair elections in Zimbabwe, many citizens have either fled the country's recent economic and political crisis or continued to live in fear of President Robert Mugabe's notorious secret police. Those who have organized to defy Mugabe nonviolently have done so at great personal risk. However, civic groups such as women of Zimbabwe arise and managed to defy restrictions, demanding education, medical care and food. They bring international attention to the plight of Zimbabwe's citizens, much to the anger of the Mugabe regime.

(iii) *China* : Communist China continues to suppress many public pro-democracy and free speech demonstrations, Tibetan self-determination, and Uighur autonomy.

Now one of the misconceptions about non-violent protest is that it is always used for altruistic and benevolent purpose. At times, however, unethical opportunists can incite and manipulate populations to advance their personal aims, particularly within zones of conflict for example, a corrupt politician in a conflict zone may rally his constituents to approve a law that would allow a non-governmental organization to build a road to get humanitarian assistance to a remote village; although the real purpose might be to use that road for illegal purposes or personal gain.

One of the most challenging tests of nonviolent protest involves cases of genocide. Prior to the holocast during World War II, Gandhi wrote an article in 1938 urging Jews to be steadfast and morally superior against Hitler and German oppression using the techniques of non violent action. In response, the Jewish philosopher and educator Judah Magnes wrote, "A Letter to Gandhi" saying that as much as he believed in nonviolent action he no longer saw it as a realistic alternative in the midst of such overwhelming evil. Magnes argued that the conditions in the Germany of his time were radically different than from those in South Africa and India where Gandhi's nonviolent techniques had successfully occurred. Having lost faith, he asked Gandhi to spell out precisely how satyagraha could be of practical use to the Jewish people in those dire times. He wrote, "I am too painfully conscious that I am beginning to admit that if Hitler hurls his war upon us, we must resist." Thus many people point to the numerous documented cases to nonviolent action successfully implemented during World War-II that saved the lives of many people.

CONCLUSION

Thus, it is evident from above discussed facts that Non-violent techniques can wield tremendous power to resolve grievances against an opponent to overcome authoritarianism and military occupation, achieve rights and advance human rights and democratic freedoms globally while this research article affirms the historical effectiveness of non-violent movements.

Thus, it is concluded that conflicts do not necessarily have to be resolved through violent means. Strategic nonviolent action enables anyone to play an important role in building peace in the community Now, non-violent techniques serve as an effective tool for citizens when implemented strategically. Thus it is clear that Gandhian form of protest by nonviolent technique is proving its relevance in present century in many parts of world.

REFERENCES

Ackerman, Peter and Jack Du Vall (2001), A force more powerful : A Century of Non-Violent Conflict, Palgrave-Macmillan, New York.

Ackermann, Peter and Christopher Kruegler (1994) Strategic Nonviolent Conflict : The Dynamics of People Power in the Twentieth Century. Preger, Westport.

Helvey, Robert (2004), On Strategic Nonviolent Conflict Thinking About the Fundamentals, Albert Einstein Institute, Boston.

King, Mary E. (2002), Mahatma Gandhi and Martin Luther King Jr. : The Power of Nonviolent Action, Indian Council for Cultural Relations, Mehta Publishers, New Delhi.

Sharp, Gene (2005), The Politics of Nonviolent Action, Porter Sargent, Boston.

Sharp, Gene (2005), Waging Nonviolent Struggle : 20th century, Porte- Sargent, Boston.

Sharp, Gene (2006), There are Realistic Alternatives, Albert Einstein Institute, Boston.

11

Globalization and Sustainability of Mankind

MADHUKAR PATNAIK AND HARIPRIYA BEHARA

Globalization is a buzzing word in India for about two and a half decades. The process is called LPG (Liberalization, Privatization, Globalization) which is still in progress. It not only brought various advantages, both directly and indirectly but also significant disadvantages. The recent happenings that took place across almost all the spheres of India, speaks about the ill effects of globalization introduced in the year 1991.

The most significant among all the above is the ecological imbalance and its consequences besides financial, political and social disorders. These drawbacks especially the environmental effects will have direct bearing on the agriculture which reduces the staple food output levels and poses a major threat to the per capita availability of food grains. It will also have a negative impact on the supply of raw material to the industry and reduces the supply of critical inputs such as power and energy. This leads to a fall in the employment generation and thereby destabilizes the total economy. Thus, a vicious circle is formed in the economy depicting the evils of globalization. What are the main reasons for such disastrous performance of globalization? What are the existing mechanisms available to cope up with the above situations? What is the role of policy-makers, planners and all the stake holders? These are the present issues discussed everywhere not only in India but across the globe. Hence, an attempt is made here to highlight the factors responsible for globalization and its impact.

GLOBALIZATION IN INDIA

India took the decision to adopt globalism when the economy was reeling under deep balance of payments crisis in 1990-91. Though their exists capitalism the then, the dominating mechanism was by the government only in its business activity. However, when the crisis was mainly due to insufficient foreign exchange reserves, the policy makers were forced to take a decision of opening the Indian Economy to the rest of the world, to the maximum possible extent. Thus, the new economic order was in vogue, giving scope to a variety of events to take place, in and out of the country.

The twin policies of privatization and de-regulation (liberalization) have helped to increase the pace of the globalization process. Issues such as, free market economy, level playing field, foreign exchange equation, price stability and a host of other macro parameters are discussed at length and depth in the country.

PRIVATIZATION IN INDIA

Privatization refers to keeping the governments out of commercial activities and replacing the objectives of socialism by capitalism. Since the public enterprises suffer from problems such as, delayed decision making, lack of autonomy, lack of supervision and motivation, etc., the planners have decided to invite private entrepreneurs, local and global, into the economy. Then the governments started selling off the publicly owned businesses and assets to national multinational and transnational private entrepreneurship. The competition that prevailed among the new generation entrepreneurs led to lower prices with better services and a variety of products to the customers. Undoubtedly the country is blessed with the process of privatization initially, but subsequently started suffering from too much consumerism and too ambitious nature.

The strange part of the process is that, the Indian government streamlined its businesses making them efficient and then offered for sales. The questions are, when the government is competent to set right the issues for better profits, why did not they do it earlier? And why these profit earning units are offered for sales? This show how crazy the planners were to privatize the economy and how globalization of the economy as a school of thought set into the country.

LIBERALIZATION (DE-REGULATION) IN INDIA

According to the existing business policy the government should have a maximum of 49% stake in any enterprise under necessary conditions , while the private sector must have 51-100% under normal circumstances. Thus, deregulation refers to, removal of trade restrictions both qualitative and quantitative as much as possible so that industry runs more efficiently. This also refers to the value of domestic currency exposed to the value of dollar which is earlier either pegged up or pegged down to fetch foreign currency. Now, after deregulation the domestic currency will find its own natural level in the reservoir of global currencies. Thus, the free trade policy allowed foreign players into Indian business. Of late, on the 15th July 2013, the government of India declared 100% opening of FDI into Indian business including the strategic areas. Therefore one can understand the extent of globalization as a process entered and established in a developing country like India.

IMPACT OF GLOBALIZATION

Globalization is often associated with economic development which refers the free flow of goods and services, human capital and financial capital across nations. This can be called as economic globalization which is only a part of the overall globalization. The economic globalization leads to economic growth, internal development and higher standards of living. Let us examine the same in the context of India.

In terms of globalization, the economic indicators of India have shown significant positive results initially. The entry on MNC's in large numbers, flow of FII's into its capital market, expansion and penetration of global market into its villages are some of the examples. Indian human capital moved abroad and migrated to developed nations as they could find more lucrative opportunities with international business organizations. They started moving freely between countries, finding the best fit between their skills and the needs of global employers. This paved way for huge remittances from these migrant workers into Indian economy and improved the standards of living of their own families.

In addition to the economic globalization there is cultural globalization which also needs a mention. India started experiencing a new culture of celebrating certain specific days such as Valentine's Day, father's day, mother's day etc. in addition to its usual traditional religious days. The most important aspect of cultural change that took place is in the food habits, dress culture and other health hazardous habits especially among the younger generation who are more in number.

Beyond all its great benefits, globalization also brought about certain odds into the Indian economy. There were permanent economic shifts which have disproportionate high burdens on select groups, middle and lower middle class especially. The increasing tendency among Indians to maximize their benefits lead to, cultural displacement, change in the family system, greedy and selfish nature, too much consumerism, and many more such catastrophes. Thus, it is neediness to say that the benefits of globalization have not come to India without any costs. Some are known and can be reduced while some are unknown. Among the known, some are being attended to, on priority base and the most ignored are found to be the environment, nature and ecology.

GLOBALIZATION AND MANKIND

Globalization, as said earlier, confined largely to economic convergence, leaving the aspects such as environment, biodiversity, climate change etc, which are essential for the sustainability of mankind. There were no global standards set for the above aspects, as a part of the globalization process. The destruction of natural resources like clean water, forests, arable land, ocean fish stocks, coral reefs and so on, are already causing extreme concern even in the traditionally conservative ranks of the society. The current rate of extinctions from the plant is comparable to the rate of the extinction event that took place 65 million years ago, which destroyed millions of species including dinosaurs. The earth is not able to cope up with the present increasing global demand for natural resources. The global economy is presently on a course to destroy itself through the planners' lack of ability to sustain it.

It is true to say that the rate at which globalization taking place, is really an achievement for the mankind. Due to the industrial growth and technology advancement, a significant amount of material pleasure and prosperity is available to the human being. But the stress caused to individuals and to the nature is equally important and needs a debate. Most importantly the developing part of the world, particularly India and China with huge population, cannot wait for the developed nations to invent new technologies to cope up with the catastrophe already created. Further, developing countries, mostly featured by problems such as population growth, fall in the land-man ratio and productivity levels, also started suffering from degradation and depletion of natural resources affecting the life-support system of all, in the name of globalization. Thus, the process and growth of globalization taking place in India, already posing a serious threat to the country.

GLOBALIZATION AND RELEVANCE OF MAHATMA GANDHI

Mahatma Gandhi, environment, mankind and sustainable development etc words can be called as synonyms as Gandhiji's entire life revolved around environment protection for mankind.

He not only authored voluminous writings on this but also put into practice by opposing the construction of large scale dams by leading people's movements. He was never against to industrialization but was concerned about excess industrialization and its impact on nature. In his words, Industrialization at a large scale can never over take the unemployed millions rather than it leads to serious detriment to the environment. Therefore, he suggested a bottoms-up growth model for Industrialization in India while Pandit Nehru suggested a top-down model. But the subsequent planners of this country, in the name of globalizing India, have been racing towards Industrial growth, dreaming overnight profits.

Swami Vivekananda also foresaw the dangers of Globalization as early as in 1893. According to him, "Shall India die? Then, from the world all spirituality will be extinct, all sweet souled sympathy for religion will be extinct and in its place will reign the duality of lust and luxury as the male and female deities, with money as its priest, fraud, force and competition its ceremonies and human soul its sacrifice. Such a thing can never be."

These above words of 1893, hold good even in the year 2013 as the recent examples of mis happenings at Uttarakhand and Himachal Pradesh can only substantiate Swamy's argument. Precisely, such a terrible thing is taking place in our country.

It is very much unfortunate that a place called as "Dev Bhumi (land of gods)" and where the land is fertile, has become today a grave yard. In the names of Globalization, Industrialization, commercialization and development, a newly formed state started its journey pathetically. The huge loss of human resources is definitely because of its development plan incompatible with its natural resources. Thus, the process of Globalization in India did not even spare places of worship as it is said that the nature of Uttarakhand is disturbed to construct a hydel project for the sake of developing the area and rest is the result. This is not the present situation in India alone. The present day world is facing different kind of natural disasters lika landslides, earthquakes, tsunamis, coastal erosions, volcanoes, fire, etc. All these have received a substantial attention of experts in the field of science & technology and the policy-makers across the globe.

J.C. Kumarappa, about six decades ago only, stressed the need for "Economy of Permanence" over the destruction of natural resources. It is interesting to know that Mahatma Gandhiji, nine decades ago highlighted the importance of environment and opined that the village and cottage industries are more needed for achieving the "Economy of Permanence". According to him, production should be by masses not by mass production. He also advocated labor intensive strategies in labour surplus economies like India. But today, Indian industry is engaged in downsizing and right sizing of labor paving way for more technology oriented production processes. Mahatma Gandhi discussed all these at length in his contributions, *Hind Swaraj*, *Harijan* and *Young India* and emphasized the need of Khadi and Village industries during the 1920"s itself. But his ideas were not given sufficient attention and the road to development has led to the deterioration of the nature. As James M.C. Hall rightly pointed out, the human being has become the most dangerous organism that the planet has ever hosted. It is apt to recall one of the basic and profound tenets of Gandhian Philosophy in his own words, "The earth provides enough to satisfy every one's need; but not for one's greed". Further in the words of Schumacher, "unlimited material consumption in a finite world is impossibility." It is also true, according to the official statistics on the levels of pollution and the number and frequency of natural calamities, that in the near future, many cities in the world may suffer from inadequate surface and ground water resources, if the nature is left to itself without proper care.

CONCLUSION

India had the distinction of being world's largest economy

during the Christian era as its share was 32.9 percent in the world GDP. Surprisingly, it is less that 1.0 percent according to the estimates. (1.2% in 2006). There were no clear explanations for such performance in the literature, except for the changes the country undergone on different lines, Period of war, coloniolisation, urbanization, modernization, westernization, globalization, etc.) the latest among them was the contemporary globalization which brought several changes in Economics, social, cultural and political spheres of the Indian economy. In spite of all these changes, the major challenge remained is "sustainability". There were unevenness and inequalities everywhere. Intellectuals and elites in recent times have been suggesting several measures, the most common being the protection of nature.

Globalization is proved to be a double edged weapon, a boon and equally bane if, not handled properly. Intellectuals, planners, political leaders and a host of experts from other areas, have been recalling the memories of Gandhian Ideology and accepting that equitable and sustainable development is possible if the country imbibes the vision and value of Gandhiji. His theory of Economic Equality suggests that human beings shall always have the means to supply all their natural needs but definitely not beyond the natural level. Efforts are to be made to evolve policies that promote a right understanding on the manmade relationship.

References

Srinivasan, T.N. (2002) : Economic Reforms and Global Integration (PDF), Jan. 2002.

Rai, Saritha (2004) : "World Business Briefing–Asia: India, Trade Restrictions Eased", *The New York Times.*

Gangadhara Mohapatra (2012) : Globalization and Changing India: Counters current.org, www.bolofi.com

Pathak, Avijit, 2003, Post war-Thinking : Need for Egalitarian Globalization Mainstream, 41(22) 2003 (17 May) : pp. 11-12.

Singh, Yogender, 2000: Culture Change in India, Jaipur, Rawat Publications.

Trilok, N. Singh and D. Venkat Reddy, Editorial note. *International Journal of Earth Sciences and Engineering* (ISSN 0974-5904).

E. Berman, J. Bound, S. Machin : Implications of Skill Biased Technological Change : International evidence: *Quarterly Journal of Economics*, Vol. 113, 1998, pp. 1245-79.

E.F. Schumacher (1997): Roots of Economic Growth.

K.R. Nayyar : Politics of Sustainable Development, *EPW*, May 1994.

Dr. Zafar Mahfooz Nomani, "Environment, Sustainable Development and Globalization" : A plea to Indian Legislature.

Further Reforms needed to sustain Fast Economic Growth—WTO *Trade Policy Review of India*, 2007.

Next Big Spenders : India's Middle Class, The Hindu on live (2008)

The Environment crisis and Relevance of Gandhi www.mkgandhi.org

"Globalization and the Crisis of Environmental Governance in India"—by A. Kothari (2008) @ whereis.mit.edu

Hind Swaraj, Harijan and other literature authored by Sri Gangrede, Dr. Anil Dutta Mishra etc. all @ Library, Centre for Gandhian Philosophy and Human Development, GVP Degree College, Visakhapatnam-45.

12

Concept of Conflict

A Gandhian Perspective

BIRAJA SHANKAR RATH

INTRODUCTION

Larger part of Gandhi's life was spent in leading India's struggle for freedom and in attending to diverse socio-economic problems. This preoccupation of Gandhi was not a matter of choice or preference but was logical and inevitable. At the first instance, therefore, one wonders whether Gandhi was able to spare enough time and attention to the larger problems of conflict and peace. But, though confined to the locale of his own land Gandhi spoke, wrote and functioned in a way that transcended the limitations of space and time. He has left behind him a rich legacy of innumerable writings containing ideas that are surprisingly striking in their freshness, permanent relevance and world-wide appeal. There was an element of eternity in whatever he said and his constituency embraced the whole mankind. A Japanese scholar aptly pays his tribute. "Gandhi stands at the converging points of culture in the contemporary world and is therefore universally significant as a symbol over and beyond cultures in the contemporary world. This symbol indicates the only meaningful destination of man or mankind". (Kasai, 1981: 89)

Gandhi did not set out to elaborate on the theory of conflict and peace. But one can infer his ideas on this topic from the rich collection of his writings. This inference is easier than otherwise implied because his approach towards all problems-individual, national or international–was integral and interrelated. His entire philosophy forms a coherent whole and is based on a simple value system comprising of truth and non-violence.

Gandhi defies any classification so far as any exclusive school of thought is concerned. Any search for an internally consistent and systematized body of Gandhian thought would prove elusive. He had no time and little patience with theoretical formulations.

He was in one sense a conservative, in another, a philosophical anarchist; he was on the one hand a socialist, and on the other a capitalist, and yet again he was a primitive communist. For each of these assertions some evidence can be culled from his writings and speeches. He belongs at once to all these camps and to none of them. For whatever else may be said of him, Gandhi was not a political theorist. He entered the practical realm suggested by one political creed only to make his own constructions and move on to the next." (Bondurant, 1959: 146)

Nevertheless Gandhian contribution centers upon the role which Satyagraha as a technique of action, together with the philosophy of conflict which lies behind it may play in social and political system based upon them. Gandhi's Satyagraha as a type of struggle may be viewed as a contribution to the uniting of religion and politics, as a contribution to the forms of revolutionary struggle, or as a kind of social behaviour intended to help the individual achieve greater fulfilment.

A GANDHIAN APPROACH TO THE CONTEMPORARY SOCIAL CRISIS

There are certain outstanding features of the world system which point towards disaster of one kind or another overtaking humanity: the threat to the survival and well-being of humankind, the threat of war with weapons of increasing lethality, the unspeakable impoverishment of vast masses of people, the massive violations of human dignity deriving from discrimination on the basis of religion, colour, gender, class, caste, nationality etc., the threat to life sustaining capacity of the earth and so on. These have taken mankind to such a formidable predicament that it seems well nigh impossible to return to normal or rationally ordered life within the framework of modernity.

From one perspective, these threats are being perceived as global problems requiring global solutions. From another, they are problems that we confront in our daily lives—individually, in our families, in our villages, towns and cities, in our nations and in our regions. That is, we are faced with violence, economic needs, violations of dignity, deteriorating environments and divisiveness in circle of our lives from the individual to the global.

Gandhi had clearly foreseen this predicament, the oncoming disaster as early as 1909 in his *Hind Swaraj*. And throughout his life he continued to warn against it and showed the way to avert or steer clear of it through his ideas and experiments with truth and non-violence. In *Hind Swaraj* Gandhi had characterized modern civilization as a 'disease' and a 'nine days' wonder'. Even thirty years later in 1938 he said, "After the thirty years which I have since passed, have since nothing to make me alter the views expounded in it". (Quoted in Gangal, 1987: 20). Earlier in 1927 he had forewarned the 'civilized' west that "a time is coming when those who are in the mad rush today of multiplying their wants...will retrace their steps and say "what have we done?" (*Ibid*: 20-21). Barely two weeks before his death in January 1948, Gandhi had made the rather prophetic statement, "...this (modern) civilization is such that one has only to be patient, and it will be self-destroyed." (*Ibid*: 21)

Though not the only cause, nevertheless, a major cause for this increasing threat to human survival and well-being, is our continued acceptance of violence, i.e. our willingness to kill. Our historic readiness to kill for security and revolutionary changes has brought us to a mental and technological state in which each one of us has become vulnerable. As ancient wisdom warned us and as Gandhi taught, 'violence begets violence'. We are faced with prospects of infinite ingenuity in discovering new ways to destroy each other.

All the major problems in the world today are due to the violence-accepting culture that pervades across the spectrum of nationality, religion, race, caste and gender. If fact, all the above cleavages among mankind are more or less united on the issue of acceptance of violence, if not as the best method, but at least as a fait accompli. A serious analysis of the major problems that confront us will lead to violence in both thought and action as a major initiator and exacerbetor.

Our willingness to kill contributes to our economic deprivation in many ways. It directly diverts morality, intellect, science, labour, capital, resources and technology from service to human needs to serve human greed for a section of self seeking people. The gigantic global military establishments that we have created contribute to deprivation by preventing the need responsive structural changes within and among nations.

Secondly, our commitment to violence to pursue and realize freedom and justice for the deprived put these cherished values in permanent jeopardy. The violent fighter for freedom and justice today becomes tomorrow's deadly threat. All the terrorist groups operating now have their origin in the adoption of an ill-conceived method to realize the desirable goal of freedom, equality or justice. The cause of their struggle becomes so overwhelming that the violent method that they adopt is generally overlooked by those who patronize and sympathize with them. One righteous atrocity generates another till it reaches a Frankensteinian proportion to engulf a substantial section including the supporters and sympathizers into a hate filled environment of death and destruction.

Thirdly, this continued commitment to violence threatens to kill the life sustaining capabilities of the earth. The vast military consumption of fossil fuels and the wastes produced by nuclear power contributes to present and long range environmental contamination. The resource depletion and toxic wastes produced by industries that are deemed necessary to produce weapons and services for modern warfare further contribute to environmental devastation. So great is the environmental destructiveness of global militarization and associated disrespect for ecological vitality that according to the warning given by Barry Commoner, "We are in a suicidal war with planet and that planet inevitably will win". He warns that "survival depends equally on ending the war with nature and on ending wars among ourselves.....To make peace with the planet we must make peace with the people who live in it". (Commoner, 1990:243)

All these problems while seeded in acceptance of violence also reinforce each other and lead to more violence. Militarization, for example, increases insecurity, accentuates poverty, violates human rights, degrades the environment and divides mankind. Likewise an aggressive pursuance of rights and justice, increases militarization, deviates from the path of economic development and leads to depletion of environment. Our inability to protect environment leads to what is called ecological war, retards sustainable development and also often leads to suppression of rights of those like tribal and other natives who have traditionally drawn their sustenance from forest.

GANDHIAN THEORY OF CONFLICT

After this brief presentation of problems which generate conflicts, a discussion on Gandhi's ideas on conflict will facilitate a more comprehensive discussion on his technique of conflict resolution. The theory of conflict underwent significant modulation in the nineteenth century, first under the influence of Charles Darwin and later, of Herbert Spencer. The biological formula of Darwin sought to impart a halo of scientific finality to the conditioning character of the 'struggle for existence' in the evolution of the species. He perceived that the struggle for existence among species operated as a mode of 'Natural Selection' by which the undesirable was eliminated and the more fit sustained. "This preservation of favourable variations and the rejection of injurious variations, I call Natural Selection". (Darwin, 1968:31) The underlying principle here, as in the case of the later sociological interpretations of Darwin's theory, is the basic notion that as there are contending elements in nature so there are conflicting ideas and interests among men. To Darwin, therefore, struggle is the fundamental law of the universe, the implication being that conflict is a constant phenomenon and the cause of evolution.

Darwin uses the term struggle for existence in a 'large and metaphorical sense'. "I should premise that I use the term struggle for existence in a large and metaphorical sense, including dependence of one being on another and including (which is more important) not only the life of the individual, but success in living progeny". (*Ibid.*: 116). The whole stress of his thesis is on the process of struggle and he has completely ignored the unifying element of co-operation as a factor in the evolution of the species.

The Darwinian system led to, what is its natural, though not entirely legitimate result, i.e., the militarist interpretation of the history. Some of the followers of Darwin see selection as something which renders the inexorable law of heredity a source of progress which produces the good through suffering, an infinitely greater good which far out balances the obvious pain and evil. The evident suggestion in this line of thinking is that we should regard all scientific and humanitarian efforts to mitigate social conflict as not only uncalled for, but even harmful. It is an exhortation to us that if we once realize that this law of inheritance is as inevitable as the law of gravitation, we shall cease to struggle against it. The ideal attitude therefore is to let nature take its course.

Gandhi, while admitting that there are 'repulsions enough in Nature', differs radically from the Darwinian sociologists when it comes to his explanation of conflict in the physical as well as in the human world. He stands in sharp contrast with those who regard struggle as the fundamental law of creation. To him, struggle is neither a ceaseless process of evolution, nor a universal phenomenon. Conflicts which cause struggle are but unfortunate moments in the history of the human race. As such they are relatively unimportant in the course of the life of human society.

Though there are repulsions enough in Nature she lives by attraction. Mutual love enables Nature to persist. Man does not live by destruction. Self-love compels regards for others. Nations cohere because there is mutual regard among individuals composing them. Some day we must extend the national law to the universe, even as we have extended family laws to form nations–a larger family. (Gandhi, quoted in Shridharni, 1939:219)

Gandhi, here, clearly perceives a fundamental unity in the universe and society which sustains order and life. Prince Kroptokin, the Russian biologist, was led to similar conclusions from his observations of insects and animal life in the jungles of central Asia. His doctrine of 'mutual aid' which is based on compilation of evidence from the same field of investigation as that of Darwin, is in harmony with Gandhi's perception of the fundamental unity of all existence. Thus, conflicts are neither inevitable nor irreparable. They are only temporary irregularities in the order of things or brief squalls in the even flow of life.

The Gandhian position that there is nothing natural about violent instincts in man has solid roots not only in ethics but also in science. Twenty distinguished scientists drawn from diverse disciplines such as anthropology, ethnology, psychology, etc. brought out on 16th May 1986 a declaration titled 'Seville Statement on Violence'. They declared that:

> First, "it is scientifically incorrect to say that we have inherited a tendency to make war from our animal ancestors....."
>
> Second, "It is scientifically incorrect to say that war or any other violent behaviour is genetically programmed into our human nature ......"
>
> Third, "It is scientifically incorrect to say that in the course of human evolution there has been a selection for aggressive behaviour more than for other kinds of behaviour....."

Fourth, "It is scientifically incorrect to say that humans have a violent brain......"

Fifth, "It is scientifically incorrect to say that war is caused by instinct or any single motivation....."

We conclude that biology does not condemn humanity to war and that humanity can be freed from the bondage of biological pessimism and empowered with confidence to undertake the transformative tasks needed in this International Year of Peace and in the years to come. Although these tasks are mainly institutional and collective, they also rest upon the consciousness of individual participants for whom optimism and pessimism are crucial factors. Just as 'wars begin in the minds of men' peace also begins in our mind. The same species who invented war is capable of inventing peace. The responsibility lies with each of us. ('Manifesto of Nobel Prize Winners' Quoted in G.D. Paige, 1991: 433-34).

Thus departing from the Darwinian interpretation of conflict Gandhi seems to have come quite close to the Hegelian position that:

Every relation be viewed from two opposite aspects i.e., from the point of view of two terms it relates. Each term regards the relation as internal to itself and the other term as external to itself. An antinomy results which can be solved only by reinterpreting the situation and by looking at both terms and their relation from the point of view of a wider relation.....But one antinomy is solved in order to make way for another. Opposition breaks out between the terms on a higher level. (Sidney Hook, 1936:67)

Hegel, however, made his interpretation and left the rest, as it were, to the inexorable march of history and the last analysis, to the formulation of historicists. The Gandhian philosophy, accepting the dynamics of dialectical situation and taking man as the measure of reason, centers upon a technique whereby one or both sides of a conflict can resolve the antinomy into a reinterpretation.

The dialectics of both Hegel and Marx miss the heart of the problem of social and political conflict. "Hegel discovered reason in things themselves, equated real with rational and understood the progress of history in terms of the dialectics as a method of logic". (Bondurant, 1959:198-199) Marx, while striving for an empirical approach allowed the dogma of the class struggle and the absolutism of his philosophy of history to strangle the development of dialectics at a level where it could enter into a technique of action. In contrast, the dialectical approach of Gandhian philosophy of conflict provides dynamic control in the field of action through the fashioning of a technique for the 'creative resolution of conflict'. The term 'creative resolution of conflict, implies that in Gandhian terms peace is a positive concept and not the standard Western negative concept construed in 'resolution of conflict' as 'absence of conflict'. Conflict resolution to Gandhi means not the elimination of maladjustment, rather the progress towards more meaningful adjustment. This is achieved only when violent relationship is transformed into nonviolent relationship where the energies of the opponents are utilized in a higher integration or sublimation.

Victory in the conventional sense of attaining the goals declared from the beginning becomes less important than improving the parties and their relation through the conflict. The conflict becomes a medium for mutual education; together they may learn how to transform conflicts upward so that they can be handled non-violently and creatively. They come out of the conflict not only unscathed, but with higher capacity for conflict transformation capacity and it all works out even with something better than their original goals.

It is important to see how this creative resolution of conflict comes about. Here the Gandhian attitude towards a conflict situation provides the answer. The conflict is not regarded by Gandhi as an antagonistic relation between two human beings of two classes in which the important thing is to weaken the opponent but rather it is regarded as a situation in which the system binds the parties together. Gandhi views conflict as actually an invitation to social and constructive intercourse rather than an invitation to mutual elimination. Naturally his invitation to intercourse is, at the same time, an invitation to change the system. Gandhi, thus, is of the opinion that a conflict should not be a signal for rage and anger, for aggressive words and aggressive action. "To him a conflict was a challenge, a challenge that here was something to be done. While at the same time it offered possibilities of contact with a human being with whom you stand in an interesting and significant relation" (Galtung, quoted in Pran Chopra, 1972:203). This calls, more than ever, for an increase in the personal contact with the opposite party.

The fundamental Gandhian idea is that one should be aggressive not against the opponent but against the condition. The opposition should be directed against the antagonism, not against the antagonist. Gandhi expressed his fundamental attitude to an opponent in an open letter to the British written during his campaign for civil disobedience in July 1921. He wrote,

Some of my Indian friends charge me with camouflage when I say that I do not hate Englishmen, while we may hate the system they have established. I am trying to show that one may detest the wickedness of a brother without hating him......I claim to be a fairly accurate student of human nature and a vivisector of my own failing. I have discovered that man is superior to the system he propounds. And so I feel that you, as an individual, are infinitely better than the system you have evolved as a corporation....Here, in India, you belong to a system that is vile beyond description. It is possible, therefore, for me to condemn the system in the strongest terms without considering you to be bad and without imputing bad motives to every Englishman. You are as much slaves of the system, as we are." (Quoted in Theodor Ebert, 1967:103)

Thus, Gandhi has a distinctive approach to the 'enemy'. He distinguishes between the people on the one hand and their policies and system on the other. Sometimes he describes this as the difference between the evildoer and the evil itself. The 'enemy' is also seen as a victim of his own system, a view which is usually interpreted from a moral perspective. Whatever the origins of the distinction may be, it is clear that from a strategic point of view, it was very effective. This approach deliberately encouraged the British to oppose policies of the British Government in India and to work for Indian independence. The nonviolent character of the Indian national struggle made it much easier and very much more likely that Indians would in fact receive assistance from within the heart of the Empire itself. "In other words support for the Indians within Great Britain was not simply a result of special qualities of the British, or even the Labour Party, but at least as much or more so the result of the Indian reliance upon the non-violent technique to fight the British Raj." (Sharp, 1970: 262)

Anatol Rapoport (1989) shares this Gandian perception of conflict. He identifies three types of struggles and differentiates among them. He calls them 'fights', 'games' and 'debates'. In the 'fights', the opponent's presence is an unwanted one, a nuisance and so has to be eliminated. But in the 'games' an opponent is essential and his strength is also valued. Rules of the games are followed with cooperation and everyone tries to do his best. The opponent speaks the same language whose interest may be opposed but who exists as a rational being. His inner thought process is important. In the 'debates' the opponents direct their arguments at each other. The objective is to convince the opponent and to make him see things as one sees them himself. Debate is that category of conflict in which the problem of convincing another, that is, the problem of changing another's outlook is the central aspect. Rapaport's 'debates' lead the opponents towards more rationality and humanity and the first stage of Gandhi's 'satyagraha', the Gandhian technique of conflict resolution is characterized by persuasion through reason.

According to Gandhi the problem of peace and conflict should be considered within an entire philosophy of life. War and peace are not isolated problems that can be resolved incrementally or through some piecemeal strategy. Gandhian starting point with regard to peace and war, as to all other problems is the individual. Gandhi believes that any philosophy of life, in order to have any meaning at all, must commence with man as the being to which all truth is related. A study of conflict should also commence with individual on the focus "for, unless the individual wields the weapon of destruction there can be no war". (Gangal, 1960:12)

Conflict, according to Gandhi, has its root in the human lives which are often divided into watertight compartments- religious, moral, social, economic, political, individual and collective. From these different levels we have devised different sets of moral values. Often these values conflict with one another. However, life refuses to be compartmentalized. Gandhi writes, "The whole gamut of man's activities today constitutes an indivisible whole. You cannot divide life social, economic, political and purely religious into watertight compartments". (Quoted in Ramachadran & Mahadevan, 1970: 240) The evil, man does in one field of human activity, has its affect on the entire gamut of his activity.

The contradicting values that we have prescribed for ourselves to be followed at different levels of activity, are very evident. In social life we honour the man who is truthful, non-interfering, modest and affectionate. We honour greatly the man who, at his personal inconvenience, serves his neighbour. In the political and especially in the international field we expect the nations and its agents to be selfish, proud, overbearing, cruel and aggressive. As a matter of fact a nation sacrificing its real and fancied interests will not only be considered foolish but also morally deprived. In this field, truth, justice, fair play and fellow-feeling are at a discount. While in social life we denounce hate and violence, the successful use of it in the political field is not only not condemned but also upheld. While an individual murderer pays with his life for the crime, a politician or an army general responsible for arson, loot and mass murder, gets the honour of the patriot and of the hero. Violence unleashes the lowest and the basest of the human passions; but it does this under the guise of bravery, self-sacrifice, patriotism and even altruism. Gandhi admits though that there are situations in which violent resistance, when offered on behalf of a just cause, would seem to be instrumental to the development of certain highly moral qualities, such as courage, self-sacrifice, endurance, discipline, etc. Nevertheless as violence has been steadily growing in destructive power so it has also been steadily growing in intensity. If we continue to use it, its end is bound to be "the moral ruin and reduction of the human beings to robots". (Gandhi NVPW II, 1949: 410) The individual citizen is, thus, unsuspectingly betrayed into antisocial and murderous conduct of which he would be ashamed in his individual and social life.

For Gandhi, the lag between man's moral development and social capabilities on the one hand and his technical skills and potentialities on the other is mainly responsible for the growth of overt violence, overkill capacity and dehumanization. Moreover, the institutional means which have been evolved to realize great human ends, being out of tune with the true nature of man, solve one type of problem and create much more complex problems of other types.

Because of these contradictions of moral values in human life, according to Gandhi, violence permeates all levels of human life - the individual, the family, the village, the society and the state and the national and international. Conflict is, thus, a direct result of this violence and it follows, therefore, that a state of non-violence is a state of peace.

Gandhi was also quite awake to another aspect of conflict, i.e., the economic aspect. Though not a Marxist, he shares some of the basic postulates of Marxism. Without using the Marxian terminologies or those of the later Marxian scholars like the dependency theorists Gandhi spells out in clear terms how the dominant power penetrates the industrial, economic and cultural life of the dependent society thereby imposing its economic and cultural imperialism. Gandhi writes, "The British have exploited India through its cities, the latter had exploited the villages. The blood of the villages is the cement with which the edifice of the cities is built". (Quoted in D.N. Pathak, 1983: 924) The mechanism of this exploitation, Gandhi foresaw quite rightly, would be the transfer of high cost western technology ill-suited to the local conditions of the developing countries. Technology, according to Gandhi, is not neutral by nature and carries within itself a whole cosmology, a message, a code and a structure. To use Johan Galtung's phrase, "Transfer of Western technology is a structural, cultural invasion". (*Ibid.*, 923) Introduction of western technology is a Trojan horse bringing along with itself the concomitants of centrality, verticality, exploitative matrix of man-over-man and man-over-nature relationships. This realization about western technology as an instrument of dependency relationship came much after Gandhi had warned us precisely on the same lines decades before.

Gandhi's entire approach to development is in tune with his integrated world view of man, his own self, man-nature and man-society relationships. Development, to him, means constructive programme i.e., the way by which society has to be reformed and made fit for swaraj or self-rule. The two key concepts in the Gandhian approach to development are swaraj and swdeshi. Swaraj stands for the moral autonomy of the individual as also the political, economic and moral autonomy of nations. Swadeshi stands for the self-reliance of the basic units of society where, up to a point, production is for use and not for exchange. It means non-exploitative relationships between and among nations, avoidance of dependence and elimination of disparities between the rich and the poor. For Gandhi, swaraj is the end and swadeshi, its only legitimate means. In his quest for swaraj through swadeshi Gandhi not only shows his deep understanding of the subtle ways of exploitation at every level of society including the exploitation of the colonial and non-colonial societies; but also displays a keen interest into the far-reaching effects of industrialization based on western technology, especially upon the developing world and in a developing country, upon the marginalized sections.

Thus, it may be seen that Gandhian view sharply departs from the modernist view over the chain causation between science and technology on the one hand and development on the other. To Gandhi, it is development, its pattern and structure that should and must engender technological development. The modernist view which lies behind the whole scheme of technology transfer is that backwardness of the developing countries can be removed by planting western 'developed' technologies in the developing world. Till recently the modernist view reigned without any substantial opposition. This has resulted in the end of the very process of development in the developing countries because of the fact that the import of technologies has set a pattern of development which has created more problems than it has solved.

Gandhi believes that it is the pattern and structure of development which should determine and produce appropriate technologies. That is why he is opposed to the indiscriminate use of machines and is afraid of the distortion of the very process of development. Gandhi's fears have proved to be only too real. It is significant that *The Economics*, a biannual journal of German contribution to economic science, has openly recognized that the Western model of growth as implemented in many countries in the Third World:

> With their doctrine of forced industrialization and neglect of domestic agriculture and small scale industry have led to grave consequences. The developing nations are realizing through practical experience that a much better method would be to build up a system of social market economy patiently from below through decentralized decision-making. (Quoted in Shriman Narayan, 1978: 29-30)

Gandhi may have appeared to be a little too insistent that the right causation must be accepted–the causation from development to technology and not the other way round. But he has been vindicated.

A conflict, in Gandhi's view, is regarded as the confrontation not simply of two parties, but between two sets of relative truths. And, therefore, no party has a right to employ violence to achieve its goal which is, at most, a relative truth, certainly not absolute truth. Conflict resolution to Gandhi means realization of higher truth which can only be achieved by the synthesis of the two relative truths which, again, must necessarily be achieved through non-violent means.

References

Bondurant, J.V. (1959). *Conquest of Violence: Gandhian Philosophy of Conflict*. Oxford University Press.

Chopra, Pran (1972) (ed.). *The Sage in Revolt, A Remembrance*, Gandhi Peace Foundation: New Delhi.

Commoner, Barry (1990). *Making Peace with the Planet*. New York: Pantheon Books.

Darwin, Charles (1968). *The Origin of Species By Means of Natural Selection or the Preservation of Favoured Races in the Struggle for Life*. London: Penguin Books Ltd.

Gandhi, M.K. (1949). *Non-violence in Peace and War*. Vol. 2, Ahmedabad: Navjivan Publishing House.

Gangal, S.C. (1960). *The Gandhian Way to World Peace*, Bombay: Vora and Co. Publication Pvt. Ltd.

Hook, Sidney (1936). *From Hegel to Marx: Studies in the Intellectual Development of Karl Marx*, London.

Kasai, Minoru (1981). Gandhi and the Converging Points of Cultures: India, Japan and others.

Narayan, Shriman (1978). *Towards the Gandhian Plan*, New Delhi.

Paige, Glenn D. (1991). Gandhi's Contribution to Global Non-Violent Awakening. *Gandhi Marg*, Vol. 12.

Pathak, D.N. (1983). Gandhi's World View. Intimations of a Peaceful World Society, *Gandhi Marg*, Vol. 12, No. 1, January, pp. 918-26.

Ramachandran, G. and T.K. Mahadevan eds. (1970). *Quest for Gandhi*. New Delhi: Gandhi Peace Foundation.

Rapoport, Anatol (1989). *The Origins of Violence*. New York: Paragon House.

Sharp, Gene (1970). Gandhi as a National Defence Strategist, *Gandhi Marg*. Vol. 14, No. 3, pp. 254-73.

13

Globalisation and the Perspective of Legal Education in India

RAJIB BHATTACHARYYA

INTRODUCTION

Globalization has been a subject of debates and discussions from numerous perspectives. There is no doubt that globalization has profound implications for the future of higher education worldwide. Inevitably, the need for raising academic standards, creating a better research environment, developing sound infrastructure, formulating good governance models, creating better career opportunities, and promoting professional advancement of academics are all central issues for formulating the necessary policies for higher education.[1]

Globalization has posed multiple challenges to the future of legal education in India, but it has provided an opportunity to challenge the *status quo*, which is an essential condition for seeking any reform. India has huge challenges to confront in promoting legal and judicial reforms, with a view to establishing a rule-of-law society. The role of lawyers and judges will become critical for addressing future challenges of governance. In this regard, the training that is imparted to future lawyers and judges in our law schools needs to be thoroughly re-examined to suit the social and economic transformation that is underway in the country.[2]

In India, legal education has seen many phases of reforms both during and post-British era. Initially during the British era, when India in all academic spheres: be it Science and Technology, Medicine, Engineering or Law, had its own traditional way of imparting education. This methodology had least empirical impetus and research oriented curriculum. There was no impact of any educational reforms which were being undertaken outside the country. After the British advent and their circumvention of Indian traditional systems, education felt the largest impact and legal education was the first in line. This was probably because lawyers was one such prominent class of citizens who posed a serious challenge to the arbitrary, imperialist British regime due to the fact that they could analyse and foresee the implications of British policies and the thus the future of their own country. During this phase, legal education was primarily westernised and it lost its pan-Indian character. Before commenting whether that proved beneficial for the indigenous system or not, it can be said that before the Indians could realise that the glamour of western education has eroded their inherent capabilities, they had come too far in accepting the English way of imparting legal education. Thus, the result was mixed approach towards the legal education because Indians could never reject what they were being offered in the westernised form neither could they fully part away with their traditional way of imparting education.[3]

Globalization has been a subject of debates and discussions from numerous perspectives. There is no doubt that globalization has profound implications for the future of higher education worldwide. While the debate relating to foreign universities coming into India or private investment in higher education is very important, it is critical to examine how India as a country will face up to the competition posed by institutions worldwide in attracting Indian students for pursuing educational opportunities abroad. Inevitably, the need for raising academic standards, creating a better research environment, developing sound infrastructure, formulating good governance models, creating better career opportunities, and promoting professional advancement of academics are all central issues for formulating the necessary policies for higher education.[4]

Legal education in the context of globalization falls into three main categories:[5]

1. Importing foreign students to home law schools for LLM and research degrees.

2. Exporting domestic law schools' programmes to foreign countries, sometimes in conjunction with a host institution.
3. Creating global law schools that attempt to appeal transnationally.

IMPORTING FOREIGN STUDENTS

Recruiting foreign students to postgraduate programmes at the LLM or PhD level is the typical method of supplying legal knowledge to students outside one's own borders. The Inns of Court have carried this out for many years often educating the political leaders of Commonwealth countries (e.g., Nehru in India; Lee Kuan Yew in Singapore). Although this type of educational programme has fallen into desuetude, it has been replaced by the forceful marketing of university LLM courses which are often highly specialized. Indeed, LLM courses fulfil two sets of needs: one is a general approach to the host country's legal system—e.g., courses on English or American law—the other is to supply legal skills in specific areas such as human rights, banking law, or alternative dispute resolution.

EXPORTING DOMESTIC LAW SCHOOLS

In part to maximize revenue and tap into new markets a number of universities from countries such as the US, UK and Australia have established campuses in overseas locations especially in the East, e.g., Singapore, China, Malaysia, and Japan. One such example is New York University School of Law's arrangement with the National University of Singapore.

CREATING GLOBAL LAW SCHOOLS

In recent years there have been moves by established law schools to create a global faculty. The most notable example is New York University which set-up its Hauser programme in the mid-1990's inviting a "global" faculty and student body.

The influence of globalization on legal education can be summarized from the following principles:[6]

1. Globalization and the rise of technology in the field of legal education.
2. The move from polycentric to monocentric modes of education and paths of entry into the legal profession.

3. The re-professionalization of the legal profession as a result of the growth of the large law firm and new forms of regulation as in, for example, the UK and Australia.

SIGNIFICANCE OF LEGAL EDUCATION[7]

'Law is the cement of society and an essential medium of change'. The significance of legal education in a democratic society cannot be over-emphasized. Knowledge of law increases one understands of public affairs. Its study promotes accuracy of the expression, facility in arguments and skill in interpreting the written words, as well as some understanding of social values. It is pivotal duty of everyone to know the law. Ignorance of law is not innocence but a sin which cannot be excused. Thus, legal education is imperative not only to produce good lawyers but also to create cultured law abiding citizens, who are inculcated with concepts of human values and human rights. We must have a legal education which can fulfil the need of the society and country as well. We are no longer *laissez-faire* but a welfare State and in welfare society law plays a very important role in every affair of human being. Law serves as an important instrument to achieve socio-economic development. Today law is not viewed merely as an instrument of social control but also an instrument of social change. The aim of legal education should be not only to produce good lawyers but also create cultured, law abiding citizens who are inculcated with concepts of human values and human rights who can serve humanity in various capacities such as, administrators, law teachers, jurists, judges, and industrial entrepreneurs, etc. As far as creation of good advocates and solicitors is concerned, the legal education should aim at equipping them with legal techniques and professional skills. An Advocate must be tolerant, must listen patiently other man's point of view and not hazard opinions without some basis. He should be rational, secular keeper, willing to work hard, competent to communicate having good expression, must have critical understanding of human institutions and values. Legal profession is objectively in the position of producing Statesmen. This is due to two reasons:

(1) Lawyers belong to an independent profession. They are not subordinate to the government or to anyone else.

(2) They are directly in contact with society in its entirety as they have to deal with all kinds of problems of people from all sections of society, unlike say, doctors who are

confined to technical problems. Hence lawyers are the people who are most conversant with the problems of society as a whole.

A well administered and socially relevant legal education is a *sine qua non* for a proper dispensation of justice. Giving legal education a human face would create cultured law abiding citizens who are able to serve as professionals and not merely as business men.

The quality and standard of legal education acquired at the law school is reflected through the standard of Bar and Bench and consequently affects the legal system.

EVOLUTION OF LEGAL EDUCATION IN INDIA[8]

In ancient India law was understood as a branch of Dharma. It is difficult to draw a distinction between secular law and religious ordinances in Ancient India. The Vedas were the original sources of law, and the Smritis announced the message of Vedas and Smritikars were great jurists. Smritikars, commentators and Nibandhakars [essayists] were the legal guardians of law. King made laws were also interpreted, thus, the commentators were virtually law-makers. Sadachara, Custom, Nyaya or Yukti were the base of legal process in Ancient India. The King was advised by a Sabha which had both advisory and executive functions. The parishad was an expert committee comprised of ministers of officials, generally Brahmans, who advised the King authoritatively on law.

The concept of Dharma, in the Vedic period, can be seen as the concept of the legal education in India. Although there is no record of formal training in law, the dispensation of justice was to be done by the king on the basis of a self-acquired training. Justice was also administered by the King through his appointees who in turn were persons of known integrity and reputation of being fair and impartial. The guiding force for the King or his appointee was the upholding of the Dharma.

In the later period, the britishers came to this country for the purpose of trade, which they started through a company, popularly known as East India Company formed in 1600 in England. In the beginning the courts were presided over by merchants who were having very rudimentary knowledge of law, but later on legally trained persons were put for the job.

First British court was established in Bombay in 1672 by Governor Gerald Angier. First concrete step in the direction of organizing legal profession was taken through Regulating Act of 1773 which empowered to enrol advocates and Attorneys-at-law to the Supreme Court. The Supreme Court was established in Fort William in Bengal through a charter issued in 1774. At that time Indian Lawyers had no right to appearance in the Courts. The position was same when the Supreme Courts with the same jurisdiction and power were established at Bombay and Madras later. The Bengal Regulation VII of 1793 which created for the first time a regular legal profession for the company's courts, which allowed the appointment of Vakils or native pleaders in the courts of civil judicature in the provinces of Bengal, Bihar and Orissa. In 1861, three High Courts were established at Calcutta, Madras and Bombay. At this time three bodies of practitioners viz., advocates, Attorneys and Vakils were in existence. Advocates were the barristers of England or Ireland but the Vakils were Indian Practioners. Bar Councils Act, 1926 unified two grades of legal practioners, the Vakils and Pleaders, by merging them in the class of advocates. It also provided for making rules for giving facilities of legal education and training.

The pattern of legal education which is in vogue in India was transplanted by the English; after the establishment of their rule in India. Formal legal education in India came into existence in 1855 when the first professorship of law was established at the Government Elphistone College in Bombay and Madras and Hindu College at Calcutta. At that time the primary aim of legal education was to equip law students so that they could help the lower courts and the High Courts in the administration of justice by enrolling themselves as Vakils or becoming judicial officers, and thus serve the interests of the Administration. As majority of the population was rural and illiterate, the need was felt to bridge the gap between the existing law and the uneducated masses crying for justice, by rendering importance to formal legal education. Initially a law school had to be a self-financing institution, and if possible a money making concern so that it could feed the teaching of other disciplines in the University. There is no tradition of legal research and academic legal training. In the year 1857, legal education was introduced as a subject for teaching in three universities in the presidency towns of Calcutta, Madras and Bombay. Thus, a beginning of the formal legal education was made in the sub-continent. The language of the British statutes being English, so any Indian who learnt English could study law and was considered qualified to practice the profession. At that time law classes were attached with arts colleges. However, if one aspired to something higher, he could go to England and join the Inns court, provided one could afford it.

NEW CHALLENGES TO THE LEGAL EDUCATION IN INDIA[9]

Half a century ago, the main purpose of university legal education in India was not the teaching of law as a branch of learning and as a science but simply to impart to students a knowledge of the black letter law, that is, certain principles and provisions of law to enable them to enter the legal practice exclusively for local needs. Gradually this perception changed and the process of reform in law and legal education was initiated. The real break came in 1990s when the new challenges posed by scientific and technological revolution and greater interaction between nations, trade in goods and services, information technology and free capital flow across international boundaries made the world a global village. Consequently, the concept of "local practice" widened to that of "transnational practice" in the context of globalization and opening up of most of the economies of the world.

Roscoe Pound directed to particular attention new aspect of the lawyers' role in modern society. He said that the worldwide economic unification is challenging the self-sufficiency in the systems of law. He pointed out that law transcended local and political limits and has become an economic necessity. He said, "Even more the development of industry carried on with instrumentalities and under conditions increasingly dangerous to life and limb and under conditions creating ecological problems and the mechanizing of every activity of life likewise threatening injury to everyone, have been creating new legal problems calling for revision of the old doctrines and finding out a new means of promoting and maintaining a general security......thus the science of law must be increasingly comparative. Whether we are dreaming of a world law or thinking of further development of our own law, to suit to the worldwide problems of general security in the present and immediate future, the methods of jurist must have a base of comparison. Comparative law and international law have achieved such vital importance in current life that they have become an essential part of legal education. The lawyer of today has to play a role in influencing world policies and building up the future of mankind."

How should the legal profession and legal education respond to the new challenges? Never before in history has the need for sound thinking and planning on all issues been felt so intensely as today.

Unless the topics of universal application are integrated into legal education in developing countries, our lawyers and those of other countries would not be able to compete in the transnational marketplace. In the present day, an innovative programme of integrated interdisciplinary legal learning and in the new areas such as Comparative Law, information technology, intellectual property, corporate governance, human rights, environment, and international trade law, investment, and commerce, transfer of technology, alternative dispute resolution and space is important. Comparative Legal education for professional excellence is needed in these and other areas on a global basis.

The world's problems require international co-operation and solutions, especially after the initiation of the liberalisation and globalisation process in today's world of increasing international trade and inter-dependence. The recent trend is that most of the agreements are construed internationally and the member, countries are obliged to implement them at the domestic level. It is necessary for lawyers to understand the political, cultural and social influences on the legal systems of other countries and, by using that knowledge, to forge strong relationships between parties. Some observations of David Gerber are apposite in this context. For instance, Gerber calls for greater attention to theory in the broad sense of conceptual structure, because theories are the mechanisms for structuring information and knowledge effectively. The object of the entire exercise is to structure knowledge about foreign legal systems. Analogous to this viewpoint is the model suggested by Ugo Mattei. He argues for a classification of legal systems, which he refers to as taxonomy of legal systems for the purpose of learning from each other by rethinking the traditional boundaries drawn in the context of changing nature of global politics. This situation necessitates revisiting the classic categorisation of legal systems as civil, common and socialist.

GLOBALISATION AND LEGAL EDUCATION IN INDIA[10]

The term 'globalisation of law' refers to the degree to which the whole world lives under a single set of legal rules. Such a single set of rules might be imposed by an international body, adopted by global consensus, or arrived at by parallel development in all parts of the globe. In today's world of increasing international trade and inter-dependence the need for transnational law has increased many fold. As more and more countries open their economy, either partially or completely, there is a growing need to recognize and work towards a uniform system of law. This process of globalisation is evident in all facets of law—the importance of Comparative LegalEducation.

India is at a significant stage now positioned for a role as a major global player. Considering the growth of India in areas of technological and financial sectors, it is important to reflect upon these developments and assess the need to study transnational law and Comparative Law. It can be said that in recent times the value of Comparative Law has been appreciated, however it is not yet been made a compulsory course. Recommendations of the National Knowledge Commission of India (NKC) also emphasize that legal education should meet the needs of trade, commerce and industry in the context of growing internationalization of the profession. The NKC constituted a Working Group in order to propose some key reforms in the field of legal education in India. The Working Group comprised of experts, who are members of the Bar, the Bench and academia. The Chairman of the Working Group is Justice M. Jagannadha Rao. The Working Group of the NKC recognizes *inter -alia* the importance of the study of Comparative Law, with the purpose of creating lawyers who can deal with differing legal systems and cultures, while remaining strong in one's own national legal system.

The emergence of Law Schools in India and two decades of their functioning might have done a lot good to the profession and fraternity of lawyers superficially. But the roots of the legal education in India have been weakened. Law schools might have commercialised or marketed the legal intelligentsia but it has miserably failed to familiarize the budding lawyers with the real social conditions of the country. Therefore it can be stated as 'Globalisation and Legal Education at Crossroads'. It is not a negative impact of globalisation on legal education in India but the failure to fully adapt with what globalisation demanded from the Indian education system.

Following are some of the reasons explaining the loggerheads between globalisation and Indian legal education with some recommendations.[11]

Reforms in the Senior Secondary School Curriculum

Since the roots of India legal system being weak, reforms in the school education should be the first in line to revamp the legal education in India. No doubt, the school students study a bit of legal provisions and rights available to them as a part of the subject of

Social Studies up to their secondary standards. This part of syllabus should be made a separate subject with an aim to increase the legal literacy amongst youth. The way Environmental Science has been made a separate subject and it has served beneficially by making youth aware of the environment around them, legal literacy can also pave way for a better sensitised and sensitive youth towards their nation's legal system. A common notion among children is that the Indian legal system is shallow and faulty. They need to be told that it is not the system rather the implementation which is faulty. India has the best of laws and can be the best managed democracy if they are implemented in letter and spirit.

Law Courses should be Integrated with Other Academic Fields

Now, in the times when legal education has sprawled to all others academic spheres, Indian education cannot afford to be general in approach. A mere law degree would not suffice the need for expertise in specific areas.

Thus, new courses should be initiated which focus upon collaborations between law and other spheres which law can cater to. Intellectual Property Rights, Business Administration are a very few areas which have already been integrated into law degrees. To name a few more, legal-medico issues, core technological areas, Geographical dimensions are such components of today's world where law is frequently taken into consideration, thus initiating specific courses of law integrated with these academic areas will create an expertise for the target specific dispute resolution and policy making.

National Law Universities and Indian Institutes of Technology: A Comparison

Though National Law Universities were mooted in India on the pattern of IITs which are the Centres of Excellence in the field of science and technology under the aegis of Union Government, they have not been treated at par with IITs to cater to the legal fraternity as Centres of Excellence.

IITs are established under a central legislation whereas National Law Universities are established under the state legislations of their respective state. This largely effects the funding of institutions. IITs get a large chunk of funding from the central government whereas there remains a paucity of funds in the National Law Universities. In order to remove this barrier, all the National Law Universities need to be brought under a central legislation with a common name Indian Institute of Law (IIL) and not the separate names of each National Law University.

An Apex Research Governing Council for all the National Law Universities

One of the main objectives of establishing National Law Universities was to enhance the research output and quality from the legal fraternity which could assist the social policy making in the country. This was again necessitated by the globalisation because globalisation had made research a primary component of advancement and also a parameter for assessment. By way of globalisation, the quantitative analysis gave way to qualitative analysis which in turn was always based upon the research levels. This is not the case only in the education sector but all other spheres like Information Technology, Manufacturing, and Pharmaceuticals etc.

Unfortunately, National Law Universities have failed to live up to those expectations. With the exception of National Law School of India University, Bangalore which is the oldest National Law University in the country, all other institutions have not been able to give expected quality research output. Even if any of them has contributed towards the socio-legal research, it gets marred by the isolation and thus non-integration with the mainstream research activity. One prime cause for this is that there is no coordination among all the NLUs to focus upon some core areas and assist and integrate for research projects. Each National Law University functions individually with intent to unsurp the other's reputation. But this attitude has not paid much to the legal education and profession. There is a dire need of a better focussed cooperation and integration among various NLUs. It can only be integration and not the negative competition which will take the Legal Research levels in these reputed institutions to new levels.

Thus it can be suggested that there should be a single Apex Research Governing Council for all the National Law Universities which should comprise of all the Vice-Chancellors, eminent members of Bar and Bench, representatives from civil society and student representatives. This council shall timely formulate the research policies for all the NLUs and distribute the tasks to each university. The Council shall evaluate the research output from the individual universities and take the corrective measures.

Association of Members of Parliament with Law School Students

The Indian democracy is marred by illiteracy of its Members of Parliament. Even if they are literate they lack the Legal Literacy. It is not mandated for them to be well verse with the Constitutional Law, Administrative Law, International Law, and other relevant legal instruments. Each bill before it is laid in the house of Parliament is sent to each MP for his/her views and comments. They are expected to go through the bill and suggest amendments which could suit their people's local needs and expectations who have selected him/her to represent them in the parliament. But due to lack of legal awareness and expertise, this laid down procedure rarely transforms into reality. This is one of the most important reasons why the people's elected representatives fail to fulfil their obligations.

Therefore, it can be suggested that the students of National Law Universities should be made to associate with the Members of Parliament. These students shall make the MPs aware of the Constitutional Law, other laws of the land and also assist them in analysing the bills to be discussed in the house. This will also serve as a real time internship for students. This also cures the commercialisation of Indian legal education propelled by globalisation.

Collaborations between NLUs and other institutions like TISS, ISRO, etc.

It can be recommend that both the IITs and NLUs should cooperate in such overlapping areas of study where each of them can contribute to the other's skill enhancement. Moreover, institutes like Tata Institute of Social Research (for socio-legal research), ISRO (space law), Indian Institutes of Management (for Corporate Laws and Human Resources) and many others if come into association with the National Law Universities can be of great benefit in creating world class institutional infrastructure for such studies. All such policies and decisions can be taken under the aegis of Research Governing Council suggested above. The representatives of collaborating institutions can also be inducted as members of the Council. This innovative initiative would serve the demands of globalisation.

Unplanned Expansion of Law School Brand

The orgy of making legal education in India more globalised, more and more National Law Universities are being established even when the already established ones are not able give the expected results. The current focus should be towards fixing the existing gap between what globalisation demands and what is being done in the National Law Universities. The focus should be towards innovating new methods and solving the existing loopholes some of which have been explained in the preceding text.

Booming National Law Universities in each nook and corner of the country will weaken the NLU brand and lessen the quality. It does not mean that the number of such excellent institutions should never be increased. But once the existing ones cement their existence by fulfilling all the objectives with which they were established, only then this brand reach should be expanded.

Moreover, the new National Law Universities should be planned in such areas where there is no advent of legal education as yet. This will help heralding a new era in the Indian higher education.

Social Sensitivity of the Course Curriculum

Another gap which has been left in the aftermath of globalisation is the sensitivity of Law School curriculum towards Indian society. Globalisation has made the study curriculum more commercialised while completely ignoring the societal needs of the country. This is again a very important reason of Law School graduates not becoming the actual social engineers because they are not sensitive enough towards the social objectives needed to be achieved in the country.

The curriculum in the National Law Universities should be more inclusive of social problems of India with the students being made to solve real time typical social problems. Another important part of the curriculum should be compulsory rural research. It serves no purpose to the nation with students thriving for corporate internships only. They should be made to intern with village panchayats compulsorily. This will make them more inclined towards the local needs and aspirations of the society.

Bill Referrals to the National Law Universities

The globalisation of legal education has made the students addicted to corporate laws and corporate internships. In this race of corporate honchos, the brains of National Law Universities do not serve the nation. The bills to be introduced in the Parliament or the State Legislative Assemblies can be referred to the National Law Universities for in-depth research and recommendations. This can be the best service to the nation. This will be a learning experience for the students as well as the laws framed would be more sensitive towards the societal need and problems as well.

RECOGNIZING THE NEED FOR MODERNIZATION OF LEGAL EDUCATION[12]

The conventional role of a lawyer is to step in after the event takes place, in order to resolve dispute and dispense justice to the aggrieved party. In the changed scenario, the additional roles envisaged are that of policy planner, business advisor, negotiator among interest groups, experts in articulation and communication of ideas, mediator, lobbyist, law reformer etc. In this the era of information capitalism, economic liberalization and WTO, legal profession in India has to cater to the needs of a new brand of legal consumer/client namely the foreign companies or collaborations. The law colleges are required to make strategic plans, that set out a clear vision of justice delivery and also address the emerging realities of the market. Goal of the law schools should be to build a system of legal education that is able to meet the new challenges and for this purpose we should encourage the following steps:

Encourage Clinical Legal Training

In the past it was sufficient for those reading laws to restrict their knowledge to the theories of law, codes or decided cases. However, in order to meet the new challenges of the present legal system, it is imperative that the law schools provide clinical legal education.

'Justice' must become central to the law curriculum and community-based learning must give the desired value orientation in the making of a lawyer. This concept of justice education in the field of legal education means that the law school curriculum should entail certain programs like Lok Adalats, Legal Aid & Legal Literacy and Para-legal training.

The complementary teaching methodology of learning by doing and the conventional classroom teaching, through the law school clinics, help in developing the advocacy skills in the law students. 'Mock' trials and Moot court competitions, structured as court trial; client interviewing and counselling sessions; legal research; editing of law journals; legal drafting and conveyancing; court visits, etc. in the curriculum is one of the ideal ways to facilitate performance based education. It is a means of improving in students the basic skills such as the skills of critical thinking, presentation skills, participation skills, the skills to work as a team, the leadership quality, in addition to the boost in students knowledge of law.

Even though, in tune with the time, Clinical Legal Education holds an indispensable position, still its acceptance, existence and development in present legal education system, is at its nascent stages. Albeit the Bar Council of India, constituted under the Indian Advocates Act, 1961, is endowed with the responsibility by Parliament to prescribe and maintain the standards of legal education in consultation with State Bar Councils and universities teaching law, the curriculum adopted at various law schools has not been structured to give adequate time for clinical training programs. The divergence between law in books and law in action calls to strike a balance between the law curriculum and the teaching methods. The monologue lecture scheme adopted in law schools, where practical training is either totally neglected or marginally implemented at the level of Moot Courts, Court visits and legal research will not make good lawyers in todays scheme of legal education.

Most of the Universities due to lack of infrastructural support and lack of funds have failed to establish a clinic in the Law Schools which would facilitate the students to carry out experimental learning of law. It is pertinent that the University Grants Commission facilitates, by funding, the establishment of functional clinics and for promoting the programs like Lok Adalats, legal aid and legal literacy, client interviewing and counselling, etc.

Even those law schools where the clinics do exist, the results are fruitless, for the reasons of lack of resource faculty who have the competence and knowledge in clinical training. The teachers associated with the clinical education should preferably have some practical experience in law. Association of retired judicial persons, as visiting faculty would be instrumental in selecting suitable clinical experience for the students and enhance amongst the students the commitment to learn.

Other constraints that curtail the law schools to foster higher standards of clinical legal education is the high teacher-student ratio. Law being an interactive discipline there should not be more than 20 students to 1 teacher, so as to ensure adequate supervision, right guidance and extensive practical learning. There should be regular refresher courses organized by the authorities—'training the trainers'.

Promote an Inter-disciplinary Approach of Law with Other Social Sciences

A person who studies law must have some proficiency in country's history, political theory, economics and philosophy, to enable him/her in becoming agents that participate in institutional changes.

Encourage Proficiency in Languages

Command over spoken and written language, effective oral skills, diction and extensive reading are pre-requisites that go without saying. Knowledge of a foreign language is important to be a lawyer in the global economy. Law students should be provided with the opportunity to learn a foreign language of their choice.

Personal Characteristics

Lawyers, solicitors, legal executives all need good intellectual ability, the ability to assimilate and analyse facts quickly. Law students hence need to develop their ability to distinguish the relevant form the irrelevant, screen evidence, and apply the law to the situation under scrutiny.

The law students are further required to enhance the ability to argue, explain and convince points of law. They need to maintain their complete integrity of character and need mental and physical stamina in order to cope with the long hours, travelling and stress.

Promotes Acquaintance with New Technological Developments

Law schools and universities should be able to provide e-courses on the shelves. The teachers should put course materials on the Web, conduct on-line tests/assignments and grade students. Web-sites can lead learners to virtual class-rooms. Teachers and students should be oriented to look at the Web as an information provider. Law teachers should switch over to what is called as 'comparative method of teaching'. The law students should be mobilised to evaluate the existing or prospective draconian laws, participate in discussions on the latest developments and required amendments.

CONCLUSION

Legal education is an investment which if wisely made will produce most beneficial results for the nation and accelerate the pace of development. Of late the role of a lawyer in a common law system is more than a skilled legal mechanic; he acts as a harmonizer and a reconciler. The legal education granted at the law schools should be aligned to the conventional and contemporary needs of the legal profession.[13]

The guiding question remains: what kind of lawyers or law graduates are to be produced by the institutions of higher learning in law. It is important to attend to this question, which is to be addressed before we revisit the curriculum and suggest some changes for making international law as a discipline more effective and influence students to read the subject in detail. For a major part of the law course, Comparative Law is an optional paper in the curriculum in Indian Universities. It is prudent and desirable to teach this subject. This exercise to a large extent will influence the purpose of international law teaching and methodology. It is precisely at this point that learning Comparative Law can prepare students for effective participation in an increasingly global and diverse legal profession. Further, students can enhance their legal skills, collaborative learning and leadership.[14]

With the growth of international and regional legal orders, an understanding of the forms and methods of comparative legal study has become essential to all those wishing to understand and engage in current legal debates. Amidst this scenario, it is necessary to transform legal education in response to present and future needs. The debates and theories relating to legal systems are important to be a compulsory part of the legal curriculum. It may be said that the purpose of Comparative Law is not to unify the different laws and legal cultures of the world, but to understand the multiplication of these laws, different traditions and cultures and in the process to get acquainted with the unfamiliar legal systems of the world. In this effort, lawyers and legal scholars will learn to appreciate the similarities and differences in systems of the world and will tend to look at issues in a rational manner. This situation will further the enrichment of understanding of the layers of complexity in a society.[15]

The increasing demand of lawyers in a globalised world has given a fresh impetus to the study of international law in India. Therefore this demand requires the present curriculum and pedagogy related to international law and teaching be revisited so as to set some new standards in the field of international law training in the universities and national law schools.[16]

We have been looking at the globalization of law along a number of factors. The global distrust of hierarchical authority and concentrated public and private power generates growth in administrative law, constitutional, and other rights law, and in legal regulation of economic enterprise. The global desire to protect the individual generates growth in personal injury, consumer protection, environmental law, and even family law. The globalization of markets and business enterprise generates the growth of a worldwide law of business transactions. The global multiplication of exterior business relationships and the growth of arms-length regulatory styles fuel a growing demand for lawyers and their involvement in more and more social, economic, and political relationships. Having stressed on the need for globalization, we need to adopt our domestic structure to be able to keep pace with the movement of globalization both in terms of legislation and in terms of legal education and practice.[17]

After all, the 21st century lawyer should have a good understanding of the transnational legal environment because international concerns and agreements in a century like India are pervasive and encompass virtually all branches of human activity—from the ocean floor to the planets climate to outer space. The legal educators/practioners need to be more aware of the changes and should be pro-active in changing to meet the challenges in today's globalized world.

Notes and References

1. Global Legal Education In India: Opportunities And Challenges, Halsbury's Law, Sponsored by Lexis Nexis, April 2009, at lexisnexis.com, written by Professor C. Raj Kumar is the Vice-Chancellor of O.P. Jindal Global University and the founding Dean of Jindal Global Law School.
2. *Ibid.*
3. Reforming Law School Education in a Globalised India by Kshitij Bansal, Edited version of this Article was originally published in Lex Witness Live, available on http://ipanglobal.org/index.php/2012-10-22-20-54-13/articles-opeds/87-reforming-law-school-education-in-a-globalised-india browsed on 02.08.2013 at about 7 p.m.
4. Globalisation and legal education, C. Raj Kumar, Associate Professor of Law at City University of Hong Kong and Chief Executive Officer of Legal Education and Research Society, Published on *The Hindu*, Monday, August 06, 2007 available on http://hindu.com/2007/08/06/stories/2007080650041000.htm browsed on 05.08.2013 at about 7 p.m.
5. Legal Education in the Global Context: Challenges from Globalization, Technology and Changes in Government Regulation, John Flood Report for the Legal Services Board, University of Westminster School of Law.
6. *Ibid.*

7. The Impact of Globalization in Legal Education In India—by Adv. Devadas T.M., LL.M. IIIrd Semester, Nuals, available on http://www.answeringlaw. com/php/displayContent.php?linkId=1276 browsed on 12.08.2013 at about 7 p.m.
8. *Ibid.*
9. *Ibid.*
10. *Ibid.*
11. Reforming Law School Education in a Globalised India by Kshitij Bansal, Edited version of this Article was originally published in Lex Witness Live, available on http://ipanglobal.org/index.php/2012-10-22-20-54-13/articles-opeds/87-reforming-law-school-education-in-a-globalised-india browsed on 02.08.2013 at about 7 p.m.
12. The Impact of Globalization in Legal Education in India—by Adv. Devadas T.M., LL.M. IIIrd Semester, Nuals, available on http://www.answering law.com/php/displayContent.php?linkId=1276 browsed on 12.08.2013 at about 7 p.m.
13. *Ibid.*
14. *Ibid.*
15. *Ibid.*
16. *Ibid.*
17. *Ibid.*

14

Protecting Human Rights in a Globalized World

An Overview

MALABIKA TALUKDAR

> *"Human rights are what make us human. They are the principles by which we create the sacred home for human dignity. Human rights are what reason requires and conscience commands."*
>
> —Kofi Annan
>
> Former United Nations Secretary-General[1]

INTRODUCTION

Would globalization enhance the implementation of human rights as stated in the Universal Declaration of Human Rights (1948) and the subsequent United Nations agreements, particularly the covenant on civil and political rights (1966), the covenant on economic, social and cultural rights (1966) and the declaration on the right to development (1986)?[2]

Attempting an answer to this question is not an easy task, mainly because of the different and contradictory connotations of the term globalization.[3]

If globalization is conceived as turning the whole world into one global village in which all peoples are increasingly interconnected and all the fences or barriers are removed, so that the world witnesses a new state of fast and free flow of people, capital, goods and ideas then the world would be witnessing unprecedented enjoyment of human rights everywhere because globalization is bringing prosperity to all the corners of the globe together with the spread of the highly cherished values of democracy, freedom and justice.[4]

On the other hand, if globalization is conceived as turning the world into a global market for goods and services dominated and steered by the powerful gigantic transnational corporations and governed by the rule of profit then all the human rights of the people in the world, particularly in the south would be seriously threatened.[5]

Literature on globalization, in general, by both the so-called advocates and opponents of globalization is abundant. However the critics of globalization lay much more emphasis on its impact on human rights, particularly of the poor people and of the developing countries. Their analysis and conclusions are usually supported by facts and figures drawn from international reports and statistics to prove that human rights have been adversely affected by globalization. They usually relate one or the other aspect of human rights to one or the other aspect of globalization, such as relating poverty in developing countries to debt or relating unemployment to privatization, or relating health deterioration to the monopoly of medicine patents. Or they enumerate the aspects of deteriorations in human rights, such as impoverishment and lowering standards of living, increasing inequality discrimination, deprivation of satisfaction of basic needs such as food, clean water and housing, illiteracy etc. and explain these facts by globalization in general through making comparisons between the state before globalization (usually before the 1990s) and after it, such as stating that "progress in reducing infant mortality was considerably slower during the period of globalization (1990-98) than over the previous two decades.[6]

In recent years, globalization has become an intensely-debated issue at all levels of society across the world. Despite no specific and accurate definition offered to describe this phenomenon, people are all aware of its business-driven character which spills over a tremendous aura that has shaped the global trend to an unprecedented homogenized culture. It further portrays our daily life as living in a world where interactions across borders appear significantly greater and faster than in the past, and which can be attributed to certain advancements in technological, social, and economic organization of humanity. Regardless of its multifaceted character, globalization has been dominantly associated with economic context which connotes recent evolution in the nature of the global economy reflected in the rapid development in the level and speed of economic transactions, primarily, across geographical boundaries and territorial borders. This evolution has been brought about by a range of factors among which include, mainly, advancement in technology and liberalization. Indeed, too much has been made of the phenomenon of the globalization in its economic dimensions. It is as if economic dimensions of globalization have acquired a status higher than human values or even above fundamental human rights, which are going to be seriously affected by current global trends.[7]

In an age of globalization, the struggle for human rights has become more complex and challenging. While protections for human rights are increasingly passed by governments and international bodies like the United Nations, grave threats to and gross violations of human rights are also on the rise.[8]

The world's financial capital is ever more integrated, and wealth is ever more centralized in the hands of financial elites and institutions. Realizing social and economic rights, especially eradicating hunger and unemployment, is becoming increasingly difficult. Bringing conflicts to a just and durable resolution is more daunting with the increased capacity of individuals, governments and their military forces, and other groups, including paramilitary, to organize and unleash violence. These groups have access to more sophisticated communications technology and more deadly instruments of war than ever before.[9]

Ending violence and wars, and checking impunity and disregard for international human rights and humanitarian laws, will require more than political will and moral courage. Concrete programs and mechanisms are needed to realize the totality of human rights—civil, political, social, economic, and cultural.[10]

Human rights—expressed in affirmations and declarations, treaties and conventions, laws and statutes—are products of struggles to affirm and fulfil the wholeness and fullness of life. As peoples and governments increase the catalogue of rights that are recognized and protected, protections not only increase, but so do our approximation of and striving for human dignity.

The term globalization is derived from the word globalize, which refers to the emergence of an international network of social and economic systems.. Globalization (or globalisation) is the process of international integration arising from the interchange of world views, products, ideas, and other aspects of culture. Put in simple terms, globalization refers to processes that increase world-wide exchanges of national and cultural resources. Advances intransportation and telecommunications infrastructure, including the rise of the telegraph and its posterity the Internet, are major factors in globalization, generating further interdependence of economic and cultural activities.[11]

Though several scholars place the origins of globalization in modern times, others trace its history long before the European age of discovery and voyages to the New World. Some even trace the origins to the third millennium BCE. In the late 19th century and early 20th century, the connectedness of the world's economies and cultures grew very quickly.[12]

The term globalization has been in increasing use since the mid-1980s and especially since the mid-1990s. In 2000, the International Monetary Fund (IMF) identified four basic aspects of globalization: trade and transactions, capital and investment movements, migration and movement of people and the dissemination of knowledge. Further, environmental challenges such as climate change, cross-boundary water and air pollution, and over-fishing of the ocean are linked with globalization. Globalizing processes affect and are affected by business and work organization, economics, socio-cultural resources, and the natural environment.[13]

IMPACT OF GLOBALIZATION ON HUMAN RIGHTS[14]

Globalization has its winners and losers. With the expansion of trade, market, foreign investment, developing countries have seen the gaps among themselves widen. The imperative to liberalize has demanded a shrinking of state involvement in national life, producing a wave of privatization, cutting jobs, slashing health, education and food subsidies, etc. affecting the poor people in society. In many cases, liberalization has been accompanied by greater inequality and people are left trapped in utter poverty. Meanwhile, in many industrialized countries unemployment has soared to levels not seen for many years and income disparity to levels not recorded since last century. The collapse of the economies of the Asian Tigers are examples of this. The Human Development Report of 1997 revealed that poor countries and poor people too often find their interests neglected as a result of globalization. Although globalization of the economy has been characterized as a locomotive for productivity, opportunity, technological progress, and uniting the world, it ultimately causes increased impoverishment, social disparities and violations of human rights. That is what we see today.

GLOBALIZATION, DEVELOPMENT AND HUMAN RIGHTS[15]

The relation between globalization, development and human rights raises policy and legal questions. One such question is whether globalization of market-oriented economic system is essential for development and protection of human rights? While searching for an answer to this question we should analyze how we perceive the concept of development and human rights, especially in the context of developing countries. Human rights have become an integral part of the process of globalization in many ways. The Western countries are increasingly using their view of human rights concept as a yardstick to judge developing countries and to deal with economic and trade relations to extend development assistance. At the same time globalization intensifies impoverishment by increasing the poverty, insecurity, fragmentation of society and thus violates human rights and human dignity of millions of people.

Development or economic development is widely perceived as a historical process that takes place in almost all societies characterized by economic growth and increased production and consumption of goods and services. Development is also often used in a normative sense as a multi-valued social goal covering such diverse spheres as better material well-being, living standards, education, health care, wider opportunities for work and leisure, and in essence the whole gamut of desirable social and material welfare. But, in today's globalization, the concept of development itself is interpreted differently and the concept of right to development is not taken seriously.

The Preamble of the Declaration of the Right to Development, adopted by the UN General Assembly in 1986, describes "development as a comprehensive economic, social, cultural and political process that aims at the constant improvement of the well-being of the entire population and of all individuals on the basis of their active, free and meaningful participation in development and in the fair distribution of resulting benefits". The 1990 UN Global Consultation on the Right to Development as a Human Right, stated that the right to development is an inalienable human right with the human being as the central subject to the right and that all the aspects of the right to development set forth in the Declaration of the Right to Development are indivisible and interdependent, and these include civil, political, economic, social, and cultural rights. It was further maintained that the right to development is the right of individuals, groups and peoples to participate in, contribute to, and enjoy continuous economic, social, cultural and political development, in which all human rights and fundamental freedoms can be fully realized. A development strategy that disregards or interferes with human rights is the very negation of development.

The aims and objectives of the so-called development models promoted by different governments or international development agencies are not compatible with human rights standards. A new model of development ideology is being promoted that is based on the market and its logic. Several decades of discussion on alternative development model is withering away and a dominant model of market-oriented development taking roots in that place. As a result of the globalization process, more negative effects are visible now. Global integration of the structures, processes, and ideologies produce injustice, oppression, exploitation and mal-development in society. The systematic integration of the forces that are dominant in the globalization process intensifies human rights violations.

INTERNATIONAL RESPONSES TO THE PROBLEMS OF GLOBALIZATION AND HUMAN RIGHTS[16]

Globalization has led to an increased concern about the responsibility of all international actors to ensure the promotion and protection of human rights. International institutions and scholars have responded with various proposals for strengthening the international regime. First, human rights activists and institutions have begun to posit the primacy of human rights law. The Committee on Economic, Social and Cultural Rights (CESCR) has emphasized that, "the realms of trade, finance and investment are in no way exempt from these general principles [on respect for human rights] and that international organizations with specific responsibilities in those areas should play a positive and constructive role in relation to human rights." The CESCR also asserts that competitiveness, efficiency, and economic rationalism must not be permitted to become the primary or exclusive criteria against which governmental and inter-governmental policies are evaluated.

Can the primacy of human rights be justified in international law? An argument can be posited on the basis of treaty law. The

U.N. Charter refers to human rights in its second preamble paragraph and lists human rights as the third of its purposes in Article 1, after maintenance of peace and security, and the development of friendly relations among nations based on equal rights and self-determination of peoples. The Charter not only makes human rights an aim of the organization, it obligates all member states to take joint and separate action with the U.N. to achieve universal respect for and observance of human rights and fundamental freedoms, as in Articles 55 and 56. Article 103 of the Charter provides that, "in the event of a conflict between the obligations of the members of the United Nations under the present Charter and their obligations under any other international agreement, their obligations under the present Charter shall prevail." This "supremacy clause" has been invoked to suggest that the aims and purposes of the U.N., maintenance of peace and security, and the promotion and protection of human rights, constitute an international public order to which other treaty regimes must conform.

The second response to globalization is found in efforts to insist on state responsibility for the behavior of non-state actors. As far as human rights are concerned, this means the state is responsible for its acts and its omissions. The Restatement of U.S. Foreign Relations Law makes it clear that a state violates international law if it commits, encourages, or condones genocide, slavery, torture, or inhuman or degrading treatment. Complicity in human rights violations between state and non-state actors is a growing subject of interest and litigation.

The next question posed is whether or not a state is responsible for the acts of international organizations in which it participates. The International Covenant on Economic, Social and Cultural Rights (ICESCR), Article 2(1), provides that each state party will "take steps, individually and through international assistance and cooperation" to achieve the rights in the Covenant. This means that voting in the World Bank or IMF for programs or policies that will lead to human rights regression in one or more states could be deemed to violate the voter's obligations under the Covenant.

Traditional interpretations of the ICESCR, Article 2, permit states to determine how and when they allocate resources for the realization of economic, social, and cultural rights. However, in its General Comment No. 3 on the nature of the state parties' obligations under the ICESCR, the CESCR declared that concrete legal obligations are imposed by the Covenant under Article 2. State parties are obliged to realize minimum standards relating to each of the rights utilizing available resources in an effective manner. Violations can occur either through commission or omission.

The jurisprudence of the CESCR also recognizes "minimum core obligations" on the part of state parties that have to be fulfilled irrespective of resource or other constraints. In determining whether a state party has utilized the "maximum of its available resources," attention shall be paid to the equitable and effective use of and access to available resources. States also may be responsible if they fail to exercise due diligence in controlling the behavior of non-state actors, such as transnational corporations, over which they exercise jurisdiction, when such behavior deprives individuals of their economic, social, and cultural rights.

The CESCR has consulted with multilateral institutions, specialized agencies, and non-governmental organizations (NGOs) in developing its approach to the issue of globalization. Other treaty-based human rights mechanisms have also shown concern over rising economic disparities that impact on their individual mandates. For example, the Committee examining periodic country reports under the Convention on the Elimination of All Forms of Discrimination Against Women (CEDAW), has shown great concern over the evidence of the feminization of poverty and the impact of economic policies on the rights of women.

A number of U.N. specialized agencies have also addressed the question of globalization. The ILO has long tackled the phenomenon. From the Copenhagen Social Summit in 1995 to the 1998 Declaration on Fundamental Principles and Rights at Work, the ILO has pressed for an international consensus on the content of the core labor standards that provide a social floor to the global economy. In 1998, the ILO adopted the Convention concerning the Prohibition and Immediate Action for the Elimination of the Worst Forms of Child Labour (Convention No. 182). It also adopted its Declaration on Fundamental Principles and Rights at Work together with a follow-up procedure based upon technical cooperation and reporting. The principles have been incorporated into codes of conduct by the private sector and also used as a basis for action by various regional communities, such as the Southern African Development Community, MERCOSUR, and the Caribbean Community. U.N. bodies and specialized agencies, such as the U.N. Children's Fund (UNICEF), the U.N. Educational, Scientific and Cultural Organization (UNESCO), the Office of the U.N. High Commissioner for Refugees (UNHCR), and the U.N. Environment

Programme (UNEP), have all carried out work that has implications for the overall response by the U.N. to the phenomenon of globalization.

In a third approach, the international community has been moving towards greater ascription of individual responsibility for human rights violations, both by state and by non-state actors. While states remain primarily responsible for ensuring the promotion and protection of human rights, increasing attention is being given to the responsibility under international law of inter-governmental organizations, business enterprises, and individuals. In this regard, the international legal system can no longer be described as one governing state alone. The Universal Declaration of Human Rights opened the door to this development by providing, in Article 30, that, nothing in this Declaration may be interpreted as implying for any state, group or person any right to engage in any activity or to perform any act aimed at the destruction of any of the rights and freedoms set forth herein." Conceptually linked to this, the preceding article stipulates that, "everyone has duties to the community in which alone the free and full development of his personality is possible."

That multilateral mechanisms have a unique role to play in meeting the challenges and opportunities presented by globalization and that the process of globalization must not be used to weaken or reinterpret the principles enshrined in the Charter of the U.N., which continues to be the foundation for friendly relations among states, as well as for the creation of a more just and equitable international economic system.

International conferences also have called on international financial institutions to pay greater attention to human rights, through promotion and through assisting in the development of benchmarks to monitor compliance and remedies to respond to violations. In particular, "social safety nets should be defined by reference to these rights and enhanced attention should be accorded to such methods to protect the poor and vulnerable in the context of structural adjustment programs." Social monitoring and impact assessments, similar to that done for the environment, are recommended to international financial institutions and to the WTO. Labor unions have called for including core labor standards in the future WTO work program.

International organizations have taken up several problems where trade and human rights are linked, in the process enhancing global governance by bringing together state and non-state actors. If the behavior of non-state actors violates international norms directly applicable to their conduct, they may be held responsible to their victims. Efforts to hold corporations accountable for conduct occurring in overseas operations have recently become prevalent in U.S. courts.

The ILO remains the key institution concerned with the rights of workers throughout the world. To the extent that other organizations have become involved, the ILO seeks to determine whether or not their standards conform to those of the ILO and adopt a similar human rights approach. The ILO Tripartite Declaration of Principles Concerning Multinational Enterprises and Social Policy addresses the obligations of four groups: the enterprises themselves; workers' groups; employers' organizations; and governments. Its aims are to encourage the positive contributions of multinational companies to economic and social progress and to minimize the negative consequences that might accompany their activities. The Declaration provides that all four groups should respect the Universal Declaration of Human Rights and the two U.N. Covenants on Human Rights. The ILO also surveys the positive and negative effects of multinational activities based on information from workers, employers, and governments.

The U.N. Declaration Against Corruption and Bribery in International Commercial Transactions encourages social responsibility and ethical behavior, calling on partners to international transactions to observe the laws of the host countries, and take into account the impact of their activities on economic and social development and protection of the environment and human rights.

Yet another response to the intersecting issues of globalization and human rights has been to utilize market mechanisms and other forms of private regulation to impact corporate behavior. Pressure from international and national groups, as well as perceived long-term interests, have led many companies to take up the issue of human rights.

The final approach concerned with enhancing human rights in a globalized world is one that has broad implications for global governance generally. It seeks to enhance non-state participation in international organizations and other for a concerned with international regulation.

The U.N. Millennium Declaration resolves to give greater opportunities to the private sector, NGOs, and civil society in general "to contribute to the realization of the Organization's goals and programs." The U.N. Global Compact Initiative aims to develop policy networks of international institutions, civil society, private sector organizations, and national governments to further human rights. The Initiative has taken up such issues as trade in diamonds in zones of conflict, corporate social responsibility generally.

CONTRADICTORY BASIC ASSUMPTIONS OF HUMAN RIGHTS AND GLOBALIZATION

An emerging feature of the new global context is the rise and increasing participation of peoples' and citizens' organizations in leading the establishment of just, participatory, and sustainable communities. This new context must be celebrated; it is one venue of counter-globalization. The so-called "civil society," especially through non-governmental organizations, is increasingly present in forums where grassroots advocacy and global governance are at stake. Through the presence of non-governmental organizations in all levels of governance—local, national, regional, global—globalization is challenged in multiple ways, from the local and the global. Human rights monitors, themselves a threatened group of defenders, have increased in the ranks of civil society.

The following are some of the human rights issue wherein globalization contradicts with their very essence in protecting the needs and dignity of every individual.

Children's Rights and Well-Being

The United Nations Convention on the Rights of the Child expresses this same concern for the child. The convention extends the basic concept of protection to the level of human rights. The Convention affirms that the rights described in the Universal Declaration of Human Rights are rights that belong also to children.

Children's rights are human rights. United Methodists worldwide must continue to urge their governments to implement the convention, and for the United States to ratify it.

Women's Rights and Empowerment

Gender equality is critical to the development process. The process of globalization may have resulted in new avenues of growth, but due to unequal distribution of its benefits women have been adversely affected in many cases. It calls for creating opportunities for women to be part of this development process. Merely enacting legislation will not help. What is required is its proper implementation.[17]

According to a United Nations Development Fund for Women's report, over the past two decades the process of globalisation has contributed to widening inequality within and among countries, coupled with economic and social collapse in parts of Sub-Saharan Africa and countries in transition like in Eastern Europe and the former Soviet Union and financial crises in Asia and Latin America. The process of globalisation must be reshaped so that it is more people-centred instead of profit-centred and more accountable to women.[18]

Migrant Workers

While globalization heralded the swift movement of capital across national borders, the movement of laborers seeking work in richer countries of the world has been slow and increasingly restricted. Transnational corporations have moved to poor countries where labor is much cheaper and workers' organizing is either weak, suppressed, or altogether banned.

The underlying causes of migration are twofold: first, economic competition which forces industrial economies to hire cheap labor in order to remain competitive in the global market, and second, to resolve structural imbalances in the local labor force on the part of the labor-sending countries.

Migrant workers continue to be discriminated against and abused, especially those who are undocumented in their host countries. Women migrants are particularly vulnerable to exploitation especially when they work in gender-specific jobs that consign them to various forms of sexual, domestic, and menial work. Studies show that the majority of migrants are uprooted because of the lack of jobs at home, or because jobs pay extremely low wages. While globalization has spawned more capital and spurred greater production, workers' wages have been kept low and below a livable wage even in those countries whose governments have a prescribed minimum wage.

Migrants' rights are human rights. It is tragic when migrants, whose rights have already been violated in their home countries, find their human rights also violated in their foreign host countries. Invoking host country laws rarely works in their favor. United Methodists should urge their governments to ratify and implement the United Nations International Convention on the Protection of the Rights of All Migrant Workers and Members of Their Families. This Convention will be an instrument to protect, secure, and ensure the human rights of migrant workers and their families.

Indigenous Peoples: Toward Self-Determination

Globalization threatens the human rights of indigenous peoples, including their aspirations for self-determination. Exploration and colonization have led to rapid appropriation of indigenous peoples' lands and natural resources, and the destruction of their sciences, ideas, arts, and cultures.

Indigenous peoples demand respect of their right to their culture, spirituality, language, tradition, forms of organization, ways of knowing and doing, and their intellectual properties. Indeed, it will be hard for indigenous peoples all over the world to exercise their fundamental human rights as distinct nations, societies, and peoples without the ability to control the knowledge they have inherited from their ancestors.

Right to Education

The right to education has been also adversely affected by the privatization policies and the turning of education into a profit generating enterprises in the developing countries. Due to the reduced governmental expenditure on education the quality of public free education has suffered a lot. Investors established educational institutes covering all the range from kinder gardens to universities offering better but much more expensive quality of education for the elites and motivated mainly by profit. However most developing countries still suffer a high rate of illiteracy and graduates of the governmental low quality educational institutions are not well prepared for the labor market so they suffer unemployment.

Right to Development

There is almost a consensus over the fact that the human rights are much more adversely affected by globalization in the south or the so-called developing countries. One of those adversely affected fundamental rights is the right to development. "When countries loose their right to regulate the entry, behavior and operations of foreign investment in the interests of their own people, it is not difficult to appreciate why it is bound to result in an impairment of the right to development.

Right to Healthy Environment and Sustainable Development

Human rights holism must be read in the light of environmental and ecological justice because man can survive only under appropriate environment and ecological milieu where under sustainable development and growth with justice may be possible. In this context, apart from the numerous UN instruments, we may have to recall the Summit assemblages where the world's visionary statesmen, sensitive scientists and committed NGOs have met to advance the cause of social justice in its many dimensions. Among the most important concerns for which considerable effort is necessary bears upon the twin values of environment and development. The Stockholm Conference of 1972 stressed the paramount importance of environmental conservation. Indeed, India has made various enactments like the Water Act, Air Act, Environment Protection Act, Environment Tribunal Act, etc. Mere laws, without being monitored in performance, may prove a flop and so, the United Nations Conference on the Environment and Development was held, followed by the Rio Declaration which is of paramount importance as it sets out the famous Agenda 21 (3-14 June, 1992, UNCED). The Rio Summit sought to build upon the past with the goal of establishing a new and equitable global partnership through the creation of new levels of cooperation among states, key sectors of societies and people, working towards international agreements which respect the interests of all and protect the integrity of the global environmental and developmental system, recognizing the integral and interdependent nature of the Earth, our home, some excerpts will help.

Culture of Peace and Peace-building

In this era of globalization, the icons of war are more prominent and the arsenal of killing machines is more lethal than ever before. Our images of peace and the implements that make for a just peace most often are stymied by these icons and arsenals.

There is need of a comprehensive international legal system, capable of change as conditions require, in order to prevent and resolve conflicts, to protect rights, to hold accountable those who disturb peace and violate international law, and to provide fair and effective review and enforcement mechanisms, respect for the inherent dignity of all persons and the recognition, protection, and implementation of the principles of the International Bill of Human

Rights so that communities and individuals may claim and enjoy their universal, indivisible, and inalienable rights.

CONCLUSION

The key international legal developments that appear to be emerging as a result of globalization, as discussed above, seem to be the following. First, human rights institutions and activists are asserting a primacy of human rights law over other fields of international law. Whether or to what extent this assertion will be accepted remains to be seen. Second, the international legal personality of inter-governmental organizations is seen to carry with it the obligation to conform to general international law norms, above and beyond the requirements of the constituting charters or constitutions of the organizations. Third, the imposition of responsibility for human rights violations on non-state actors appears to be increasing. This all leads to asking: does the state need strengthening?[19]

Globalization has created centers of power that are alongside, even in competition with the power of states. Accountability for human rights violations and prevention of future ones must today and in the future take into account these non-state actors: the media, corporations, and international organizations such as the WTO and the World Bank. States and their agents are no longer the only or sometimes even the key actors responsible for ensuring that human rights and freedoms are guaranteed. As recent international developments have shown, there are multiple avenues to respond to this problem. The first is to strengthen the state and to insist on its responsibility for ensuring that non-state actors do not commit human rights violations.[20]

From the preceding analysis, it is fairly evident that the phenomenon of globalization, primarily through its economic dimensions has numerous implications for the promotion and protection of all human rights. This implies that there is a need for a critical reconceptualization of the policies and instruments of international trade, investment and finance. Such reconceptualization must cease treating human rights issues as peripheral to their formulation and operation. The institutional mechanisms developed to establish norms and resolve disputes in the context of overlapping jurisdictions and conflicting values will in practice determine whether globalization proves to be a friend or foe to human rights. Additionally, what is also required is a more balanced approach, which ensures that human rights principles are integrated into the rule-making processes from the outset.

Notes and References

1. http://www.umc.org/site/apps/nlnet/content2.aspx?c=lwL4KnN1LtH&b= 4951419&ct=7327711 browsed on 02.08.2013 at about 8 p.m
2. http://www.countercurrents.org/ahmed210407.htm browsed on 05.08.2013 at about 6 p.m
3. *Ibid.*
4. *Ibid.*
5. *Ibid.*
6. *Ibid.*
7. http://www.ijbssnet.com/journals/Vol_2_No_19_Special_Issue_October_ 2011/33.pdf browsed on 09.08.2013 at about 3.30 p.m
8. http://archives.umc.org/interior.asp?ptid=4&mid=1016 browsed on 12.08.2013 at about 11 p.m
9. *Ibid.*
10. *Ibid.*
11. http://en.wikipedia.org/wiki/Globalization browsed on 03.08.2013 at about 10.45 p.m
12. *Ibid.*
13. *Ibid.*
14. http://www.religion-online.org/showchapter.asp?title=1559&C=1398 browsed on 07.08.2013 at about 11.45 p.m
15. *Ibid.*
16. http://lawdigitalcommons.bc.edu/cgi/viewcontent.cgi?article=1172& context= iclr browsed on 13.08.2013 at about 4 p.m
17. http://www.mainstreamweekly.net/article1351.html browsed on 10.08.2013 at about 9 p.m
18. *Ibid.*
19. http://lawdigitalcommons.bc.edu/cgi/viewcontent.cgi?article=1172& context= iclr browsed on 12.08.2013 at about 7 p.m
20. *Ibid.*

15

Human Rights, Ethics and Democracy

G.N. TRIVEDI

The conception of human rights is embedded in a range of philosophical-ethical and moral traditions of human society. It figures prominently in various discourses on how to achieve a vision of life built around the idea of enhancing human potentiality. This purpose of human upliftment does not find any exposition either in the form of glorification of individual or the celebration of collectivity. However, the articulation of human rights is clearly inclined in favour of either. The purpose of the study is to transcend obvious limitations of human rights discourses in order to comprehend the idea of rights in terms of its contribution to the growth of humanity. Significantly, this is a huge task given the complexity and contentious nature of human rights in today's world. Nevertheless, the task is worth taking up in order to work out connectivity between ethics, human rights and democracy.

The purpose of the paper is not to offer a proposition from among the various contending perspectives on human rights. Its primary objective is to explore the possibilities of understanding and examining human rights from the angles of ethics and democracy. It seeks to find the ethical origin of rights and their relevance to the people through democracy. This is how I try to establish links between the three specified ideas of human rights, ethics and democracy. In the light of these concerns, it is pertinent to note that analytical interpretations are employed to refine understanding through unravelling hidden and passive meanings of the issues at hand and not to arrive at final and absolute conclusions.

UNDERSTANDING HUMAN NATURE

First of all, I intend considering human nature in the way it has been explained by different philosophical traditions that emerged in the form of an ethical worldview as the basis of the explanations of human rights. Human nature has been brought into focus by highlighting its three different aspects. While the Hindu and Buddhist traditions take into account the distinct nature of individuals, the Chinese traditions emphasise it as part of cultural communities. But the western thought takes human beings as members of the human species.[1] These differing emphases gave rise to the idea of naturalism in the form of universal and particular. These philosophical traditions regard ethics as pivotal to all right and moral decisions. Since human rights primarily concern human beings, its articulation is premised on the notions of both universal and particular. Here, it is important to dwell on the ideas of human nature as explained by Prof. Bhiku Parekh when he questions the conventional understanding of social reality based on universal claims deriving from exclusive analytical understanding of human nature.[2] Fundamentally, he has touched upon four aspects of it to argue that human beings are as much a part of the human species as part of the human conditions and predicament. Briefly, I would mention all these four positions to gain a better understanding of the issue.

Besides the internal properties of human nature, external conditions constitute a factor that plays a crucial role in shaping human nature. Human beings have countless ties to the non-human world. They are subject to ecological and other constraints, and form part of the universe structured in a certain way. Human beings must work to preserve their existence. Indeed, they are shaped by geography, particular historical epoch and history. Living together with other human beings constrains them in multiple ways. These and other aspects of human existence are not internal to human beings but external or interpersonal, and form part not of human nature but of the human conditions or predicament.[3] Prof. Parekh delineates the need to consider the human predicament along with human nature to develop a better understanding of human beings.

Secondly, the traditional account of human nature is a-historical. Prof. Parekh has reflected upon the historically acquired capacities of human beings: how human beings creatively interact with the natural environment and change it to suit their needs. This shows a constant human engagement with nature to develop their capacities. 'In the course of this dialectic with nature, they change themselves and their world, develop new forms of social organisation, and acquire new capacities and dispositions. These historically acquired capacities and dispositions are institutionalised and reproduced during successive generations, and become part of their species' heritage or nature'.[4] Further elaborating this point, he opines, 'much of human nature is, thus, not a product of human nature but of human struggle. It is natural in the sense that it is acquired by virtue of belonging to the human species, but it is not natural in the sense that it is a result of the efforts of the species itself and forms part of its process of self-creation.[5]

Thirdly, there are two difficulties in discovering human nature beyond what is inherent in their physico-mental structure. 'Since human beings', Prof. Parekh puts forward, 'have always led organised lives, their nature has been so shaped by layers of social influences that we have no direct access to it in its raw or pristine form, and cannot easily detach what is natural from what is manmade or social'.[6] Further, he concludes, 'in short, human nature is not a brute and empirically verifiable fact, but an inference or a theory that is beyond any reliable corroboration. [7]

The other difficulty is the explanation of normal and social phenomena appealing to human nature to strengthen moral claims of such an explanation. The explanatory category of human nature is deliberately employed to delegitimise other understandings and to develop alternatives. This is surprisingly also adopted by various scholars. Turning to human nature for the purpose of explaining might not be objectionable if it is put to critical scrutiny with a dose of scepticism.

Fourth and finally, 'human beings are actually embedded in that they are born into, raised in and shaped by their cultural communities'.[8] All the factors of human creativity, geographical conditions, historical experiences and so on enable different societies to develop different systems of meaning, ways of looking at the world, ideals of excellence, traits of temperament and forms of moral and social life, giving different orientations and structures to universally shared capacities and desires and cultivating wholly new ones of their own.[9] Prof. Parekh finally comments: 'cultures are not super-structures built upon identical and unchanging foundations, or manifestations of a common human essence, but unique human creations that reconstitute and give different meaning and orientation to those properties that all human beings share in common, add new ones of their own, and give rise to different kinds of human beings. Such human beings are culture creating and capable of creative self-transformation, they cannot passively inherit a shared nature in the way as animals do.

HISTORICAL TRAJECTORY OF HUMAN RIGHTS THEORY

The Universal Declaration of Human Rights by the UN in 1948 forms the basis of respect for human rights globally and any violation of these rights invariably becomes the cause of concern, condemnation and ultimately sanction. But, this final stage of universal declaration is followed by long philosophical traditions in both pre-modern and modern times. This section presents a brief account of this long journey of human rights' theory.

The antecedents of human rights may be traced to the philosophical and dramatic writings. For example, the playwright Sophocles (495-406 BC) provided an early defence of the individual's right to resist state repression.[10]

Plato (427-348 BC) was another Greek philosopher who 'set an early version of universalism in ethical standards, implying fair treatment to all persons, whether they are citizens or not'.[11] Plato's disciple, Aristotle too focussed on the role of political community in ensuring justice and rights to its members. Roman Philosophers Cicero and Seneca also talked about the wise and rational man as the citizens of the world.[12] Cicero 'provided the philosophical foundations for later theories of natural law, when he advocated for a general set of universal principles which should transcend local civil laws'.[13]

Needless to say, the European enlightenment marked a watershed in the evolution of human rights and making a fundamental break with the past dominated by the idea of divine rights of the king. Thomas Hobbes (1588-1679) prepared a new basis of individual's allegiance to the state by focusing on the pre-social nature of the human being. To him, human beings are selfish and quarrelsome and absolutely relentless in showing aggression towards each other. This trait of human beings entails the process of social contract among the inhabitants of the state of nature and subsequent establishment of a powerful state. The raison d'être of the creation of the state is to provide security to each and everybody. The right to security, thus, became the paramount concern of both the state and the people. This basic right to security, to Hobbes, is the legitimate basis of the sovereign state and if the state fails to perform this mandatory duty then it loses the legitimacy of its existence. It would be considered as the breach of contract and therefore people have every right to overthrow it. In short, Hobbes recognized people's innate right to security from the state.

In continuity with this contractual tradition, John Locke (1632-1704) does acknowledge the state as an outcome of the social contract but on an altogether different basis. His state of nature is distinctively marked by the natural rights of people. Each person enjoyed right to life, liberty and estate but the absence of an arbiter in the event of disputes to interpret natural rights necessitated the process of the creation of the state. Thus, Locke, considered as the father of modern liberalism, quite specifically emphasized the inalienable rights enjoyed by the people in the state of nature and also justified the creation and continuity of the state as long as it fulfils the purpose of its creation.

The last thinker in the tradition of social contract theory is the French philosopher, Jean Jacques Rousseau (1712-78) who distanced himself from the individualism of Hobbes and Locke in his articulation of human freedom. 'Man is born free but finds himself everywhere in chains' forms the basis of Rousseau's enunciation of freedom. The obedience to general will ensures the freedom of all as it is the sum total of real will of the people, a will of conscience that elevates people from baser instincts to a higher level of consciousness. This tradition of French enlightenment was carried forward by many other philosophers like Montesquieu, Voltaire and others. Montesquieu is credited with initiating the theory of separation of power to ensure rights to the people. He was averse to all forms of despotism, slavery and intolerance. Voltaire (1694-1778), another famous French philosopher, strongly reiterated the need of abolition of torture and degrading punishments and also 'attacked censorship by calling for a respect for freedom of opinion and expression, whatever the views or the content in question might be.[14]

Thus, the French philosophers championed the cause of political rights of man which forms one of the important tenets of contemporary human rights. Moreover, it is the German philosopher Immanuel Kant (1724-1804) who is often credited with laying the groundwork for the modern understanding of human rights as ethical practice.[15] To him, the right to freedom is an incontrovertible right. Unlike Locke, he outlines a 'manifesto for practical moral action, based on the qualitative recognition of human dignity, which has subsequently found its way into the core of human rights discourse.[16] He based his belief in justice on what he termed the 'categorical imperative' of moral action.[17] He has included three main components of moral principles–the formula of universality, the formula of the end in itself and the formula of kingdom of ends.[18]

The first formula emphasizes the need for a morality that must be impartial and non-arbitrary and based on equality. This principle of morality demands that individual should act towards other in a way they would expect and desire others to act towards them. It is the moral responsibility of all human beings to act in a way that it should acquire the status of universal law. The second formula of the end in itself establishes the moral superiority of human beings by reiterating that 'humans should always be treated as ends in themselves, and never as means to an end. It thus demands respects for all persons and affirms that morality must involve justice'[19]. The third formula of kingdom of ends 'is a principle of autonomy that demands that individuals recognize their responsibilities and their empowerment, thus affirming that morality must involve freedom'.[20]

The significance of Kant lies in the fact that he made a clear distinction between human rights and civil and political rights accorded to the citizens by the state. Hence, he formulated a triangular structure of rights–first, the civil rights of individuals within their nation states; second, the international rights of states in their dealings with one another; and third, the cosmopolitan rights of individuals and states as existing interdependently in a universal state of humankind.[21] This triangular structure of rights aims at the essential oneness of the human race. Thus, Kantian articulation of ethical basis of human rights constitutes the core of human rights discourse in the contemporary world.

The evolution of rights underscores an unending human quest for their realization. However, multiple contending perspectives and interpretations have invariably eluded a consensus.

HUMAN RIGHTS AND ETHICS: A THEORETICAL EXPLORATION

While reflecting on the aspects of human nature in this paper, many questions relating to universal nature, particular context of human nurture and growth have been dealt with. However, the extraordinary importance of human rights calls for addressing some specific key questions in the context of human rights that bear stamps of various theoretical traditions. For the purpose of convenience three important issues–universality of human rights; incontrovertibility of rights; and subjectivity of human rights are being picked up.[22] This would also follow the ethical questions concerning human rights.

The idea of universality has proximity to the Lockean notion of natural law and Kant's formulation of human freedom. This natural law is grounded in a pre-social, universal state of morality as opposed to positive law, which is grounded in official, binding, constitutional acts and precedents. The bogey of natural law has been raised primarily not to give importance to rights but to establish a philosophical basis for political constitution with specific rights to the people who have evolved from pre-social state of nature to social. This is at least the position of Locke and Hobbes. Kant, on the other hand, applied the paradigm of natural law specifically to the questions of morality and ethics. He wanted to show not only that morality is universal but that it is articulated through the behaviour of people towards one another. Thus, Kantian position provides the basis of good society.[23]

The concept of natural law is a hugely contested one. The prospects of some higher kinds of rights in pre-social stage seem not to make any sense. Is there any use of having rights in absolute loneliness? What can one do on a deserted island if left alone? Such formulation of rights is meaningless. Besides, the explicit individualism of Kantian project has been questioned by the communitarians and post-modernists.

There is the emergence of a neo-Kantian tradition to re-establish the universal foundation of human rights.[24] John Rawls and Habermas are the two thinkers who have made attempts to rescue Kantian philosophical tradition. They separate natural law from the idea of universality. Both these philosophers ground these universal perspectives in everyday actions.

Rawls has coined the term 'moral constructivism' to define this perspective which seeks to defend the search for underlying universal ideas and show how these abstract principles relate to everyday life and are, indeed, constructed and interpreted through everyday actions.[25] Rawls justifies the universal morality of his original position in the acceptance of the people to create a society based on equality and justice.

On the other hand, Habermas locates these principles in the practice of everyday communication.[26] He proposes that there is an underlying consensus operating within society which could be discovered through the application of communications skills and speech. He considers this underlying consensus as truth and its discovery would lead people to freedom and justice. Thus, Habermas, instead of appealing to any abstract pre-social universal moral principle, emphasizes the need to find the ways to freedom and justice through daily action. He also does not agree with the post-modernist position of cultural relativism as it depoliticises the discourse of human rights.

As far as the issue of incontrovertibility of human rights is concerned, it deserves serious attention. In fact, it is preposterous to think that rights cannot be controvertible in any circumstances. There are many instances that demand controvertibility. If there is conflict between two and more rights then one of the rights must be given up. Similarly, 'prisoner is denied the right to freedom, so long as the prisoner has, in fact, committed a crime deserving of such punishment.'[27] Therefore, the incontrovertibility of right does not hold ground.

The third proposition of the subjectivity of human rights is equally significant. The issue of subjectivity is closely associated with the rationality of individuals and their being endowed with the autonomy of agency. It was Rene Descrates, the celebrated French rationalist philosopher, who most famously declared that humans are special form of life because we have consciousness.[28] He developed this position through recognition of mind and body. 'Kant added a practical twist to this logic, suggesting humans deserve to be treated with dignity because they have power of agency. That is, they are active thinking beings.[29] These traits qualify human beings for rights. However, there is an obvious problem with such a conception as 'rights are not contained within the individual but with his or her capacity for reason'.[30] According to this view, animals, new born babies, terminally ill patients are denied rights as they are not considered moral agents. Moreover, the subjective realm of rights in the form of individuality has been philosophically critiqued by the Marxist and religious traditions.

There is much to be gained by expanding the range and developing western thinking on rights by incorporating some of these non-western collectivist traditions.[31] While agreeing that these rights are universally valid, the Bangkok Declaration of 1993 insisted that they should be defined and applied in the light of local history, culture and religious background.[32]

APPROACHING ETHICS

Kant's project as a moral philosopher was as much about providing a framework for what might constitute ethical social action as it was about tracing the origins of universal morality.[33] Here, it is important to note that the core components like rights, good and thought of ethical system cannot be measured but these ethical concerns can be justified through their appeal to intuition as they have been emphasized by famous philosopher G.E. Moore.

Kant has also come up with his notion of intention. This intentionalism places a lot of importance on motive. Kant insisted that the moral value of any act is contained within its motive. He argued that the only moral motive is that something is done because it is one's duty to do it, because it is a right thing to do it. In the Kantian world the attempt matters, is born out of a recognition of one's duty to make it, and if made en masse, provides the building block for the good society.[34]

Kant's blend of universalism and intentionalism, thus, provides a bridge between his appeal to some abstract sense of truth and his commitment to the practice of moral behaviour. For Kant, ethics are, thus, embedded in social action. In this respect, human rights are perhaps macro structural version of aggregate ethical behaviour. The ethics of everyday social action might reside in a respect for mutual human dignity.[35] The famous French philosopher Michael Foucault too recognizes that morality has come to mean a set of values and rules of action that are recommended to individuals through social institutions. One can summarize Foucault's position in this way that all moral actions follow unified moral conduct that enables one to form an ethical subject–and all this practice passes through the subjective realm of one's self. Obviously, this entire process of becoming an ethical subject enhances the possibility of human freedom.

Thus, it would be fair to conclude that the ethics of human rights provide theoretical and practical justification for the necessity of rights. As mentioned above, the ethics of human rights is phenomenologically confirmed and therefore hermeneutically inexhaustive.

HUMAN RIGHTS AND DEMOCRACY

It is commonly held that democratic representative government is the best form of government to safeguard and guarantee the people's right. Keeping the objectives of Universal Declaration of Human Rights, the following four significant characteristics for the effective realization of human rights were conceived:

The first assumption is that the territorial state is the appropriate community for democratization. It is important to mention in this regard that the concept of liberal democracy is tied to the idea of self-governing community, a community of citizens defined by national sovereignty, the territorial nation state, self determination and domestic jurisdiction. Its impact is so wide that 'political theory has made a profound connection between democracy and the nation-states, which international theory and practice reinforce, placing democracy squarely within the domestic sphere.'[36]

The second assumption places the principle of accountability at the centre of all forms of liberal democracy. Freedom of speech, free press, independent judiciary and above all the periodic regular elections are aimed at ensuring the accountability of the government and the state.[37]

The third assumption is that democratic states continue to exercise a high degree of autonomy in making public policies to serve the interests of the people. This places government in a position to freely utilize the economic and political resources to promote the common interest in accordance with the principle of democracy. Internally, the autonomy of the state is generally believed not to be constrained though externally the relative power position of the state determines the degree of exercise of autonomy of the state.[38]

The final assumption is that the democratic state acts in the interest of the whole people, not in the interest of the particular national or global interest. There is an obvious tension between the liberal and democratic elements of liberal democracy as the latter demands the inclusion of socio-economic rights whereas the former is almost exclusively concerned with civil and political rights.[39] All these long held assumptions question the viability of the functioning of democracy within territorial boundary.

The advent of globalization is marked by the free flow of economy, ideas, cultural exchanges, social interaction and political inter-connectedness—all these processes are widening and deepening. The development of new technology enables the formation of new transnational relationships that challenged the territorial limits of democracy, raising the question of how to define the appropriate democratic community. The possession of technological capability by some groups and people frees them from the democratically constituted controls of the state.[40]

Secondly, globalisation has seen state power decline as transnational processes grow in scale and number. This is evident in the growing intensity of global economic, social and political interconnectedness that threatens the capacity of the state in its role as the guardian of the common good and the national interest. This poses a challenge to the 'economics of market' and 'politics of democracy' in many countries of the world.[41] The former is exclusive whereas the latter is inclusive. It is pertinent to note that the dynamics of market necessarily excludes people particularly those who do not have purchasing power (the poor and the deprived). But the politics of democracy entails the process of inclusion. The third potential challenge to the dominant understanding of democracy follows from the above. With the complexity of political and economic life, many traditional functions of the state are transferred to global and regional international organisations. States, therefore, surrender their sovereignty to larger political units such as the European Union, the NATO, the World Bank, and WTO. These organisations generally work in a way that greatly imperils the national interest. In such a situation, the national democratic concerns of the people are put aside that are inextricably linked with the issue of protection of human rights. Consequently, despite the state as the main protector of human rights, the dynamics of global structure greatly constrains the autonomy of the state in fulfilling its democratic demands. Instead of creating a post-Cold War world order that offers the prospects for protecting human rights through democracy and the rule of law, globalisation has created conditions for disorder, authoritarian rule beyond the territorial state, reformation of the state entity and potential for continued violation of human rights. For those who put their faith in democracy, the assertion that 'the great beauty of globalisation is that no one is in control, offers a chilling reminder that democracy at the state level will not be enough.'[42]

Now, I would like to make a few comments on the state of democracy concerning development and human rights. The main reason for promoting democracy in the less developed countries is the failure of development. This makes it imperative for the developed countries to create at least the procedural-formal democratic structure in these countries to avoid social unrest and most importantly to ensure free flow of capital in these countries. The operation of democracy in such countries is termed as low-intensity democracy , its main job is to ensure formal structure of democracy and provide free passage to global capital. In the event, these set parameters are transcended , this angers the developed world and as a result, the low intensity democratic countries face the threat of military coups. In these countries, trade unions are weak, low wages are widespread and the media censorship is common. The only professional training is provided to military and other coercive apparatuses of the state.[43]

Lastly, the discourse of development is apparently anti-democratic. The dynamics of growth through enhanced GDP is premised on the large scale displacement of people. In fact, development has become an end in itself rather than a means to an end.

In conclusion, we may argue that national forms of democracy are incapable of providing a culture of rights until we recognise the need to democratise both the institutions that operate above the state, at the global level and those below the state, at the local level.

CONCLUSION

The above discussions on human rights highlight various opinions and views on it. The idea of human rights is premised on privileging one set of rights against the other. They are articulated as civil and political rights against the socio-economic rights, individual rights against communitarian rights and so on. We are of the view that this is the outcome of the dominant understanding of human rights. In fact, the attempt to homogenise the discourses is to check a pluralist interpretation of human rights. Although the merit of a diverse understanding of rights was accepted in the Bangkok Conference organised by the UN in 1993, the gap still remains in actual practice.

The ethics of human rights and their controversial nature in the form of universal versus particular is once again the result of the hegemonic discourse of the post-enlightenment project. The distortion arising out of it is being laid bare by Prof. Bhiku Parekh. 'The most satisfactory way to arrive at consensus on universal values is through a universal or cross-cultural dialogue. The dialogue brings together different historical experiences and cultural sensibilities, and ensures that we appreciate human beings in all their richness and that the values we arrived at are as genuinely universal as is humanly possible'.[44]

Thus, there is an absolute necessity to democratise the discourses on human rights to evolve a mutually acceptable framework.

Notes and References

1. Bhiku Parekh, *Rethinking Multiculturalism*, Macmillan, London, 2000.
2. *Ibid.*, 118-21.
3. *Ibid.*, 118.
4. *Ibid.*, 119.
5. *Ibid.*
6. *Ibid.*
7. *Ibid.*, 120.
8. *Ibid.*
9. *Ibid.*
10. Darren J.O. Byrne, *Human Rights*, Pearson, 2003, p. 28).
11. *Ibid.*
12. *Ibid.*
13. *Ibid.*
14. Byrne, p. 18.
15. *Ibid.*, p. 31.
16. *Ibid.*
17. *Ibid.*
18. *Ibid.*, pp. 31-32.
19. *Ibid.*, p. 32.
20. *Ibid.*
21. *Ibid.*
22. *Ibid.*, p. 37.
23. *Ibid.*, p. 38.
24. *Ibid.*, p. 39.
25. *Ibid.*, p. 39.
26. *Ibid.*
27. *Ibid.*, p. 45.
28. *Ibid.*, p. 46.
29. *Ibid.*
30. *Ibid.*, p. 50.
31. *Ibid.*
32. Parekh, p. 136.
33. Bryne, p. 56.
34. Bryne, p. 56.
35. *Ibid.*, p. 57.
36. T. Evans, *The Politics of Human Rights: A global Perspective*, London, Pluto Press, 2001, p. 102.
37. *Ibid.*
38. *Ibid.*, p. 103.
39. Parekh, p. 134.

40. Evans, p. 104.
41. D. Nayyar, p. 362, cited in N.G. Jayal (ed.), *Democracy in India*, OUP, New Delhi, 2001.
42. Evans, p. 105.
43. *Ibid.*, p. 11.
44. Parekh, p. 128.

16

Natural Resources and Sustainable Development

Gandhian Perspective

S.B. NAKADE

INTRODUCTION

India has rich natural resources and biodiversity. Proper utilization and exploitation of natural resources will contribute to economic growth and prosperity. The Government in order to have rapid growth and to improve the standards of living of the millions of people adopted the Western model of industrialization.

Adoption of liberal economic policies no doubt has brought foreign capital for investment in industrial sector which increased economic activities for development. External pressures not only from the international institutions–International Monetary Fund and the World Bank, but also from multinational corporations are compelling the government to restructure the economic system to conform to the *laissez faire* model. Industrial units as well as foreign companies in collaboration have been exploiting the natural resources of our country for getting wealth but without caring for ethical values.

Indian economy is at cross road and facing financial crises. The stark reality is to make a choice between conserving the natural resources through constructive programmers or to destroy the resources without caring for conservation of environment and sustainable development. In such a critical situation the Gandhian theory as depicted in 'Hind Swaraj' shall provide positive solutions for economic development and that too without domination of others.

Gandhi was concerned with the poor, alleviation of poverty and eradication of poverty. He advocated the programmers to transform villages into self-reliant and self-sufficient villages. He also wanted to ensure not only higher standard of living for the millions but 'also a high standard of life' which include ethical and spiritual values of human existence.

The essence of Gandhian theory of economic development is bold decentralization of economic and political power so that plans are worked out 'implemented by and large at village level by the people and for the people.'

Gandhi's principle is that means adopted are as important as the end itself. The end does not justify the means. The means employed determine the nature of ends produced. He stated that only just and non-violent means would lead to build a harmonious society. There is inviolable connection between the means and end. This noble principle of Gandhi is relevant even today in modern times for framing and implementing the plan of conservation of natural resources and sustainable development.

NATURAL RESOURCES

Environment is a key factor for sustainable development. It includes natural surroundings with all physical conditions necessary for the origin and survival of life on the planet. It comprises all natural resources such as land, the eco-system, flora and fauna, ocean as well as environment and deposits under the land surface include all minerals–coal, iron, oil, etc.

The concept of sustainable development has four constituent parts-economic, ecological, political and cultural sustainability. Sustainable development is a mode of form of human development in which the use of natural resources meets the needs of society while preserving the environment not only for the present but also the future generations to come. The Burndtland Commission used the term 'sustainable development.' It means development that meets the needs of the present without compromising the ability of future generations to meet their own needs.

Planning for economic development should take into consideration the use of technological mechanisms that meet the present day needs and to ensure environmental protection and social justice. No doubt, now-a-days 'Gradually economic development is moving from good to better but the quality of environment is going from bad to worse.'[1] Specialized training programmes for environmental protection awareness, as well as programmes for economic, political and cultural sustainability will have to be implemented.

For world sustainability individuals will have to think 'globally and act to locally'. Lifestyle of the modern individuals is changing and a new philosophy has been identified which is coined as glocal philosophy. The key words of glocal and local are linked with each other and called as glocal for smooth development. Principles of glocal philosophy envisage creativity, connectivity and linkage between 'the local traditional values by linking them with global trends for continuous and smooth development of the individuals.'[2]

CONSERVATION OF ENVIRONMENT

Conservation of natural resources is primary concern of the society and state. In order to have quick returns people are misusing the potentialities of the nature. Forests, lakes, rivers, flora and fauna are being exploited for getting wealth without respecting the socio-economic interests of the society. In 1972, Stockholm Conference declared:

> "the protection of the environment is a major issue which affects the well being of people and economic development throughout the world."

Conserve the environment for tomorrow has become a modern slogan all over the world. Prosperity of the people is dependent upon the spirit of cooperation, contentment, peace and non-violence.

Conservation of natural surroundings has been the primary concern of the society. People will have to come forward voluntarily for the protection of natural resources if some greedy industrialists are exploiting the scarce resources of the nature. In modern times Gandhi has been considered as acknowledged prophet of environmentalist's movement. The Indian activists have struggled hard and launched movements for the protection of environment.

"From the Chipko Andolan to Narmada Bachao Andolan environmental activists have relied heavily on Gandhian techniques of non-violent protest, and have drawn abundantly on Gandhi's polemic against heavy industrialization."[3]

SUSTAINABLE DEVELOPMENT

Gandhian theory of development of economy was based upon Swadeshi principle. He emphasized upon the utilization of local and traditional and eco-friendly methods. Village cottage industries and utilization of local labour contributed to development of rural economy. He was firm in stating that earth has everything man needs only it cannot satisfy his greed.

Mother earth is one and which supports life system due to proper use of air, water, land and flora and fauna. Using machines in agricultural fields and also the use of pesticide caused damage to the fertility of land. It has also disturbed environmental balance. To protect village economy it has become necessary to protect and conserve environment on sound and scientific basis. Gandhian theory is more suitable, practical and relevant to Indian people. Attainment of self-sufficiency of villages on the basis of physical labour of able bodied persons was the goal. Basic needs of food, clothing and shelter could be fulfilled if constructive programmes are framed and implemented in villages. Those programmes should be eco-friendly.

Main object of economic development was eradication and alleviation of poverty. Poverty is considered as the worst form of violence. Full employment for the people is indispensable in order to uproot poverty. Since the capital is scarce, low-capital, full employment-oriented industries are to be encouraged and established. Western model of economic development is not suitable in India because it has brought disastrous consequences and caused environmental pollution.

ECONOMICS OF PERMANENCE

Gandhian principle was economics of permanence for all-round development. Motto of life is to live happily, peacefully and to render service to other people for their happiness and prosperity. Therefore holistic approach has to be adopted with regard to economic development. Prosperity depends upon adoption of indigenous methods followed in villages and not upon the Western model of development which is mostly based upon the tools of new technology.

In modern period critics point out that it is difficult to practice Gandhian Swadeshi principle in the midst of industrialization and exploitation of scarce resources of the nature. But it is a fact that mindless exploitation of rare resources without caring for the principle of equal distribution will create more problems in the society. Even though Gandhian principle is difficult to practice yet it is practical, beneficial to humankind in the world. Upanishad, Indian scripture says that:

> 'Get-up, wake-up and learn from the wise. As it is difficult to walk on the razor's edge so it is difficult to walk on the right path.' Hence why not to adopt Gandhian idea of 'Plain living and high thinking' so that natural resources could be kept safe for future generation to come."

Greed Economics

To acquire wealth and power depends upon mainly on the acquisition of power over natural resources and exploitation of manual labour of the working class. One who works shall eat. It is individual's duty to work honestly and earn his bread. 'Work is worship.' Exploitation of physical labour of the workers is against morality and perpetuates injustice in the society and therefore it is called as 'greed economics.' Money making becomes the sole object of some persons who want to satisfy their greed but it is detrimental to the interests of society. 'Money is not the be all and end all of life.' Gandhi has stated that:

> "An economics that inculcates Mammon worship and enables the strong to amass wealth at the expenses of the weak, is a false and dismal science. It spells the death. True economics promotes the good of all including the weakest, and is indispensable for decent life."[4]

Another aspect of 'greed economics' is that it is unjust and against social justice. Gandhi had not separated and differentiated ethics from economics. He had stated that true economics is the economics of justice. People will have to be happy and they should learn to respect others and be righteous in their conduct. They should not become rich by hook or crook because that will do immense injustice to other persons.

Economics is closely related with ethical. Social and ethical values are to be cherished and protected even in the field of economic development. Gandhi categorically stated that. "True economics never militates against the highest ethical standards just as all true ethics to be worth of its name must at the same time be also good economics."[5] Thus the individual has to be content by earning his livelihood with his labour and should not possess more or acquire wealth more than what one needs.

In the modern period environmentalists have pointed out the adverse effects of exploitation of the nature and its limited resources. It is a fact that environmental degradation is the result of over consumption of material goods, multiplication of wants and consumerist culture. Keeping in view Gandhian philosophy for improving the Indian standard of living, the state, society, civil society and non-governmental organizations will have to devise methods for sustainable development.

POWER POLITICS FOR EXPLOITATION OF NATURAL RESOURCES

In modern times capitalism has facilitated a new economic system at global level known as liberalization, privatization and globalization. In fact, in the beginning the developed countries gave financial assistance and new hopes for cooperation for the development of economy of less enveloped and developing countries. Financial assistance given to less developed states was not free of cost and it imposed heavy conditions upon their governments.

At present, governments of less developed states are unable to repay the money taken from the rich states as well as from the World Bank. They have been caught in debt trap. There is revolutionary impact of globalization in the fields of trade and commerce, agriculture, education and health care. Modern plutocrats have been exploiting natural resources in order to make more profit. Mega machines employed in the factories has created serious problem of unemployment. Ordinary farmers are being displaced from their farms under the guise of economic development. Lands of Indian farmers' have been acquired for the establishment of Special Economic Zone and also for launching of projects under public-private partnership system as well as for development of infrastructure in India.

Thousands of acres of land owned by the farmers have been acquired by the government for public purpose and a part of the land acquired is allotted to the Corporate Houses for starting heavy industries. Activists of Civil society have accused the government of treating farmer's land as commodity. Land mafia and sand mining mafia have suppressed the voices of the farmers and the poor. They have not spared even the exploitation of the bed of small or big rivers for extracting water as well as sand. The same water and sand taken out of the rivers are being sold at heavy price.

This modern phenomenon of exploitation of natural resources has created environmental problems, scarcity of drinking water, climate change and also contributed to global warming. Industrialization has also created economic inequality due to mad race for acquisition of wealth and power. The consequences of industrialization at different places are far-reaching such as ecological disasters, corruption, terrorism, violence and insecurity of life and also posed a threat to the safety of the nature meant for future generations.

Modern trend is that socialist and communist states have also adopted some of the policies of capitalism and people have been permitted to set up special economic zones for economic development. Communist state such as China has welcomed foreign investment for economic development.

Rich industrialists claim that they alone can utilize and exploit the natural resources properly. The object of capitalist class which invests huge capital to set up industries or multinational companies is to acquire more profit at any cost even at the cost of labourers by disregarding ethical values of human life. Over exploitation of natural resources caused depletion of scarce natural resources and adversely affected lives of millions of people throughout the world. Giovanni Ricoveri stated that :

> "People are also part of nature and the exploitation of nature is therefore also the exploitation of some people by other people. Environmental degradation is also the degradation of human relationships."[6]

Under the pressure of globalization the powers of government are reduced. This new system in effect has become, 'our new unelected, uncontrollable world government. One that outlaws our attempts to make things better..."[7]

Freedom of trade was in the beginning freedom of communities to carry out their trade and business equally with each other. The system of globalization has become all powerful. It has become a boon to some states and a bane to others and allowed 'A license for the big, the powerful and the rich to ride roughshod over the small, the weak and the poor..."[8]

A few decades before the establishment of IMF, World Bank and WTO the states whether developed or less developed conformed to the rules and regulations of internationalism for trading. But the rules which have been developed due to globalization have pitted one country against another country in the mad race of international competitiveness for acquiring world hegemony.

Business has a social purpose. Gandhian policy of cooperation instead of competitiveness is relevant to solve the problems of economic inequality because it puts the people before profit. Ultimately the people should wake and give a call for social change and social justice as well as for a bright future without violence, hate, inequality and exploitation.

TRUSTEESHIP SYSTEM

According to Gandhi everything belongs to God. People are the owners of land and natural resources. When an individual has acquired more wealth than what is required for him then he must act as trustee of the surplus income. Theory of trusteeship has the sanction of philosophy and religion. It should become a way of life in order to secure the welfare of all. It is in consonance with the noble principles such as non-violence, sarvodaya and love for all.

Wealth is to be created before trusteeship. Underlying principle of trusteeship is that individual who has surplus wealth should utilize it for the benefit of other individuals of the society . It is aimed at equitable distribution of income, not to possess more wealth than what is required to meet one's needs.

Ownership of trust property shall be vested in the hands of trustees and not with the state. Trustees if they betray the faith reposed in them will face wrath of the people. Masses will resort to non-cooperation and protests against them and will persuade them for performing their duties.

In ideal Swaraj people will be free from exploitation and domination by the rich class because wealth without work is considered as a social sin. It is expected that the rich people will hold wealth and talents in trust and use them for rendering social service to society. In Ishopanishad, an ancient scripture stated that:

> "All that is in the universe is pervaded by God, renounce first, therefore, in order to enjoy, covet not any body's riches."[9]

BASIS OF TRUSTEESHIP

Gandhian Trusteeship system is based upon non-violence, swaraj and equality which are inter linked with one another. Gandhi in order to establish an ideal social order, a non-violent non-exploitive and an egalitarian society made no sharp distinction between economics and ethics. Character of production will be determined by social necessity and not personal whim or greed of the rich. Gandhi stated that:

> "I must confess that I do not draw a sharp or any distinction between economics and ethics. That economics is untrue which ignores or disregards moral value. The extension of the law of non-violence in economics means nothing less than the introduction of moral values as a factor to be considered in regulating international commerce"[10]

Gandhi advocated trusteeship for the betterment of working class and for establishment of an egalitarian society wherein there will be good relations between the propertied and propertyless. He has given due recognition to divinity of man. i.e. 'Jiva is always Shiva' a man is by and large divine.

In India we have mixed economy with public sector and private sector for economic development. More than hundred big industrial units control largest share of economy. Concentration of wealth in the hands of a few plutocrats has been increasing day-by-day and the workers are under the grip of losing their rights to get adequate wages, right to negotiate with the employers for getting legitimate facilities. There is bound to be conflict between the industrialists and the workers. Gandhian theory will come to the rescue of both the employers and employees. Gandhi stated that:

> "A violent and bloody revolution is a certainty one day unless there is voluntary abdication of riches and the power that riches give, and sharing them for the common good. I adhere to my doctrine of trusteeship in spite of the ridicule that has been poured upon it."[11]

Criticism is leveled against trusteeship system. It is considered as an utopian plan and impracticable and unattainable. But there is no other fair alternative than to make sincere attempts for practicing it in order to resolve the conflicts between the rich and poor and to maintain harmonious relationship between the two. Thus, there will be peace and harmony in the society.

DECENTRALIZATION

Object of the welfare of the people cannot be achieved on the basis of centralization of political and economic power. Gandhiji supported the principle of the decentralization of the powers at village and state level. Centralization of powers as a system is inconsistent with non-violent structure of the society. It certainly curbs the initiative of the individual.

The principle of the decentralization seeks human happiness, mental and moral development. Gandhiji wanted to bring reforms in the villages in order to make them self-reliant and self-sufficient. He stated that every village should become a republic or Panchayat having full powers and be capable of managing their affairs which will be beneficial for the establishment of cultural and democratic society.

Gandhi advocated the decentralization in the field of economic development because it is a key to reshaping or reforming the existing economic system for the betterment of the people. Adoption of the principle of the decentralization the people will become self-reliant and they will be able to frame and implement the policies for the development at rural, local and national level.

GOOD GOVERNANCE

Democratic polity is based on the consent of people. Its object is to secure to all its citizens–justice, social, economic and political. Therefore, there is always a demand from the people for good governance.

A few principles of a good governance are–Accountability, Transparency and Responsiveness of the government towards the people. According to first principle those who are at the helm of affairs must be accountable to the people who are being governed by them. Secondly the functions and decisions of the persons who hold the powers of the state must be transparent for the good of people and thirdly, responsiveness on the part of administrators while discharging their public duties towards the people is indispensable for achieving the goals of democratic polity.

Good governance becomes meaningful if the citizens are vigilant and play their active role in the functioning of democratic polity. It is a continuous process to work for the achievement of sustainable human development.

Good governance depends upon the persons who administers it. It requires a set of honest men, men of strong character, men of vision and men who will have the interest of the country before them and who will not sacrifice public interest for personal gains.

CIVILIZATION

The concept of Indian civilization and meaning of modern civilization can be better understood if the people have a glimpse of Gandhiji's writings. Gandhi had explained civilization as:

> "Civilization in the real sense of the term consists not in the multiplication but in the deliberate and voluntary reduction of selfish wants. This alone promotes real happiness and contentment and increases the capacity for service."[12]

Civilization means good conduct. Attributes of goodness are universal. Gandhi did not recognize modern civilization as 'Civilization' at all. He calls it as 'Satanic'. Its goal is acquisition of material things and prosperity.

In the West people have given importance to freedom and marched on the road to attain material prosperity without caring for ethical values. Human reason has been employed to look at the material side of the world but has not considered the spiritual side. People recognized the value of reason for the economic growth and also acquired power. But the cultural and spiritual side of human beings have been given scant respect.

Indian Civilization is based on the principle of non-violence and spiritual values. People achieve their goals in accordance with dharma or rules of morality and show compassion, love and tolerance, towards others and look forward to render selfless service.

In modern times the peoples of most of the countries have realized the message of Gandhi about civilization, therefore, they are turning towards his philosophy of truth, non-violence, spiritual values, tolerance and respect for other religions. Human nature is to love to strive and to find out truth which exists everywhere.

Gandhiji's version of civilization is all comprehensive—'truth that combines the reason of the spiritual self, and the reason of secular self.[13] Ultimately the culture of non-violence, cooperation, understanding has to be developed for the pursuit of world peace and unity of humanity.

In the West importance has been given to the development of science and technology which produced tremendous power. People rely upon the machines for fulfillment of their needs. If they press a button they will have clothing and other items by their side and another time if they press another button a car will be waiting for them. This reflects the nature of civilization which neither considers morality nor religion. Rajiv Vora remarked: "Godless reason and reasonless religion are two curses of modern times."[14]

In the West people are highly advanced and follow hedonism. Craze for the satisfaction and multiplication of wants and consumerist culture lead to global warming. Means to achieve the ends i.e. high growth and material prosperity for happiness should have been based on just and moral principles. But people are not satisfied with what they possess and use the latest products produced by machines. There is greed to have more and more wealth. Hence, they face crises. They do not have mental peace in their lives and are in the pursuit of social, nobler and ethical values.

CONCLUSION

In the world globalization has facilitated cut-throat competition. Developed states have been exploiting the natural resources of the less developed states without caring for the demand of sustainable development. Indiscriminate industrialization and urbanization have resulted in producing two civilizations–'haves' and 'have-nots' and has also posed acute problems of conservation and protection of environment.

Adverse effects of power politics at national and international levels for acquiring wealth and power have to the restrained. Amidst crises people have to have recource to Gandhian principles which are valuable and relevant even today. The government, wealthy industrialists corporate houses, civil society, non-governmental organizations will have to strive hard to practice these valuable principles–dignity of the individual and guarantee of decent quality of life, free and fair trade and business based upon cooperation and not upon competitiveness, fair use of natural resource and empowerment of the individuals especially of women and children.

Adoption of Gandhian philosophy which is based on truth, non-violence, peaceful, co-existence, decentralization of economic and political power, eco-friendly sustainable development, tolerance, minimization of wants instead of multiplication, good means to achieve noble ends and holistic attitude towards different civilizations will pave the way for establishment of 'Vasudhev Kutumbakam.' It will give guidance and inspiration to the individuals for self-realization, self transformation and for rendering selfless service for the betterment humanity and ultimately to continue the pursuit of truth of humane and human existence and also of the Nature.

Instead of adoption of power politics for exploitation of natural resources for improvement of the standard of living of the individuals throughout the world then why not to explore solution for implementation of Gandhian principles of peaceful co-existence, cooperation and non-violence in order to translate the motto of the World Bank 'Our dream is a world without poverty' into reality.

In the end I quote the words of Mahatama Gandhi and close my speech : Gandhiji Stated.

> "While living a simple and peaceful life in Sevagram village, I aspire not only to identify myself with humanity, but even to be in tune with the Infinite."

References

1. Mohd. Muzammil, "Economy and Society: Need for Sustainable Development," *University News*, Special Issue on Research in Higher Education Institutions for Sustainable Development, (April 29-May 05, 2013), p. 136.
2. Deepali Tyagi and Sujeet Kumar Mishra, 'Glocal Philosophy for Sustainable Development *University News*, Special Issue on Research in Higher Education Institutions for Sustainable Development, (April 29-May 05, 2013), p. 148.
3. Bindeshwar Pathak, 'Gandhian Approach to Environmental Sanitation, Anil Dutta Mishra (ed.) Gandhian Approach to Contemporary Problems (1996), p. 176.
4. S.B. Kumar, 'Environmental Problems and Ghandhian Solutions', (2002), p. 83.
5. *Young India*, 13th Oct., 1921, p. 325.
6. Shreeya Kashyap,'Grisis of Capitalism: Environmental Degradation, South Asia Politics, *Monthly Journal*, November (2012), p. 30.
7. Anita Roddick, Speech delivered at The International Forum on Globalization, Seattle, 27th Nov., 1999, Hywel Williams (ed.) Great Speeches of our Time (2009), p. 267.
8. *Id.*, at pp. 267-68.
9. Pyare Lal, Mahatma Gandhi, The Last Phase Vol. 2, (1956), p. 624.
10. Neeru Kapoor, Trusteeship : Moral and Spiritual Approach to Economics', Surjit Kaur Jolly (ed.), Reading Gandhi (2006), p. 193.
11. Shriman Narayan, Towards the Gandhian Plan (1978), p. 57.
12. Pascal Alan Nazareth, Gandhi's Outstanding Leadership, (2007), p. 118.
13. Rajiv Vora, Gandhi's Dialogue on Civilization, Anand Sharma (ed.) Gandhian Way (2007), p. 218.
14. *Ibid.*, at p. 217.

Index

BASIS OF TRUSTEESHIP

Gandhian Trusteeship system is based upon non-violence, swaraj and equality which are inter linked with one another. Gandhi in order to establish an ideal social order, a non-violent non-exploitive and an egalitarian society made no sharp distinction between economics and ethics. Character of production will be determined by social necessity and not personal whim or greed of the rich. Gandhi stated that

> "I must confess that I do not draw a sharp or any distinction between economics and ethics. That economics is untrue which ignores or disregards moral value. The extension of the law of non-violence in economics means nothing less than the introduction of moral values as a factor to be considered in regulating international commerce"[10]

Gandhi advocated trusteeship for the betterment of working class and for establishment of an egalitarian society wherein there will be good relations between the propertied and propertyless. He has given due recognition to divinity of man. i.e. 'Jiva is always Shiva' a man is by and large divine.

In India we have mixed economy with public sector and private sector for economic development. More than hundred big industrial units control largest share of economy. Concentration of wealth in the hands of a few plutocrats has been increasing day-by-day and the workers are under the grip of losing their rights to get adequate wages, right to negotiate with the employers for getting legitimate facilities. There is bound to be conflict between the industrialists and the workers. Gandhian theory will come to the rescue of both the employers and employees. Gandhi stated that:

> "A violent and bloody revolution is a certainty one day unless there is voluntary abdication of riches and the power that riches give, and sharing them for the common good. I adhere to my doctrine of trusteeship in spite of the ridicule that has been poured upon it."[11]

Criticism is leveled against trusteeship system. It is considered as an utopian plan and impracticable and unattainable. But there is no other fair alternative than to make sincere attempts for practicing it in order to resolve the conflicts between the rich and poor and to maintain harmonious relationship between the two. Thus, there will be peace and harmony in the society.